COMMUNITY MATTERS

An Exploration of Theory and Practice

Margot Kempers

Fitchburg State College

Burnham Inc., Publishers

Chicago

President: Kathleen Kusta
Vice-President: Brett J. Hallongren
General Manager: Richard O. Meade
Project Editor: Sheila Whalen
Design/Production: Tamra Phelps
Cover Illustration: "Old Town-Wells St." by Dan Siculan
Printer: Sheridan Press

Library of Congress Cataloging-in-Publication Data

Kempers, Margot.
　Community matters : an exploration of theory and practice / Margot Kempers.
　　p. cm.
　Includes bibliographical references and index.
　ISBN 0-8304-1568-8 (alk. paper)
　1. Community. 2. Community life--United States. I. Title.

HM756.K45 2001
307--dc21   2001035703

Copyright © 2002 by Burnham Inc., Publishers

All rights reserved. No part of this book may be reproduced in any form without permission in writing from the publisher, except by a reviewer who wishes to quote brief passages in connection with a review written for broadcast or for inclusion in a magazine or newspaper. For information address Burnham Inc., Publishers, 111 North Canal Street, Chicago, Illinois 60606.

Manufactured in the United States of America

10 9 8 7 6 5 4 3 2 1

The paper used in this book meets the minimum requirements of American National Standard for Information Sciences—Permanence of Paper for Printed Library Materials, ANSI Z39.48-1984.

CONTENTS

ACKNOWLEDGMENTS   vii

PREFACE   ix

Chapter One
COMMUNITY MATTERS—AND STUDYING THEM   1

Chapter Two
POLITICS AND LAW IN COMMUNITY   17
The Maine Indian Land Claim

Chapter Three
TRADITIONS AND CHANGES   41
*Unitarian Universalism and
the "Welcoming Congregation"*

Chapter Four
CHANGING SPACES AND PLACES   63
Rent Control in Cambridge

Contents

Chapter Five
PUSHING THE LIMITS OF COMMUNITY 81
Rejuvenation Efforts in Waterville, Maine

Chapter Six
"IT AIN'T OVER TILL IT'S OVER" OR
"IT'S ONLY JUST BEGUN" 101
Boston's West End and Celebration, Florida

Chapter Seven
(RE)CREATING COMMUNITY? 117
The "Virtual" Communities of Cyberspace

Chapter Eight
HOW MUCH DOES COMMUNITY
MATTER ANYWAY? 133
The Liberal/Communitarian Debate

Chapter Nine
IS COMMUNITY EVEN POSSIBLE? 147
Postmodern Considerations

Chapter Ten
COMMUNITY THEORIZING AND
COMMUNITY LIVING 161
Questions and Lessons

BIBLIOGRAPHY 171

INDEX 185

ACKNOWLEDGMENTS

The list of people who helped me think through and complete this project is indeed lengthy. Members of the communities described in this book deserve my greatest thanks, and I hope they are pleased with what I have presented here. Among the many individuals who shared their community insights with me are Jim Ashton, Jim Campano, Jane and Bill Cullen, Alice Hartwell, Sally Harwood, George Keller, Elea Kemler, Winnie and Steve Kiersted, Ken LaFleur, Larry Lemmel, Jennifer Logan, Kathleen MacKay, Hal Melvin, Faye and Jim Nicholson, Lerin Peters, Kit Porter, Clair Prontnicki, Jody Rich, Jay and Ray Rogers, Ruth and Gerry St. Amand, Michael Sullivan, Phyllis Taylor, Severn Towl, Mike Turk, Lloyd P. Wells, Meg Wickes, Rosemary Winslow, and Nancy and Dave Wynne.

The Bunting Institute at Radcliffe College provided the kind of supportive environment I needed to focus my interests in community matters. Sharing questions and ideas with my fellow sisters during the 1991 academic year was exciting and intellectually rewarding. Fitchburg State College has supported this project by funding release time for research and writing in both the 1994 and 1999 academic years. I also received great help from the college librarians, and again would like to thank Janice Ouellette and Jean Missud for their cheerful assistance in tracking down some very elusive quotations and sources.

Numerous friends and colleagues contributed to this project by reading all or parts of the manuscript and by offering suggestions that invariably improved the final project. I am grateful to Gregg Carter, Arch Horst, Nancy Kleinewski, Jason Nwankwo, and Shirley Wagner, and especially to Egon Bittner and Maury Stein. Their careful comments, as always, deepened my understanding of community and society. Harriet Alonso, Elsa Dorfman, Gabby Friedler, Jan Teresko and Karen Wolf

Acknowledgments

remained interested in my work over the years, and their enthusiasm helped convince me that I was on the right track. I must acknowledge each of my running "buddies," all of whom simply urged me to go faster.

Richard Meade of Burnham Publishers recognized and understood my goals in writing this book, and I appreciate how he steadily encouraged me to achieve those goals. I also have special thanks for Stan Kaplan and Sheila Whalen, each of whom took charge in preparing final versions of the manuscript for publication.

Family, like community, matters. In mine, we four "Kempers kids" have developed a tradition of claiming that any one individual's accomplishments are the direct consequence of the other siblings' influence. Thus, I duly acknowledge that I owe it all to Natasha, Peter and David. Finally, I thank my husband Fred Scholz for his loving support. This book is dedicated to him.

PREFACE

My desire to understand community matters is rooted in an experience I had as a graduate student in the mid-1980s. During an afternoon meeting in which I was to explain my proposed dissertation research on the experience of group or community rights in American law, I felt my confidence growing as committee members nodded their heads in general approval. Then one professor with whom I'd worked particularly closely asked for my thoughts on what constitutes and characterizes community. This direct query floored me. The details of my instant anxiety attack and the specifics of my garbled response have since faded, but I still can recall the humility that frequently confronts individuals made aware of a reliance on unexplored assumptions. And the nagging question still remains: what is community?

This book responds to that question, and it also builds on several ideas I emphasize in my teaching. I always encourage my students to look for examples of general concepts and, whenever possible, to consider personal experiences as relevant examples. I additionally encourage students to explore how individuals and groups produce, maintain, and change their social conditions and processes—such as "community"—in response to specific contexts involving societal pressures.

Community Matters is also a response to what I perceive to be contradictions between recent academic thinking about community and communities as they are lived. On the one hand, late twentieth century debates have challenged the likelihood, and even possibility, of genuine community life. On the other hand, however, numerous examples of contemporary communities challenge such theoretical skepticism by reaffirming the dynamic and desired qualities of shared existence. My approach is to present both sides of this controversy within an analyti-

Preface

cal framework that underscores process and context. Students and instructors may want to begin with the case studies in chapters 2 through 7, or they might choose to start with the theoretical arguments presented in chapters 8 and 9. Either way, it is my hope that readers will come to agree with the simple claim that, indeed, community matters.

Chapter One

COMMUNITY MATTERS— AND STUDYING THEM

> [T]he concern for the community, its values, properties, and means of access, is the major intellectual fact of the present age. (Nisbet 1962, 30)

This book is about what matters in community and about how community matters. My initial claim is that the social phenomenon that we have come to recognize as "community" is fundamental and unavoidable. We spend our lives in communities: some we join or leave or create almost at will, while others claim us at birth and continue after we die. Regardless, these varied kinds of attachments are important for each of us because they help identify who we are and where we belong. In short, *community* matters.

My second, related claim is that the varying concerns and activities that unfold in those entities we know as communities are similarly important—for what their content reveals and for what they imply about investigative methods. These community *matters* provide insight into how we are connected to and implicated in the lives of others, and they reveal the unpredictable and creative character of community. Given this, *community matters* also indicate the need for a particular analytic approach, one that begins with the understanding that community is a dynamic process.

Why Study Community?

This is a timely examination because both how we live our lives and how we think about our lives have changed considerably in the last half

Chapter 1

century. The interrelated changes have been sometimes invited and often demanded by a host of interrelated technological and social forces. Consider, for example, some of the recent sets of developments that have helped shape our "new" United States.

First, a range of social movements in the 1960s pushed for reform in many of the mainstream beliefs and institutional practices that formally defined what it meant to be an American. Civil rights activists, women's rights advocates, and many other grassroots organizations pushed the system to expand opportunities for participation and inclusion. Even though many of the goals of these movements have yet to be achieved, the movements were successful in legitimating the reality of alternative visions and possibilities for citizens of the United States.

Numerous scientific inventions and technical innovations also stimulated change by contributing to a sense of uncertainty about how we should live our lives. New developments in such areas as surrogate mothering, computer communications, organ transplants, genetic engineering and the prolongation of life have given rise to "new issues . . . for which traditional rules can no longer guide conduct" (Wolfe 1990, 9).

Additionally, the acceleration of global relations and world economic interdependence has directly affected the quantity, quality, and location of jobs in the United States. Career opportunities, work conditions, and living arrangements that seemed secure even a decade ago are in a state of flux. Individuals and groups have seen their economic positions change dramatically; some have been advantaged, others disadvantaged. Among all, though, there is a "quietly growing acceptance that the global context, the international marketplace, the world system collectively" are the source and context for the many rapid changes facing us (Flanagan 1993, 11).

Another important transformation involves changing immigration patterns that are altering the national profile. This "coloring" of America, which simultaneously threatens the hegemony of a long-dominant white majority and offers hope to previously marginalized racial and cultural minorities, illustrates the urgency of the national need "to reconfigure [our] understanding of ethnic, racial, and cultural relations" (Duster 1993, 253).

These kinds of processes and events, while not affecting everyone in the same ways, have already altered what many people think and do. Given their potential for creating new, previously unimagined opportunities for people to bond together, it's likely they will further transform

Community Matters—and Studying Them

our world. Especially noticeable are ongoing changes in public and collective concepts of identity and belonging. An awareness that these are public (political) issues rather than private (personal) concerns is growing among "the many wildly various cultures of this country produced through and around class, race, ethnicity, sexuality, geographic location, and ideology" (Chang Hall 1993, 163); this politicization is challenging traditional accounts of who's who, and who belongs, in America.

The "identity politics" that began in the 1990s recognizes conflicting sources of identity, and comprehends that the political identities that guide our lives reflect both "other-induced distortions" (Taylor 1994, 37) and "our abilities to create ourselves" as well as our places in society (Hirschmann 1992, 290). In other words, although unique identities are frequently "ignored, glossed over, assimilated to a dominant or majority identity" (Taylor 1994, 38) and while individuals and communities can be forced into a homogeneous mold that is untrue to them, it is possible to recover and develop authentic identities that will provide the basis for creative and fulfilling lives. The term "multiculturalism" has come to be associated with the promises and methods of identity politics.

Advocates of multiculturalism proudly celebrate difference as a hallmark of our culturally plural society, and proclaim diversity an essential quality of our national heritage and of our collective future. However, they are vociferously opposed by others who argue that this sort of movement only divides society and destroys basic national values. At issue in this debate is a vexing question: should our public institutions orient themselves to *universal* needs common to all (for example, income, education, health care, civil rights, political liberties), or should our public institutions recognize and respond to *particular* interests of communities distinguished by race, religion, ethnicity or gender? The question, put another way, is what should Americans acknowledge and emphasize? *Similarities* among individuals or *differences* between communities?

A well-publicized and particularly acrimonious version of this either/or debate has flourished on the campuses of American colleges and universities, where "passionate adversaries . . . have reduced the matter to good guys and bad guys battling an evil citadel or defending a sacred one" (Duster 1993, 234). Multiculturalists advocate curriculum reform through the inclusion of new approaches and multiple perspectives in core requirements. This, they claim, will enable students to develop a more accurate understanding of our national history and culture (Andersen and Collins

Chapter 1

1995; Thompson and Tyagi 1993). However, a variety of critics contend that multiculturalism's "politically correct" agenda signals the end rather than the regeneration of intellectual growth. According to these commentators, multiculturalism lowers academic standards, "silences" some students through the imposition of particular points of view, and encourages relativist, or uncritical, thinking (Bloom 1987; D'Souza 1991; Schlesinger 1992).[1]

The tensions and hostilities between the varied participants in the campus "culture wars" reveal that there are real disagreements regarding the nature and value of higher education. However, the adversarial and binary framework of the debate means that both positions are defined in mutually exclusive and mutually exhaustive terms. There is no common ground to be found in this sort of dichotomous argument; the end result is an intellectually bankrupt polarization. What might help to stimulate genuine dialogue is a more complete characterization of multiculturalism, as well as a broader conception of its options and goals (Duster 1993).

In a formative essay tracing the historical contours of the controversy surrounding multiculturalism, Charles Taylor (1994) clarifies why this struggle is so important for communities.

> The demand for recognition . . . on behalf of minority or "subaltern" groups, in some forms of feminism and in what is today called the politics of "multiculturalism" . . . is given urgency by the supposed links between recognition and identity, where this latter term designates something like a person's understanding of who they are, of their fundamental defining characteristics as a human being. The thesis is that our identity is partly shaped by recognition or its absence, often by the *mis*recognition of others, and so a person or group of people can suffer real damage, real distortion, if the people or society around them mirror back to them a confining or demeaning or contemptible picture of themselves. Nonrecognition or misrecognition can inflict harm, can be a form of oppression, imprisoning someone in a false, distorted, and reduced mode of being. (Taylor 1994, 25)

The struggle is about community markers, markers that point to who we are, where we do and don't belong, and why we should treat each other in specific ways. At stake is the redefinition of community and the renewal of community ties.

Community Matters—and Studying Them

What Is Community?

Community is one of the most enduring themes in the social sciences. It is also one of the most elusive because of its inherent variability. For example, community can be created by chance or choice, on a basis of common residence or shared beliefs. Additionally, while the survival of any community requires interaction, commitment, and responsibility among its members, these "ingredients" can be combined in many ways and in many contexts. Another source of variation stems from a community's constant struggle to balance a range of interconnecting elements and values including: shared history and culture, identification, interdependence and cooperation, differentiation and division of authority, individuality, active involvement, and coherence (Selznick 1992, 361-65).[2]

In short, community encompasses many different types of collectivities (Hillery 1955; Lyon 1987; Blackwell 1991). Although there is no clear consensus on the precise definition of community, there is general agreement that "community" appropriately describes a variety of characteristics and circumstances. The term is applied to particular people and places as well as to more abstract experiences, social relations, and aspirations. Its meanings are multiple, ambiguous and sometimes contradictory.

Notice, for example, that this everyday term is invoked to minimize differences, highlight shared benefits and emphasize mutual obligations. This sense of community, illustrated by the image of "our human community," supports the notion that we are all bound together, committed "to a common good that transcends individual interest" (Hummon 1993, 149). Here community means that "we are all one"—it is a condition and reward of being human.

However, opposition and isolation are also central qualities of community. People distinguished by a history of exclusion and hardship—for example, lesbians or people with HIV/AIDS—also build community on the basis of their unique experiences. Community ties can make it easier for an individual to survive, and thrive, in a hostile world. At the same time, though, dominant groups or communities can constrain this sort of solidarity by continuing to isolate "defensive" communities and by enforcing divisions between distinct communities. Clearly, there are high costs involved in community (Weiss 1995).[3]

Regardless of how it is conceptualized, a "peculiar evocative force"

Chapter 1

is attributed to community. Community mobilizes the energies of very diverse people, and thus it's not surprising that actions taken in the name of community conflict (Van den Abbeele 1991). Community is frequently the rationale for developing symbolic and physical boundaries to keep outsiders "out" and insiders "in."[4] Conversely, community is often identified as the means or reason for surmounting the many barriers that keep people apart. In fact, since the 1960s the very idea of community as place and specific people has been used to integrate unorganized groups into political life. The term "community" has been used to justify both social unity and social separation.

Communities can be planned or spontaneous, rooted in past experiences and also built on future hopes, established on the basis of place as well as on a foundation of ideas. Community membership can be empowering and confining, nurturing and coercive, stable and unpredictable. Individuals frequently flourish in communities, but community does not always foster individuality. Variable and elastic, community is made meaningful in a wide variety of often contradictory settings.

The fluid conceptions of community testify to long-term upheavals that have, in the last several centuries, reshaped the environment of social life. In the sense in which it was originally used, the idea of community described a condition of existence in which the presence of specific others in one's life was a fundamental fact of survival. In communities of past centuries, according to W. I. Thomas, everyone was so involved in everything that the community "was practically the whole world of its members" (Thomas 1923/1994, 157). In such communities of necessity, an individual's identity could be comprehended within any one relationship. This grounding of identity provided the foundation on which common interests could flourish.

Since then, however, revolutionary changes associated with industrialization, urbanization, and bureaucratization combined to eclipse much of the previous material basis and the consequent "given-ness" of community life (Stein 1972). Community research initially tended to focus on one angle of this societal transformation: that life as it is now undermines community as it once was. However, there is much more to the story and, as sociologist Barry Wellman has observed, "community has never been lost" (Wellman 1999, 2).

A growing body of research supports the ideas that our technology-dominated, individually-oriented world order actually creates new

Community Matters—and Studying Them

possibilities for community, and that community is still—while perhaps in different ways—an important factor in individual identity and collective well-being (Allen and Dillman 1994; Bell 1994; Cuba 1987; Rheingold 1993). If traditional forms of identity-grounding, all-encompassing communities have weakened, individuals have increasingly been able both to interact with others on the basis of a variety of social roles and to experience new freedoms. Increasingly, community *is* "up to us" in the sense that we are confronted by both responsibilities and opportunities "to make community: to find it, build it, or encourage it to grow in our fragmented world" (Godway and Finn 1994, 1).

The important reversal that has taken place is that shared interests and aspirations, rather than emerging out of community as in the past, now frequently serve as a foundation for community.[5] Today, being or not being a member of a given community increasingly involves personal choices and voluntary activities. However, greater options and increased independence seem not to have diminished the appeal of community. People seem to yearn for connections with others, perhaps because community is both a condition and product of affiliation and interaction.

This paradoxical situation in which people are both free from and still reliant upon community is the focus of Mary Waters' study of symbolic ethnicity among white middle-class Americans. She observed that many descendants of European immigrants sort and shift among various ethnic categories, sometimes blurring the distinctions between categories, as they search for their own identities. Even though ethnicity seems to matter "only in voluntary ways," Waters recognizes that it meets a fundamental need. Even when it is optional, "people cling tenaciously to their ethnic identities" (Waters 1990, 147).[6]

The communities that people yearn for and live in are not fixed entities. People continually make and remake their communities as they act and interact on the basis of what community means to them (Cohen 1985). The following observations about the production and consequences of culture apply as well to this social accomplishment of community:

> A group finds itself sharing a common situation and common problems. Various members of the group experiment with possible solutions to these problems and report their experiences to their fellows. In the course of their collective discussions, the members of the group arrive at a definition of the situation, its problems and

Chapter 1

possibilities, and develop a consensus as to the most appropriate and efficient ways of behaving. This consensus thenceforth constrains the activities of individual members of the group, who will probably act on it, given the opportunity. In other words, new situations provoke new behavior. (Becker 1982, 520–21)

Like culture, community is not simply a quality of social life that people passively receive or pass on (Cohen 1985). Rather, communities constantly evolve, emerging out of the thoughts and actions of members who, over time, "gauge their actions according to what other community members expect of them" (Allen and Dillman 1994, xvi) at a given time and under the conditions at hand. It is helpful to think of community as a symbol, one that allows those who use it to interpret it in accordance with their own experiences. Communities are works in progress, open to revision because "its meaning varies with . . . members' unique orientations" (Cohen 1985, 15).

While this dynamism implies an enormous range of community possibilities and outcomes, there are constraints. First of all, while community members may well have different understandings, they are united by the belief that they share a general way of understanding or doing things that distinguishes them as members from nonmembers. Secondly, every community is molded by hopes and fears of members and non-members, as well as by economic conditions and political arrangements at local, national, and international levels (Wellman 1999). Finally, these sorts of constraints are themselves also limited; they do not determine any particular form or consequence because they themselves are "processual, contingent, and enacted" (Hall 1994, 304).

To be concise, community is the sum total of how, why, when, under what conditions, and with what consequences people bond together. This "appropriately" general working definition of community (Selznick 1992, 358) reinforces two key propositions. The first concerns action. A community does not just respond passively to external conditions and changing circumstances. Rather, as a community is given shape and new form by its members and the surrounding environment, it is at the same time exerting influence over members and the environment. Every community exists in reflexive relationships with its members and with social structures; they construct and reconstruct one another.

The second, related proposition concerns context. Human actions and the ways we understand them are shaped by our experiences and by

Community Matters—and Studying Them

available opportunities and resources. This observation that we make our own history under circumstances not of our own choosing (Marx 1869/1968, 15) reminds us that what we do cannot be divorced from the situations in which we act. This means that thoughts and interactions, and their resulting consequences, need to be interpreted within their socially structured contexts. This embeddedness of social relations and actions was recognized initially by the founders of sociology (Kalberg 1997), and the importance of contextualized analyses has been reemphasized by a variety of scholars.

For example, Martha Minow (1990) reviews how American law treats the "differences" of disability, race, ethnicity, religion, gender, family, and age. She argues that it is only by paying attention to context that we can see how rules that appear to be neutral actually end up burdening some people (particularly those who are unlike those who make the rules). What this means for Minow is that just treatment for all is achievable only if we think about difference and relationship in new ways and learn to recognize relevant differences between people in different contexts.[7]

A similar "call to context" comes from philosopher Elizabeth Spelman (1988), who insists that gender can be understood only in the context of race and class relations. Abstracting gender from this larger context prevents us from seeing that the specific experiences and actions of each woman are directly connected to her racial identity and class position. Reminding us that our social context is one in which class and race are extremely significant, Spelman further argues against analyses that isolate gender because they end up ignoring, or worse, supporting race and class privilege.

In a joint analysis of different meanings and uses of context, Minow and Spelman (1990) urge a renewed awareness of how context affects actions as well as the thinking of those who study such actions. Their claim is that because "we are always in some context," (1,605) the issue is not whether context matters, but rather "what context matters or what context we should make matter at this moment" (1,651). Paying attention to context does not mean getting lost in the unique, isolating details of a single event, but rather "means identifying structures that extend far beyond the particular circumstance" (1,651). Furthermore, attention to context is a reminder not only "of the human relationships in which we exercise our reason" (1,648), it also is a reminder that "acknowledging the human situation and the location of a problem in

Chapter 1

the midst of communities of actual people with views about it is a precondition to honesty in human judgments" (1,649). Ultimately, they suggest, "the reminder that we are all in context might lead to different understandings of who and what we are all about" (1,652).

Another example of contextualizing research is found in Carol Gilligan's work in psychology and moral development. Her pioneering research (1982, 1990) on how women and men analyze and resolve moral problems uncovered two distinct orientations: an ethic of justice orientation (concerned with rules and individual rights); and an ethic of care orientation (concerned with maintaining connections). Both orientations are found in male and female responses to moral problems, but the ethic of care is found more frequently among women.[8] To discover why this is so, Gilligan explored two critically important dimensions of context. The first is the particularities of the situation requiring a moral resolution, and the second is the particular moral orientation of an individual. Both of these dimensions affect how an individual perceives a situation and what option an individual chooses to resolve it. Gilligan's research demonstrates that only by bringing context into analysis can we make sense of some of the differences between women and men.

The importance of context has been a familiar theme in community studies, and it has been recently re-emphasized in Barry Wellman's *Networks in the Global Village* (1999). This collection of community network analyses illustrates the many ways that large-scale social systems influence and are influenced by the communities embedded in them. Around the world, systemic constraints and opportunities mold community life as, simultaneously, communities shape their larger social environments.

Increasingly, these kinds of concerns about the significance of context in social relations are articulated in disciplines ranging from philosophy, history, anthropology, and psychology to education, political science, law, speech and communications, and environmental studies (Hinchman and Hinchman 1997). This shift is characterized by both an avoidance of general theoretical explanations and a focus on narratives or stories that reflect both personal and collective experience and that therefore embody specific values and world views (Ross 1996). These narrative accounts emerge as storytellers select, simplify, and rearrange events in their everyday lives with the aim of explaining social reality. More significantly, each attempt to identify patterns is directly influenced by the narrator's circumstances and experience. The narrative turn builds on the assumption that context provides the foundation for understanding.

Community Matters—and Studying Them

These cross-disciplinary examples of contextualizing research illustrate how behaviors and meanings are produced as people interact with each other and how structural conditions are involved in what human beings say and do. They support a definition of community as both context-shaped and context forming, as well as the observation that the context of community life is vital to its content (Cuba 1987). Examinations of community-in-process need to build on these basic insights.

Finally, this conceptualization of community as interaction shifts attention away from spatial characteristics through its emphasis on social elements. This seems particularly appropriate at this stage in human history when transportation and communications technologies have minimized geographic borders and distances (Wellman 1999). Community *is* essentially about people and relationships—socially defined relationships that are often nurtured, sometimes ignored, frequently fragmented, and always evolving.

Interpreting Community

Given the numerous conceptualizations of community, it's no surprise that many different research approaches have been developed. The approach used in any given research project relies on a specific definition of community and serves the purposes of a particular line of inquiry. Among the approaches used are those that focus on community as people, as spatial arrangements, as shared institutions, as interaction, as networks, as power structure, and as social systems (Warren 1988). In each case, different aspects of community are highlighted.[9]

Studying the *process* of community requires a special perspective, one that acknowledges the ambiguity, diversity, contradiction, and complexity of community and that recognizes the dynamic, constructive qualities of human interaction. The distinctive, "down-to-earth" approach labeled symbolic interactionism responds to these concerns. This unique approach assumes that group life is characterized by "novel, unexpected, and often unpredicted outcomes" and that these outcomes help account for "the continuous, ongoing changes" in individuals, communities, and societies (Meltzer and Manis 1994, 185).

Symbolic interactionism studies how people produce their worlds through interaction with others. The focus is on how people do things together and what is produced. Interactionism has a rich and diverse

Chapter 1

intellectual heritage (Blumer 1986; Denzin 1992; Reynolds 1994), and is itself a conceptual approach that comes in many forms. In fact, "[d]epending on which author one reads, there are between 2 and 15 varieties or *flavors* of symbolic interactionism" (Herman and Reynolds 1995, 4). All, however, explore the dynamics of social interaction. Bridging the variations are a series of basic, unifying, and interrelated propositions about human experience and social context.

The interactionist view is that we live in a world of concrete and abstract things (ranging from teapots and cars to events, specific people, religion, and scientific principles) and that we respond to these things on the basis of the subjective meanings that these things have for us. The meanings we adopt and assign are modified through our interactions with others, which are all under the influence of our linguistic, gender, kinship, political, economic, religious, cultural, scientific, and moral experiences. These socially produced and socially conditioned meanings, in turn, help (re)shape our social worlds.

Guided by these ideas, interactionists study how individuals act with others in mind, sharing and interpreting meanings and altering behaviors in the process of interacting (Blumer 1986; Herman and Reynolds 1994). Interactionists emphasize the significance of actual, lived, ordinary experiences, and also emphasize that interactions and relationships cannot be understood "except as contextualized" (Hall 1994, 304). Community, a form of interaction, is understood as an emergent production,[10] "a negotiated order which emerges as people try, collectively and individually, to solve the problems they encounter in concrete situations" (McCall and Wittner 1990, 64). Rejecting abstract and monocausal theories about community relationships (Denzin 1992), an interactionist approach acknowledges the existence of multiple explanations because it assumes that people understand and act on "things" in many different ways. Finally, an interactionist approach to community pays attention to how people define the situations they are in, what they say, and what they do. The goal is "to understand 'community' by seeking to capture members' experience of it" (Cohen 1985, 20).

Increasingly, interactionist analyses focus on social structure, social organization, power, history, class, and gender (Denzin 1992, 59–60; Hall 1994). Newer interpretive versions of interactionism study the production of shared, cultural meanings that first become encoded in everyday life, and that then help to "create" the people who use them (Becker and McCall 1990; Denzin 1992, 1993). Such attention to social context

Community Matters—and Studying Them

helps clarify how the choices we make and the actions we take mesh with past understandings and shifting institutional forces.

This understanding of community as an emerging, context-dependent phenomenon raises several important questions. Specifically, if every community is a unique entity with a specific set of meanings, is it possible to learn anything about community in general? Additionally, if community is always unpredictable and ambiguous, can we ever reach any definite or certain conclusions?

An important observation that responds directly to the first question is that the uniqueness of each community does not preclude connections between communities. Even if "situations are never identical in structure, they can be abstracted and typified, and used in sense-making" (Fine 1992, 104). Actually, the open-ended definition of community presented here—community as process—provides a "vital medium through which similarities and differences may be more fully recognized, investigated, and appreciated" (Prus 1995, 437). Comparing how communities are united by similarities and differences broadens our understanding of what unites and divides us.

The second question is more unsettling. Because "[s]ocial life is complicated, after all, in its endless collision of structure and accident" (Fenstermaker 1997, 209), we cannot be absolutely certain of what will occur as community unfolds. Consider the following:

> Nothing *has* to happen. Nothing is fully determined. At every step of every unfolding event, something else *might* happen. To be sure, the balance of constraints and opportunities available to the actors, individual and collective, in a situation will lead many, perhaps most, of them to do the same thing. Contingency doesn't mean people behave randomly, but it does recognize that they can behave in surprising and unconventional ways. (McCall and Becker 1990, 6)

All appears to be uncertain, perhaps even unknowable. However, the very quality of human affairs—filled as they are "with erroneous intersections . . . [and] therefore with unanticipated consequences" (Tilly 1996, 594)—invites attention to how we correct our mistakes, respond to unexpected outcomes, and continually make and remake order in our lives. The difficulty of formulating general predictions on the basis of past behaviors stems from the fact that behaviors always occur in particular contexts and involve specific people. An interactionist approach to community as process recognizes that knowledge and

Chapter 1

truth are themselves tentative and emergent social constructions. Still, careful descriptions of how things are worked out in community life help clarify some of the conditions and actions that have shaped life as we know it today.

This chapter's emphasis on process and context invites open-ended examinations of social actions and community experiences. The next six chapters do just that. Each descriptive analysis, guided by the assumption that a key to understanding community is found in the stories of those involved in community matters, focuses on a contemporary example of community-in-action and community interactions. Chapter 2 traces the legal battle waged by several tribal groups in Maine in an effort to regain ancestral land. Chapter 3 summarizes the history of the Unitarian-Universalist Church in order to establish a basis for understanding one congregation's attempt to expand its membership to include lesbian, bisexual and gay persons. The rise and fall of rent control in Cambridge, Massachusetts are analyzed in chapter 4, and the civic renewal program in a mid-Maine town is described in chapter 5.

These distinctive community stories reveal a common characteristic: the present is given meaning and is thus shaped both by how the past has been understood and in relation to hopes for the future (Bruner 1997). Innovative communities as well as new understandings of community are discussed in the next two chapters. The "death" and "birth" of community are considered in chapter 6, with the examples of Boston's Old West End and Celebration, Florida. Chapter 7 outlines some of the recent sociological thinking about the virtual communities of cyberspace.

Following the case studies, the discussion of both significance and substance of contemporary community is refocused. Chapter 8 introduces the liberal-communitarian debate regarding the importance of community, while Chapter 9 reviews postmodern arguments about the very feasibility of community in our society. The final chapter summarizes both the challenges and implications of a contextualized interactionist approach to community and sketches an agenda for further research.

Notes

1. An important discussion of the legal battles that have been waged against political correctness in the name of free speech is found in Kors and Silverglate (1999).

2. Selznick's summary is as follows: ". . . the key values at stake in the

Community Matters—and Studying Them

construction and nurture of a community [which] constitute a complex set of interacting variables [are] historicity, identity, mutuality, plurality, autonomy, participation, and integration" (Selznick 1992, 361).

3. Allen and Dillman (1994) make a similar observation in their study of rural community in the contemporary information age: "maintaining community exacts a price, just as does commitment to other social systems" (Allen and Dillman 1994, 210).

4. "Neighborhood," a term frequently used to describe a specific geographically-based community, shares with "community" this two-sided quality of inclusion and exclusion. See *City of Memphis v. Greene*, 451 U.S. 100, 123, 126–7 (1981), summarized by Derrick Bell in the following manner:

> . . . the city of Memphis, at the request of a white neighborhood association, closed a street at the border between a white and a black neighborhood, forcing residents of the black neighborhood to take an alternate route to the city center. Blacks claimed the barrier's creation of racially separate neighborhoods was barred by the Thirteenth Amendment's prohibition of "badges of slavery" that in this instance reduced property values in the black community for the benefit of the white neighborhood. The Court held that legitimate motives of safety and residential tranquility justified the closure, and that the blacks had not suffered a significant property injury by the action. (Bell 1987: 171)

5. Antony Black, in *Guilds and Civil Society in European Political Thought from the Twelfth Century to the Present* (Cornell University Press, 1984) presents a more nuanced picture in his elegant discussion of community life as emerging out of fellowship, mutual aid, personal freedom, and legal independence "balancing, harmonizing and cross fertilizing each other" (237).

6. Waters' argument is that symbolic ethnicity persists because it provides a desired sense of connection and facilitates a sort of self-determination, but also because it conveniently "fits" with prevailing racist beliefs (Waters 1990, 147–68).

7. Related arguments are found in Engel 1993 and Becker 1998 (esp. 132–38).

8. Additionally, the ethic of care is representative of a "different voice" that has been largely ignored in psychological concepts of decision making.

9. Lyon (1987) explains the correspondence between approach and topic of research in this way:

> Broad research questions on large-scale social change, industrialization-modernization, and the quality of local life in a mass society lend themselves to the *typological approach*. Conversely, more specific, more technical questions about city placement, population growth, density, and land use

Chapter 1

are particularly well-suited for the *ecological approach*. *Systems theory* has direct applications for community development because of its ability to locate the local community systems within the larger network of national systems. And when dealing with the interpersonal relationships within a community, systems-based *network analysis* is particularly effective. Finally, the *conflict approach* has proven popular for the analysis of local economic problems such as the recent urban fiscal crises. (Lyon 1987, 90–91)

10. An emergent production or event is one that contains novel, unanticipated features. See Meltzer and Manis 1994.

Chapter Two

POLITICS AND LAW IN COMMUNITY
The Maine Indian Land Claim [1]

> The past influences the symbolic definition of the present, the definition of the present is influenced by inferences about the future, and the events of the future will reconstruct our definitions of the past. (McHugh 1986, 24, cited in Meltzer and Manis 1994)

The evolution and resolution of the Maine Indian Land Claim is a many-angled story about community survival and cultural change. Each version of this story begins with particular assumptions about the best approach to the subject and what the key issues actually are. The complicated accounts reveal some of the broad contours of this legal and cultural event, but the frequently contradictory interpretations demonstrate that there really is no definitive "God's eye vision" (Hollinger 1994) of the claim.[2] My goal in this chapter is to examine how the unfolding events of the land claim—as told by tribal members—simultaneously reinforced and changed community relations.

Between September and December 1985, I conducted 35 in-depth, open-ended interviews with members of the Passamaquoddy and Penobscot tribes. The interviews lasted from twenty minutes to four hours, with the average length just under two hours. My first interviews were with elected tribal leaders who had been closely involved with and largely supportive of the final settlement. These initial contacts suggested others. Guided by tribal members, I developed a network of contacts: some were for and some against the settlement; some had been tribal administrators; most others had not served in official capacities

Chapter 2

for either tribal community. The men and women with whom I spoke ranged in age from their early twenties to over eighty, and their opinions were equally diverse.

The flexibility and durability of community are repeatedly illustrated in the descriptions of the land battle offered by members of the Passamaquoddy and Penobscot tribes. Their recollections reveal that the tribes' experiences overall were influenced by legal rules that set parameters and shaped possibilities, and that the unfolding litigation and negotiations were significantly affected by what tribal members held valuable and believed possible. Tribal members came to understand in very practical ways that the rule of law is not apolitical (Minow 1993; Norgren and Nanda 1996).

At the same time, viewpoints on what should have been done and what the outcomes meant varied among individual tribal members. In short, each tribe—and on another level, the Passamaquoddy and Penobscot tribes together—illustrates that community is characterized by agreement and dissension, differences and similarities, solidarity and coercion. Such tensions—regarding inclusion and exclusion and between the individual and the collectivity—define community life.

The Claim in Context

Since the beginning of this country's history, most Native American tribes have been subject to federal authority and jurisdiction. Although state reservations have existed in New York, South Carolina, Michigan, Florida, and Texas, administration there has been shared with federal authorities. Maine was exceptional in having a separate bureaucracy and body of legislation concerning its native population (Taylor 1972). The guardian-ward relationship that is typically found between the federal government and Native American tribes simply did not exist in Maine.

In Maine, the indigenous populations lived on reservations that were exclusively and completely administered by the state. The roots of this tribal-state relationship extend to treaties signed in the late 1700s by tribal representatives and officials from the state of Massachusetts, which at that time included the area now known as Maine. With statehood in 1820, Maine assumed all treaty obligations owed by Massachusetts to tribes living within the borders of the new state and until the 1960s continued to fulfill treaty provisions agreed upon in 1796 (which

Politics and Law in Community

included 150 yards of blue cloth, 400 pounds of powder, 100 bushels of salt, 36 hats, and a barrel of rum annually). This unique arrangement shaped tribal life in Maine and proved to be a crucial issue in the development and resolution of the tribes' land claim. Research into the legitimacy of these initial treaties—and thus of the state's power over tribal affairs—provided the essential underpinning for the land claims made by the Penobscots and Passamaquoddies (O'Toole and Tureen 1971; Ghere 1984).

The Passamaquoddy Tribe has two reservations. One reservation area, known as Indian Township, is located in the eastern part of Maine near the border with New Brunswick, Canada. In the mid-eighties, approximately five hundred tribal members lived there, either along the shores of Lewy Lake on a stretch of U.S. Route 1 (known as "The Strip") or seven miles out through the woods at Peter Dana Point on Big Lake. A second Passamaquoddy settlement, Pleasant Point, is located some fifty miles southeast on Route 190 between Perry and Eastport. In 1985, approximately six hundred Passamaquoddies made their home on this 100-acre promontory that extends into the Western Passage of Passamaquoddy Bay. This second settlement was established in 1851 as the result of divisions in the Passamaquoddy tribe over leadership, cultural traditions, and schooling. The state of Maine intervened in these disputes, and one result was that the tribe subsequently agreed to hold elections for a chief and council members on each reservation.

The Penobscot Nation reservation is located inland, twelve miles north of Bangor, on a 315-acre island in the Penobscot River. The 1984 Penobscot Tribal Census recorded a membership of 1,725, but in 1985, only about 550 tribal members lived on the Indian Island reservation. The shared history of the Passamaquoddy and Penobscot tribes includes paternalistic and often hostile treatment from the nonnative, white population in the state. Conflict with outsiders has stimulated intertribal solidarity, and there has always been considerable intermarriage. Still, while most members acknowledge the intimate ties between the tribal communities, virtually all also emphasize the cultural distinctions and boundaries that separate the two tribes. This tension between autonomy on the one hand and commitment or belonging on the other is also played out at the individual level, among the members of each tribe. What tribal members recalled about life before the land claim and about the ongoing effects of the claim movement reflect these tensions.

One of the most frequently made observations was that the claim

Chapter 2

movement grew out of historically established, collective goals. A second was that the claim accelerated an ongoing series of changes that had already begun to distance the tribes from a fondly recollected, intensely communal way of living. Repeatedly, I was told by Passamaquoddies and Penobscots alike that nearly all tribal members grew up surrounded by misery and poverty. At the same time, most said they grew up believing that their communities owned large amounts of land which had been promised to them by the federal government (Ray 1974; but see Ghere 1984). The reality of the harsh conditions of reservation life did not erode the longstanding conviction that the tribal land claim was legitimate. As one Passamaquoddy explained,

> It was *our* land . . . we should have [had] something to say about it. For years the state had maintained control over our lands. In the late 1800s the state parceled up lots of our land along Route 1 and attempted to sell them. A tribal member stopped this, but the state circumvented the issue of ownership by leasing such lots for 999 years "on our behalf."

In February 1964 the Tribal Council of the Passamaquoddy Tribe in Indian township broke its centuries-old silent acquiescence to state authorities. The Passamaquoddies believed that a white man was illegally building on lands owned by the tribe and asked the state to exercise its authority by stopping the construction until the ownership of the land was resolved. They also requested discussions on the larger issues of the questionable appropriation by the state of 6,000 acres of tribal land. (This initial request was based on the position that of the 23,000 acres promised to the Passamaquoddy tribe by Massachusetts in 1794—a promise that Maine had agreed to uphold—only 17,000 remained in tribal hands. However, this figure was dramatically increased in the final claim to 12 million acres of land.) Every tribal member who spoke with me agreed that it was this 1964 move by the Council that initiated what was to become, in the early 1970s, an extremely complicated and politically sensitive lawsuit.

State officials were neither supportive of nor sympathetic to the Passamaquoddies' concerns over land. Notwithstanding, tribal interest in the land issue grew, sparked by the nation-wide attention to civil rights during the 1960s. Tribal members repeatedly emphasized that it was during this time, when so many groups were organizing and fighting for claimed rights, that many became fully and actively conscious of

Politics and Law in Community

social injustices that they had endured all their lives and that had been perpetuated for more than two hundred years. These were years of individual and collective awakenings. Encouraged by a national climate of activism, many Passamaquoddies and Penobscots began to explore how to change their own situation.

Several members of the Indian Township community spoke of the mid-sixties as an important period of transition for Native Americans in general. Across the nation, many tribes became actively involved in efforts to improve the social and economic standing of their members. Similarly, Maine Indians began to organize for desperately needed improvements in housing, health, and employment in particular. Such activism led to federally-funded reform programs that began to produce results by the late sixties; such changes affected the various communities independent of the land claim activities. The appearance of new reservation housing with electricity and modern plumbing contrasted sharply with still vivid memories of reservation children dying of starvation just twenty years earlier.

While no one regretted the end of such tragedies, other aspects of the "good old days" were missed. Nostalgic views of a past spent in closely-knit communities contrasted with perceptions that the community was now breaking down. As several Passamaquoddies observed,

> Back then Indians didn't knock [on doors] . . . old Indians still don't. Canoes used to be left out for general use and general care . . . now there is vandalism. In the past children were free to play anywhere on the reservation and all adults were responsible for reprimanding and guiding them. Today, while the permissiveness is still there, parents get angry if their children are disciplined by others.

It's difficult to know how these sorts of memories colored individuals' recollections about the land claim.

One Penobscot long involved in efforts to better her tribe was sharply critical of these early reform efforts, for she felt that they actually reinforced dependence on non-Indians and prevented the tribe from becoming self-sufficient. While she agreed that both tribes had a sense of what was needed, she felt that the lack of technical expertise required to achieve new goals led many tribal officials to turn to non-Indians for guidance. She believed that some of the Indians in power during this period were corrupted by the "new money" and that they had come to understand how to milk the system *and* to take advantage of the tribe

Chapter 2

simultaneously. Her conclusion was that greedy individuals took advantage of the situation and exploited both the source of assistance (the federal government) and the recipients of such assistance (the tribes).

Until recently, the Maine Indian reservations were socially isolated and economically marginalized. The Indian Island community is clearly set off from the mainstream, even though it is located less than a mile from a fairly active urban center. For many Penobscots, the most significant event in the recent past was the 1950 construction of a bridge to connect Indian Island to Old Town. Before this federally funded, single-span steel bridge was constructed, the only access to the island-based Penobscot reservation was an Indian-run ferry service. But in 1950 "the bridge went up . . . and the community began to change."

The influence of white society spread quickly as more whites came onto the island; new roads were built, sewage and electrical systems were installed, and perceptions of life changed. Before the bridge, everyone shared and pulled together, and joys and sorrows were experienced collectively. A Penobscot woman emphasized this point:

> When a family man was unemployed it was no disgrace but simply "hard times." To help such a family through these hard times neighbors would organize "pound parties"—everyone took the best of what they had in their own cupboards and made dishes which were then shared communally.

"Before the bridge," the island community was poor materially but, according to many accounts, rich and strong spiritually. A number of Penobscots insisted that the community spirit began to weaken when the physical boundaries of their community were made porous by the bridge. But others challenged this, arguing that community attachment remained strong during these transitions.

Relations between the Passamaquoddies and the majority, white society were also changing during that time. In the mid-fifties when the state constructed a causeway across the Bay, between the Pleasant Point community and Eastport, and built a highway through the middle of the reservation, neither community was consulted on the plans nor paid for land taken up by the highway. These roadway projects did more than increase the exposure of Passamaquoddies to outside influences; they also reinforced the tribal perception that the state treated Indians unfairly.

Passamaquoddies and Penobscots were actively engaged in community development before the land claim was initiated in 1964. The

Politics and Law in Community

real significance of the claim was that it triggered the beginning of the end of the tribal communities' isolation. In general, the claim represented a tangible as well as symbolic break with the past.

Formulating the Claim

On June 2, 1972, the Passamaquoddy Tribal Council filed suit with Judge Edward Gignoux of the First District Federal Court in Portland.[3] This suit was based on the premise that the treaty of 1704, in which the tribe had ceded all but 23,000 acres of their aboriginal lands to the Commonwealth of Massachusetts, had never been approved by Congress in accordance with the Nonintercourse Act of 1790. It asserted, therefore, that the Passamaquoddies still owned more than twelve million acres of land which were currently "home" for some 350,000 Maine citizens (O'Toole and Tureen 1971; Clinton and Hootoop 1979).

The Tribal Council requested both a declaratory judgment that the tribe was entitled to federal protection under the Nonintercourse Act and a preliminary injunction ordering the U.S. government to file protective action on the tribe's behalf against the state of Maine. The petition requested that the U.S. government become involved *before* July 18, because that was the expiration date for a statute of limitations on the filing of claims for damages arising from wrongful use of Indian lands. Once this deadline passed, "what was perceived as a major monetary claim would have been barred" (Vollman 1979, 8) and the Passamaquoddy case would become moot.

Penobscots also had long believed they had a legitimate land claim case against the state stemming from violations of the Nonintercourse Act. In fact, land claim activity was not new to the tribe. In the 1950s the Penobscot Nation, convinced it had been defrauded of ancestral lands, hired a lawyer to research its land claims. At that time, however, the Eisenhower administration was introducing the policy of tribal termination, and the Penobscots and their counsel acknowledged that obtaining a fair hearing of their claim would be virtually impossible. At the time, the Penobscots considered but did not pursue the possibility of approaching the United Nations.

In late June, the Penobscot tribe voted to join its claim with that of the Passamaquoddies pending the outcome of the initial suit. On July 1, 1972, the U.S. Department of Justice complied with the Federal District

Chapter 2

Court's orders that it involve itself as plaintiff in the Passamaquoddy controversy by filing a $150-million protective suit against the state of Maine on behalf of the Passamaquoddy tribe. Several weeks later the department acknowledged that its obligations as guardian extended as well to the Penobscot tribe by filing a second suit, also for $150 million, on behalf of the Penobscots.[4]

On the surface, the dispute in *Passamaquoddy v. Morton* was quite straightforward. The Tribal council claimed that the Nonintercourse Act applied to them and that there was a trust relationship between the tribe and the federal government. The Department of the Interior, on the other hand, asserted that the tribe had never been recognized and that therefore there was no such trust relationship. If the Act did not apply, then the federal government had no legal obligation to pursue action against the state of Maine on behalf of the tribe. Conversely, if the Act was found to apply, the tribes could be considered for federal recognition and thus for the specialized funding that accompanies such status. Also, the federal government would be legally responsible for bringing suit against the state of Maine for its violation of the constitutional provisions and for restitution to the Passamaquoddy tribe.

While the dispute appeared simple, the potential consequences of this case were complicated and without precedent. If Gignoux ruled in favor of the plaintiffs, a land claim of unprecedented magnitude could be pressed in court with the federal government acting as guardian-plaintiff. If, however, Gignoux ruled against the tribe by agreeing with the defendants that the Nonintercourse Act applied only to federally recognized Indians and thus not to the Passamaquoddy tribe, the tribe's ability to litigate its claim successfully would most likely be destroyed.

In January 1975, Judge Gignoux handed down his decisions regarding *Passamaquoddy v. Morton*. He affirmed the applicability of the Nonintercourse Act to the tribe and ruled that a trust relationship did exist between the tribe and the federal government under the provisions of the Act. Gignoux's declaratory judgment was understood by both the tribes and state officials as a clear victory for the Passamaquoddies. The decision was upheld by the First Circuit Court of Appeals in December, and no further appeals were made.

The *Passamaquoddy v. Morton* decision established that the tribe(s) *did* have a legal claim to huge sums of land and capital in the state. Thus, by early 1976 the federal government was in the position of having to determine the extent of its trust relationship with both the Pas-

Politics and Law in Community

samaquoddy and Penobscot tribes. It began to explore the eligibility of the Maine Indians for federal recognition and thus for the various federal benefits administered by the Bureau of Indian Affairs (BIA). Simultaneously, the Justice Department began to review the ramifications of pursuing and possibly expanding the two $150-million protective actions filed on behalf of each tribe in 1972.

Four years later the Passamaquoddy and Penobscot communities altered their joint bargaining position by voting to accept the terms of a settlement which would provide the Houlton Band of Maliseets with 5,000 acres of woodland and federal recognition (Brodeur 1985). In the fall of 1980, the elected leaders of these three Maine Indian tribal groups, the state of Maine, and federal government officials reached an out-of-court settlement on the rightful ownership of more than 12 million acres of land estimated to be worth in excess of $25,000,000 (Barsh 1982). The terms of the final settlement established a $27-million trust fund for the Passamaquoddy and Penobscot tribes and allocated $55 million for the Passamaquoddy and Penobscot tribes and the Houlton band of Maliseet Indians to use in purchasing up to 300,000 acres of state land. In addition, the settlement extinguished all future claims by Maine Indians.

Tribal Factions

Interviews with members of both tribes revealed that both individualism and collectivism are understood and valued differently. The legal focus on tribes rather than on individual Indians lends formal support to continuity and consensus, as opposed to individuality and dissent, in Indian communities. However, as this study reminds us, the essential needs and "nature" of the social person and of social groups are fluid and context-dependent. Bonds which appear solid from one vantage point seem ephemeral from another. Individuals reveal themselves as both independent and self-satisfying *and* communal and associative (Svensson 1979). A community's identity can remain strong even as it develops and changes over time (Engel 1993).

The relationship between the Penobscot and Passamaquoddy tribes has developed in response to longstanding disagreements (Beem 1987; Nyhan 1987), and each tribal group has had to cope with a wide range of controversies and feuds. Unlike the Passamaquoddies I spoke

Chapter 2

with, many members of the Penobscot Nation were very quick to criticize their own tribal leadership for political maneuvering. Penobscots explained that their dissatisfaction had grown out of claims activities and settlement negotiations. When their Tribal Council voted in 1972 to join in the land claim with the Passamaquoddy Tribe, there was a general agreement on what direction the Penobscots should take: "when the claim started some were against it, but the tribe wanted it, so it went." As negotiations for a settlement progressed, however, generations-old differences seemed to resurface and divide the community into factions.

There was no agreement on the exact profiles of the opposing factions, and the categories seemed to overlap. One common explanation of the differences was that the "progressives" favored an out-of-court (and possibly monetary, as opposed to land) settlement, while the "traditionalists" wanted both land and a court trial. Other Passamaquoddies and Penobscots explained the divisions as a function of age: the young (alternatively called "progressives" by some) were for a quick settlement but the old (or "traditionalists") "who have the ability to see the long view" were against it. A third version described the traditionalists as mostly younger Indians who were "better read . . . more active in Indian issues," and the progressives as self-centered and detached from tribal values.

However, it was widely agreed that those labeled "progressives" (specifically the administrators and negotiators who controlled tribal politics and economics) did not trust the courts. Believing that an all-or-nothing gamble in federal court was too risky, the progressives sought a negotiated settlement. In opposition, "traditionalists" believed that the tribe should not compromise itself by agreeing to an out-of-court settlement. What seemed to unite traditionalists was a desire not only for a victory, but also for a battle (Merry and Silbey 1985).

This split in the Penobscot community over claims procedures and final settlement negotiations was evident during my interviews. Each side sharply accused the other of haphazard thinking, irresponsibility, and corruption. Tribal leadership called those who opposed a negotiated settlement dissidents and radicals, labels which the opposition maintained both trivialized and demeaned them and their position. Several of these "radicals," in turn, asserted that tribal negotiators lacked a certain strength of character:

> There was a legal basis for the claim, but as time passed there was a shift towards money. Near the end all that was guiding the administration and negotiations was money . . . Money became corrupting

Politics and Law in Community

... the political processes and positions were taken over by Indians interested in self-gain. Those involved in [tribal] politics were becoming more materialistic, less culturally [communally] oriented ... Steadily, tribal members and administrators sold themselves out—all for money.

Penobscot tribal leaders with whom I spoke dismissed such charges, explained the enormous complexity and risk involved in the final negotiations, and accused their "traditionalist" critics of being tribal advocates "per convenience." As one Penobscot official put it,

> Instead of voicing their agreement and then attempting to resolve differences, those tribal members who criticize the current state of affairs tend to distance themselves ... they do not participate in tribal matters, and then exonerate themselves by saying "the tribal administration did it."

Progressives felt that "the nay-sayers cop[ped] out" because they stayed away from tribal meetings while claiming that no one would listen to them. Penobscot traditionalists believed that the tribal administration had "lost the old values and skills of negotiating and accommodating varied interests and needs." Progressives firmly maintained that the settlement was the most that could have been accomplished under the circumstances and that it has provided an avenue for the tribe's growing self-sufficiency. Traditionalists are convinced that the final settlement ended tribal sovereignty, terminated the land claim, and stimulated the assimilation and cultural genocide of the tribe; for them, the settlement represents one of the biggest swindles of Native American people in the history of the country.

Both traditionalists and progressives stated that their positions evolved as the negotiations progressed, and that they always had what they believed to be a clear understanding of the consequences involved in either settling or litigating. The "looking backwards" so regularly engaged in by both traditionalists and progressives in itself has led to new assessments and criticisms, but hasn't dispelled a mutual suspicion and lack of trust. But even such deeply-felt differences are not necessarily irreconcilable, for the Penobscots describe themselves as resilient and self-sufficient. A middle-aged Penobscot mother expressed this clearly:

> The tribe was split over the settlement and went through some very rough times because of the split, but the tribe has come back

Chapter 2

together. After all, if one is committed to the community yet disagrees with what is done, the commitment should carry weight and force the unity.

Further, the Penobscots are conscious of the fact that the tribe has historically been divided into "conservatives and liberals" (Ghere 1984) and that the settlement cannot be held to blame for community dissension in general. There always have been—and most believe there always will be—divisions and splits, for new issues invigorate old quarrels and generate new disagreements. In spite of the dire warnings of some tribal members, other more optimistic members are working on shared cultural and economic activities for the tribe's present and future. Complaints about community deterioration are matched by descriptions of how new relationships have been formed and old ones strengthened. This self-identified "Penobscot outlook," characterized as it is by diverse and frequently contradictory opinions, suggests that the tribal members understood their possibilities were limited and that all choices would have some disturbing or destructive consequences.

One final example of the tension between individual and collective identity erupted in March 1980 after the Maine Legislature approved the proposed Maine Indian Land Claim Settlement Act (MILCSA) and submitted the proposal to popular vote among members of the three tribes. Although a majority of those voting favored this proposal, a small vocal group testified at the final Senate hearings held in Washington, D.C., in July, asserting that the voting procedures had not been fair and that it was erroneous to assume that Maine Indians generally supported the provisions of the proposal.[5] These complaints were not enough to block passage of the settlement act. Opposition to the settlement continued among a handful of Indian residents who refused to accept their *per capita* settlement payments at least through 1989.

Using and Beating the System

During the first years of the land claim, public awareness of the stakes involved was minimal. State politicians and non-Indian residents didn't take the Indians' legal actions seriously until the 1975 *Passamaquoddy v. Morton* decision established that their claims were valid. Almost immediately public attention became sharply focused against the tribes as individual white landowners across the state voiced their fears that the

Indians would take their homes away. There seemed to be little that either tribe could do to assuage such fears. One Penobscot summarized the feelings of many when he described the late 1970s as a time when opportunistic state politicians used the media to generate and sustain anti-Indian sentiment.

> The state and Governor Longley recognized that the situation was intolerable; the legality of the tribes' claim meant that massive swindling had taken place and that ultimately the *state* would be held accountable by the tribes, by landowners, and by large industries. So the Governor and the state sought to switch the issue from land holdings to the more emotion-laden one of jurisdiction. Officials began to argue that the Indians wanted to become a "nation within a nation."

Newspaper and television stories stereotyped the tribes and their Joint Negotiating Committee as self-interested and land-hungry; articles and editorials emphasized that the Indians' claim posed an extremely serious threat to all Maine land- and home-owners. Neither tribe was successful in countering the escalating "us against them" mentality, and the legal issues of the claim were obscured by racial hostilities. The tribes simply were not considered a credible source of information by the white majority. In the words of one Passamaquoddy:

> The hard reality of the situation was that facts didn't matter; non-Indians didn't need to be concerned with them. The lack of information and the misunderstandings [were] translated into racial bigotry. It wasn't only the South that had [racial] problems . . . during this period, whites became more suspicious and fearful of the tribes and Indians became more distrustful of whites.

Further, limited resources and the demands of everyday living constrained tribal attempts to use the media to gain either understanding or sympathy. There was general agreement in both tribes that during this period, most reporting was inaccurate. Accounts of the tribes' position were written without any input from the tribes' Joint Negotiating Committee or its counsel. State officials had a vested interest in letting such inaccuracies stand, for it was to their advantage to minimize or conceal the state's illegal actions of the past.

During the claim proceedings state politicians were capitalizing on anti-Indian sentiment and the tribes were reacting to public hostility.

Chapter 2

These dynamics in turn were influencing the proceedings. Off-reservation Indians were especially vulnerable to hostilities, but even Indians living on-reservation were subject to verbal harassment and physical violence. Over and over I heard stories about attempts to bribe tribal members into abandoning the claim, threatening phone calls, and even shootings by angry non-Indians.

Passamaquoddies and Penobscots alike believed that state and national law enforcement officials were involved in some of these episodes and that these officials further sought to cover up their illegal actions. While quick to acknowledge the difficulties of substantiating such allegations, several members argued that only sophisticated organizations "like the FBI" could have kept so many tribal members under surveillance. I asked why the FBI should have been interested in "watching" tribal members, and was told by some that involvement in AIM (American Indian Movement) activities had earned them a place on the FBI "list." Others assumed that the government spied on the Maine Indians in order to learn more about claim activities in general. Still others tended to downplay the idea of surveillance.

Gradually, tribal members became more adept at using the media and the political system to combat the white image of the Indian as adversary. Before the claim movement, according to many Passamaquoddies and Penobscots, state politicians frequently developed successful careers by spouting anti-Indian positions. In the years since the enactment of the Settlement Act there has been a steady reversal to the point where now most candidates for political offices—including the governorship—find that they need to cultivate Indian support. This turnaround is not a reflection of increased voting strength of either tribe, but of the increasing economic importance the tribes have in the state economy. Using their leverage from the settlement, the two tribes have invested in established and new businesses around the state. Because the tribes are a source of employment for non-Indian Maine citizens, state politicians have a vested interest in following tribal affairs. As one Passamaquoddy man explained,

> the bottom line in Maine is dollars and cents. Economic power means political power, and as the tribe(s) become more self-sufficient they *should* wield increasing political influence. At present, the tribe(s) have financial resources to fall back on . . . money has given Indians a "place" . . .

Politics and Law in Community

The primacy of the federal bureaucracy in the lives of Native Americans was re-established during the long negotiation and settlement process. Most of the Passamaquoddies and Penobscots were quick to acknowledge this even without making any distinction between various branches of government which historically have dominated and constrained tribal existence. The common perception is that this "system" was like a double-edged sword, cutting with and against the grain of Indian culture. Many agreed that the system had much to offer but that going after the benefits could be dangerous.

Tribal members recognized the irony of their situation; during the 1970s when they were asserting sovereignty and seeking independence, they were required to demand to be a ward of the federal government. Throughout the claims movement and settlement negotiations, tribal members realized that they had to play the legal game according to the rules of the federal government. While recognizing that the federal government "calls the shots," they did not consider this situation legitimate. The question raised by a Lakota Indian in a different context captures the general sentiment felt by individual Maine Indians: "I wonder where the white man ever got the idea that these wrongs had to be settled in his courts by his rules" (Barsh 1982, 11).

These rules were potentially advantageous to the tribes, but *only* if the tribes were able to hold the government true to its rules and then beat it at its own game. A Passamaquoddy expressed the frustrations of many when he talked about the government's ability to call the shots: "Early on in the claim the tribes were told to use the system. When they began to win within the system, roadblocks were put up and attempts were made to change the rules of the system." Others were quick to point out that some individuals within the government do not even play according to the rules of "their" own system.

The following account from a Penobscot who traveled to Washington to testify against the settlement captures the commonly-felt skepticism towards federal law and politics:

> I went to the chairman of the Senate Select Committee in charge of the hearings, and I told him that the tribe did not agree on the settlement. He told me what [we] want doesn't matter . . . he would still introduce the legislation for final settlement. He said he would do so if 50%, 75%, even 95% of tribal members were against the settlement. When I asked him what he would do if 100% were against the settlement he replied "I would jump out the window. . . ."

Chapter 2

Though skeptical, most tribal members agreed that the legal system, specifically the court system, was the proper place for the land claim regardless of the position they had taken on the final settlement. Even while admitting that courts are not always fair—especially to minorities—they agreed that the courts provided the only option open to the tribes. The legal system was the place of last resort for the tribes, for "taking over the law was impossible."

Throughout the court proceedings and negotiations, the tribes learned and relearned the importance of keeping track of changing political players and administration goals. From the beginning, tribal expectations were guarded. This wariness, as a lifetime resident of Indian Island explained, was in part a response to the legal system's adaptability; it apparently changes to suit the needs and interests of whoever is in power. Tribal members believed that they were getting their day in court not because of the legal merits of their case, but rather because they stood out (as do most Indian tribes) as an embarrassing reminder to the legal system that "equal justice for all" is a myth. Thus, even though the legality of the land claim had been established in *Passamaquoddy v. Morton*, few trusted the courts to really respond to the legal issues.

Many who in the end supported a negotiated settlement did so because they were convinced that a court trial would be disastrous for the tribe. Repeatedly, an out-of-court settlement was justified as the most prudent move:

> Gambling all or nothing in the courts would have been irresponsible (Passamaquoddy) . . . I did not want to take a chance that the Supreme Court would not be favorable towards the tribes (Penobscot) . . . I was sure that if the case had gone to a jury—and the jury probably would have had no Indians on it—the decision would have been unfavorable (Passamaquoddy) . . . If we had litigated, all would have been lost (Passamaquoddy).

What tribal leadership did take, with the advice of its counsel, was "a practical look at what [it] could get from the system." And in the final settlement, the tribes both "won" and "lost." The principled belief that the state of Maine should be pushed towards a court settlement was tempered by what one Passamaquoddy negotiator termed "the tenor of the political system and the texture of the courts at the time." There was fear that incoming President Reagan would veto any decision reached by Congress that would be favorable to the tribes, and so by late 1979, the tribes *had* to move quickly. This same Passamaquoddy maintains that a negotiated settlement appeared to be the best solution at the time, and that the tribes were fortunate to settle: "In this sense the tribes were non-traditional . . . the settlement was the only viable approach, for if the option to go to court had been taken, the ensuing pressure on the Indians could have been overwhelming. The tribes simply might have given up."

By deciding to settle, the tribes gave up the opportunity to fully test the court system. Notwithstanding, some tribal members believe that the country's political-legal establishment did respond to their claim in the settlement. In spite of what many tribal members referred to as "a centuries-old bias against Native Americans," many admitted that the system "did shift somewhat." This "shift" can be interpreted as an indication that the legal system can and does respond positively to the collective claims brought by Indian tribes or as an indication that federal rules and regulations are arbitrarily enforced and that the system consistently undermines Indian communities.

Community and Meaningful Rights

During the repeated rounds of negotiations that followed Judge Gignoux's 1975 decision and led to the eventual settlement, the theme of rights emerged repeatedly. According to several members of the Joint Tribal Negotiating Committee, "the notion of *Indian* rights and of having them enforced by law" was central to the land claim. But this notion of rights is hard to pin down. Several Passamaquoddies and Penobscots identified rights as "that bundle of stuff that enables a community to live a way of life." Many share strong feelings that the settlement negotiations have made this "bundle" smaller.

> What was lost? Rights to gather such things that make the culture viable, for example, porpoise hunting. Such rights are lost when an activity is banned, thus forcing the end of certain skills and a teaching process needed to impart such skills. Deprivation of a way of life is a deprivation of rights. Such rights are extremely important to the tribes but are not tangible and not easily grasped by outsiders.

Tribal members recognize that such intangible rights were not necessarily referred to in treaties, but that they were part of the culture. The erosion of these rights and binding ties has threatened tribal cultures. As

Chapter 2

one Penobscot weaver put it, "these rights meant you could cut ash wherever, whenever you needed it for baskets; now the state regulates this." This critical connection between activities and culture was emphasized by a Passamaquoddy raising his children at Peter Dana Point:

> In 1936 the state legislated away hunting rights for the Passamaquoddy. Consequently, the skills required for the hunting way of life were no longer passed on—they were no longer needed. This "passing on" is a critical part of the Passamaquoddy heritage . . . not just the skills themselves but the sharing and transference of knowledge. "Progress," in conjunction with the settlement, has enabled the tribe to improve the lives of its community members; buildings are modern and safe. But these same "advances" cut deeply into the old ways of the tribe. Phones are now used instead of personal visits. Time is at a premium now. So much of the culture and traditions require time [e.g., religious ceremonies] and this type of time is being eroded by the complexity and fast-pace of modernity.

In fact, neither tribe has been seminomadic or "traditional" for decades and decades, and not all tribal members agree with this particular conception of rights. Such intangible "way of life" rights are less applicable now, and yearning for them is considered by some to be idealistic and unproductive. Furthermore, others argue, the tribal governance structure does give some order to group rights concerning hunting, fishing, and gathering, and individual Indians can act on these rights in various ways. A Passamaquoddy tribal administrator explained it in this way:

> For example, water rights may mean simple fishing, or building a camp by the water, or commercial sailing. Exercise is open so long as one's exercise does not compromise another's. This same principle pertains to housing and building . . . certain [way of life] rights can be held on to in the mind, and in reality—others cannot be. An individual Indian still does have the rights to live as the old Indians did, but modern conveniences are generally too attractive.

Still, it is not easy to unravel the complex connections between cultural identification and legal rights. Traditional Indian culture has essentially evolved out of material conditions, yet these conditions have changed dramatically during the centuries-long relationship between tribes and the larger, non-Indian society. Some rights were "taken away" by government officials while others were "given up" by the Indians as they adapted to changing social and economic conditions. Although there is considerable debate over what actually has happened to many Indian rights, the crucial point is that they—and the way of life established on them—cannot be regained. Both culture and community have evolved.

Changes in the daily life of the tribes have been in large measure induced by the dominant culture, but many are the outcome of a "process in which new and old were synthesized" by tribal members into meaningful forms (Cohen 1985, 37). But even though community members have been actively involved in change, they have arrived at a crucial point. What it meant to be an Indian in the past no longer holds true in the same way today. In the past, Indian identity was inextricably bound up in life-sustaining activities such as hunting and fishing, in activities like basket-making, and communal celebrations (all central to the culture), as well as in the transmission of the skills essential for these activities. Today, many of these activities are no longer a matter of life and death for tribal members, and some activities have been regulated away by state and federal statute. The felt entitlement of an Indian tribe to specific, named "rights" has frequently been recognized by the legal system only *after* such rights have been lost through disuse, robbed of intrinsic meaning, or taken away by "legal" action.[6]

Assessing Gains and Losses

Opinions varied on the issues of how much the tribes gained or lost in the final negotiations, but virtually all agreed that the settlement was not an end in itself but rather an element in the tribes' development. "It represents one step that will be followed by others." Still, even this general agreement that the terms of the settlement have meant change for the tribes broke down in discussions over the nature and extent of change. There was even disagreement over whether the settlement did in fact result in "tangible changes," for as one Passamaquoddy pointed out, "as far as the daily living goes . . . basic survival, food on the table, [are] still the primary issue."

By some measures the daily lives of individual tribal members were not greatly affected by the final settlement. In the late 1980s, annual per-capita payments from the dividends of the $81.5 million awarded to the tribes amounted to slightly less than $500 for each Penobscot and about

Chapter 2

twice that sum for the less numerous Passamaquoddies. There was a palpable sense that many tribal members who turned against the settlement did so simply because large-scale, *individual* monetary rewards did not materialize. "Traditionalists" and "progressives" alike expressed resentment at the self-serving attitude of some tribal members who, by complaining of the loss of an Indian identity, sought to exploit "being an Indian" for personal gain.

> [M]any looked toward the claim as a way of gaining individual wealth, not as a means for the tribe to gain self-sufficiency . . . Expectations were not totally fulfilled by the settlement. After, when lives did not begin to change drastically, complaints began. It is important to figure out what the source of the discontent is . . . for many it's money.

It is true that the settlement increased the assets of each tribe, but this hasn't been easy to see. Tribal leadership initially invested much of the settlement money in long-term projects that did not offer the possibility of immediate payback. Also, many of the physical improvements completed during the 1980s were not financed out of the settlement, but rather were paid for by money granted to the tribes when they won federal acknowledgment in 1976. All these factors prompted questions about whether the tribes would realize any gains from this new "tribal wealth" and whether the new leadership would manage the new wealth well.

Clearly, though, debate over the settlement includes much more than just monetary concerns. There was a strong sense that the social quality of each community changed. On Indian Island,

> once the settlement was finalized, there was huge and rapid change. Our people are slow, and the fast changes left heads spinning . . . The settlement brought lots of differences, bad changes because of money . . . The old tribal unity has disappeared, everyone wants to get ahead . . . [In essence] the settlement has made all the Indians the same—everyone is after money . . . There is more vandalism [as] kids who grew up in the city return to the reservation. Thieves no longer take [only] what they need, they destroy wantonly.

Others said simply that the settlement changed everything: "while there is still some sharing, individuality is much more pronounced . . . Self rather than tribe has become important." Despite the communal nature of the original claim and the fact that settlement funds were

Politics and Law in Community

invested in tribal projects, some reached the conclusion that the final settlement favored individuality at the expense of shared commitments and goals. For some, "the community feeling is gone."

Changing values were cited over and over by members of both tribes as playing a key role in the tribe's futures. The settlement opened the way for the tribes to move further into the fast-paced world of big money, federal programs, and complex bureaucracy, and new problems accompany such a move. Admittedly, the sheer enormity of coping with such problems may demand attention and energy that otherwise could be focused on unique aspects of the tribal cultures. Penobscots and Passamaquoddies recognized that the survival of their communities depends on both retaining their values and modifying them in practice when necessary as their lives and circumstances change. One of the tribal leaders at Indian Island observed: "Sure there is a risk of assimilation with the new situation, but the task or effort has to be to back out of the assimilationist trap by using knowledge and by being economically self-sufficient. Values, not actual tangible cultural skills, are the essential ingredient."

Some considered values to be inextricably linked with the past, and therefore felt that even though such values are important, acting on them was problematic. So while many advocated a return to some of the old, attractive values like communal sharing and spiritualism, they also recognized that this would not be easy or even possible. The rigid opinion of one Penobscot elder—"we can't and don't want to go back to the old ways"—was unusual, for most revealed much more ambivalent opinions on the issues of cultural survival and assimilation. Many perceive themselves in the middle of a balancing act, trying to simultaneously maintain their Indian culture and adapt to modern (i.e., non-Indian) life. A younger Penobscot spoke at great length on this subject:

> There are two ways of thinking about culture, first, traditional folklore, identity, songs, etc., and second, the ability to know this *and* to use this knowledge to function in a non-Indian culture . . . There is no longer a fine line between the Indian and the White worlds. The hunting and gathering culture or way of life is long gone. Men used to be the sole providers—no more. The dependence within a family and within the community is no longer there and this would have occurred even without the settlement. Religious ceremonies used to involve all—this has been fading . . . what remains now is just a semblance of the traditional cultural way. The trappings of the

Chapter 2

outside white society are all over . . . Assimilation is inevitable because of osmosis. Look at education, knowledge, technology; the white society is all-surrounding. Every aspect of non-Indian life is found now in an Indian community. Assimilation is inevitable and the settlement has perhaps hurried us. The standard image is that the more assimilated one is the less "Indian" one is but this does not need to be true.

The accuracy of this "standard image" is not resolved. The material basis of the traditional Passamaquoddy and Penobscot cultures hardly exists any more, and that change—symbolized in the final settlement which minimized land and maximized money—has accelerated a greater integration with non-Indian society. Although Passamaquoddy and Penobscot Indians have not disappeared as a consequence, some of their traditions have come under greater threat. In the final analysis, the success of the movement and the settlement of the land claim must be measured against the ability of these individuals to function in Indian and non-Indian worlds and to strengthen Indian identity in both.

Conclusions: The Experience of Community

The Maine Indian land claim was the first of a series of eastern Indian land claims to be prosecuted (Vollman 1979; Taylor 1984). Part of its significance was that the tribes successfully pressured the "system" to acknowledge their special identities; another measure of its success was the apparent reinforcement of the notion of tribal autonomy. Unquestionably, the tribes achieved a new legitimacy by working through traditional legal channels, and this strategy resulted in potential political advantages. On another level, though, the negotiations and settlement may have compromised the very basis of the claim. After the final settlement, Maine Indians (who officially now include *only* those three tribal groups named in the MILCSA) have come under much closer state supervision. The three tribes' lands and resources are subject to Maine laws, and they themselves are henceforth under the jurisdiction of the Maine civil and criminal courts. While the tribes do retain authority over internal matters including membership, tribal government, and the right to reside on tribally-owned land, the provisions of the final settlement formalized a status for the Maine tribes that is closer to that of a municipality than that of an independent sovereign nation.

Politics and Law in Community

The legal experiences of the Maine tribal communities provide unusual and dramatic illustrations of typical phenomena. The fluid, often ambivalent quality of the communities involved in the Maine Indian land claim is not unique. Community, influenced by societal pressures and internal dynamics, is characterized both by predictable patterns of activity and by unexpected innovations. Community relations are rooted in both similarities and differences; uncertainty and flux coexist with stability, and individual need/personal desire demand equal time with collective resistance.

Assessing the costs and benefits of the settlement continues to be a community matter, one that simultaneously unites and divides. The full implications of the entire experience are still being charted (Snipp 1990; White 1990). Tribal members continue to reexamine their spiritual and cultural resources as they integrate business into their daily lives. Individual competition, previously almost nonexistent, now exists alongside community solidarity. Members' reflections about the claim and settlement illustrate how hope, conviction, and action reinforce, undermine, and redirect each other during community interaction. Always, it is within community that the individual, cultural, and institutional dimensions of social existence interlock. Still, these community outcomes remain unpredictable. The following chapter provides further insight into the continuities and uncertainties of community life.

Notes

1. An earlier version of this chapter appeared in Kempers 1989. Permission granted.

2. My own interpretation has been guided by a range of authors. I found an insightful discussion of how observer-authors' frames of reference affect their accounts of events in Native American history in Jane Tompkins' essay "'Indians': Textualism, Morality, and the Problem of History," in *"Race," Writing and Difference*, ed. Henry Louis Gates Jr. (Chicago: University of Chicago Press, 1985), 59–77. More generalized refutations of the postmodernist argument that historical knowledge is impossible appear in *Telling the Truth about History* by Joyce Appleby, Lynn Hunt, and Margaret Jacob (New York: W.W. Norton & Company, 1993) and in *The Illusions of Postmodernism* by Terry Eagleton (Cambridge, MA: Blackwell, 1996). Most recently, anthropologist Edward Bruner's explanation of the shift in the Native American "story" from cultural assimilation to cultural renewal has reminded me of the importance of locating analytical stories in their historical contexts. See "Ethnography as Narrative" in

Chapter 2

Memory, Identity, Community, ed. Lewis P. Hinchman and Sandra K. Hinchman, (Albany, NY: SUNY Press, 1997), 264–280.

3. This was actually the second suit filed on behalf of the Tribal Council. In March 1968 the tribe's lawyer, Don Gellers, initiated a suit to recover the six thousand acres of land taken from the tribe in violation of the 1794 treaty between Massachusetts and the Passamaquoddies. (Geller's clerk was Tom Tureen, who took over the land claim case in 1969 after completing law school.) Shortly after filing suit, Gellers became embroiled in his own, drug-related legal troubles and was fired by the Passamaquoddy Tribal Council. This first suit was thus never argued in court.

4. An interesting and unexplored question is how, or to what extent, the size of the Justice Department's protective suits played a role in the tribe's actions. It seems reasonable to suspect that it may have encouraged some tribal members to push directly for a court trial. See Vollman 1979.

5. U.S. Congress. Senate. "Hearings before the Senate Select Committee on Indian Affairs" on S.2829, Proposed Settlement of Maine Indian Land Claims. 96th Cong., 2nd sess., 1980.

6. However, it seems important to consider Martha Minow's observations that those who are disempowered (e.g., feminists, women and men of color, gays and lesbians) "use" rights in a very proactive sense "to translate claims so that those with more power can hear and may be compelled, by their own investment in their world, to respond" (Minow 1993, 60. See also Williams 1987; Dalton 1987; and Matsuda 1987).

Chapter Three

TRADITIONS AND CHANGES
Unitarian Universalism and "The Welcoming Congregation"

> For most of us . . . community is something we don't yet have in the way we want to have it; something lacking which we feel we need . . . Community, for most of us, means some sort of common identity in which we can maintain our personal freedom even while feeling at home with one another. (Rouner 1991, 1)

Religion responds to a human need to belong and encapsulates individuals in communities that become essential parts of those individuals' identities. It is both a private matter and a public experience, for religion helps fulfill individual identities as it confers a common identity. This integrative function is at the heart of Durkheim's classic definition of religion: "a unified system of beliefs and practices relative to sacred things . . . which unite within one single moral community called a church, all those who adhere to them" (Durkheim 1965, 62).

Participating in religious rituals and remembering stories of shared love and suffering binds individuals together, but this sort of community-making does not take place in absolute freedom. Religions and religious communities develop and persist in a context of constraints and opportunities. Churches shape the aspirations and behaviors of members as they themselves are guided by participants' thoughts and actions. Furthermore, individuals engaged in the creation and reformulation of their moral communities are also continually influenced by the wider social, political, and economic forces conditioning their lives (Bellah et al. 1991). Religious communities are thus evolving processes, the products of social interactions.

Chapter 3

This chapter examines the complicated interrelationships and emergent nature of religious community by looking at Unitarian Universalism, "the most freely unorthodox of the American religious movements" (Robinson 1985, xi). In particular, it explores how members of this liberal religion foster community change by self-consciously reinforcing community traditions.

Unitarian Universalism in the United States

The Unitarian Universalist approach to religious life is unique. This liberal faith inspires loyalty and encourages independence among its approximately two hundred thousand members nationwide. Sustenance and inspiration is drawn from such varied sources as Judaism, Christianity, and humanism; the "words and deeds of prophetic women and men"; and the "direct experience of that transcending mystery and wonder, affirmed in all cultures, which moves us to a renewal of the spirit and an openness to the forces which create and uphold life." Ultimately though, the "primary source of authority in religious matters . . . [lies with] each individual in conversation with tradition and in community with others" (Buehrens and Church 1989, x).

Unitarian Universalism has no explicit creed. It acknowledges that faith is formulated gradually and personally and is always undergoing modification. The essence of "UU" faith is captured in the following statement of purposes and principles enacted by the General Assembly in 1986.

> We, the member congregations of the Unitarian Universalist Association, covenant to affirm and promote:
>
> - The inherent worth and dignity of every person;
> - Justice, equity, and compassion in human relations;
> - Acceptance of one another and encouragement to spiritual growth in our congregations;
> - A free and responsible search for truth and meaning;
> - The rights of conscience and the use of the democratic process within our congregations and in society at large;
> - The goal of world community with peace, liberty, and justice for all;
> - Respect for the interdependent web of all existence of which we are a part.

Traditions and Changes

Church polity is primarily congregational, as the authority to exercise rule over the church resides with the membership. Thus, every local congregation and fellowship group chooses its own minister, draws up its own bylaws, establishes its own lay-led governance, and provides support for its own programs and staff, in accordance with democratic principles.

The theological freedom and individualism that characterize contemporary Unitarian Universalism evolved out of the histories of two separate religious movements that merged in 1960. They had much in common. Both Unitarianism and Universalism arose in New England in the early nineteenth century. They both rebelled against Calvinism, challenging its doctrine of predestination which held that an individual's salvation was predetermined by God before her birth. Both rejected the Calvinistic claim about the depravity of human nature and offered instead a new climate of optimism and hope. Early Universalists preached "universal salvation," and their Unitarian counterparts emphasized individual self-determination and the benevolence of God. They also rejected the concept of the Trinity, arguing that it was impossible for God to be simultaneously the Father, Son, and Holy Spirit.

Another link between the two movements was acceptance of religious freedom unencumbered by adherence to creeds. Influenced by Enlightenment thinking, both proposed to subject the Bible to historical and literary criticism and rational analysis rather than accept its teachings on faith. A review of the distinctive origins and characteristics of each clarifies another important similarity. Starting in the late 1700s, what it meant to be Universalist or Unitarian was continually renegotiated and redefined. The separate yet related historical paths of these two denominations provide a contextual understanding of the "living tradition" of contemporary Unitarian Universalism.

Unitarianism[1]

Unitarianism developed primarily within the well-established Congregational churches of the "Standing Order" in New England, as members split over theological and organizational concerns in the late 1700s and early 1800s. Initially identifying themselves simply as "Liberal Christians," the first Unitarians were an elite group of generally wealthy, well-educated, and socially important individuals who had a growing faith in the ability of mankind to control its destiny (Cassara 1970). They

Chapter 3

departed from Calvinism, which had dominated New England for nearly two centuries, arguing that the doctrines of original sin, eternal punishment, and the Trinity were both unscriptural and irrational. By the end of the eighteenth century, liberal criticisms of various aspects of Calvinism within Congregationalism had become fairly common. However, few believed that the growing diversity of opinion threatened the unity of the Congregational churches.

The seriousness of the rift between the liberals and the orthodox became clearer by the first decade of the nineteenth century. A precipitating event was the transition of Harvard College, "a veritable cornerstone of Calvinism and the New England Standing Order" (Forman 1989, 8), from orthodox to liberal control. In very close votes, the Corporation and Board of Overseers of the college chose liberals to fill several key appointments—namely, the Hollis Professorship of Divinity in 1805 and the college presidency in 1806. While instruction in religion at Harvard was officially nonsectarian, orthodox Congregationalists concluded that the college was no longer an appropriate place for its seminarians to receive training. To compensate, the orthodox founded the Andover Seminary in 1807.

The Unitarian controversy in Congregationalism intensified when William Ellery Channing delivered his famous "Unitarian Christianity" sermon in 1819. In this talk prepared for the induction of fellow liberal (and Harvard-educated) Jared Sparks as minister of the new Unitarian Church in Baltimore, Channing summarized the particular issues that united the liberals and separated them from their conservative colleagues. He first explained that the Bible had to be interpreted by reason and could not be accepted simply on faith. Embracing the name Unitarian, he then went on to argue that the correct understanding of the Scriptures taught the unity and moral perfection of God, the moral perfectibility of mankind, and universal love. Each of these positions contradicted Calvinist doctrine, and together they served to identify the liberals as a discrete theological group.

The theological positions outlined by Channing contributed to a structural separation already underway. As members of the established Congregational churches split between orthodox and liberal positions, disagreements arose over which group would retain control of the original church records, property, and buildings. In 1821 a legal ruling over such a dispute in Dedham, Massachusetts, upheld the two-part argument that those who withdrew themselves from a church (even if they were

Traditions and Changes

the majority) became uncovenanted and that those who stayed behind (even if they were the minority) retained the rights and property of the church. Given that most of the splits involved the withdrawal of orthodox rather than liberal members, this ruling meant that many formerly orthodox, "Standing Order" churches became Unitarian. In 1825 the Unitarian identity and cause were further solidified by the formation of the American Unitarian Association (AUA).

In the decades from 1835 to 1865, Unitarians sought to put their "pure and rational Christianity" into practice. Members of this numerically small denomination made enormous contributions in the areas of education, literature, and politics, and many worked to end slavery and to promote social welfare and prison reform. Unitarianism was characterized by "complete mental freedom, unrestricted reason, and general tolerance of differences, in religion" (Cassara 1970, 486). Unitarian identity seemed secure, but as Unitarians worked to change the world, attempts were made from within the ranks to change Unitarianism itself.

Starting in the 1830s, a "New School" of religious liberals who called themselves Transcendentalists challenged the standard Unitarian commitment to rationality and reason. This theologically radical group, which included such intellectual and literary greats as George Bancroft, Ralph Waldo Emerson, Margaret Fuller, Theodore Parker, and Henry David Thoreau, claimed instead that religion "was properly a matter of intuition, emotion, and faith" (Howe 1989, 44). The Transcendentalists saw and felt God everywhere, in nature and in themselves. The division between the two parties of Unitarianism was widened significantly by Emerson's 1838 address to the graduating class at Harvard Divinity School, in which he argued that organized religion (including traditional Unitarianism) was a "second-hand" force that prevented people from having direct access to God.

Emerson, a former student at the Divinity School, had chosen to resign from the ministry in 1832 rather than continue to administer some of the rituals of Unitarian services. His public address was correctly understood by his supporters and critics as an indictment of Unitarian clergy as well as a rejection of doctrinal positions. Emerson dismissed the scriptural accounts of ancient miracles as irrelevant, and instead urged individuals to seek and love God directly by communing with nature "without mediator or veil" (Howe 1989, 47).

Orthodox critics responded in various ways to Emerson's attempt to redefine the Unitarian theological enterprise. One pointed out that

Chapter 3

God could not be equated with the nature and beauty that he had created. Another argued that the pantheism of Emerson and the Transcendentalists attributed Christian qualities to what was actually just nature worship. A third criticized Emerson's substitution of personal intuition and inspiration for scriptural revelation. Although Emerson, busy building a new career for himself outside denominational affairs, refused to answer these criticisms, the controversy was kept alive by others who subscribed to Transcendentalist ideals. Each side accused the other of misrepresentation and misunderstanding.

The denomination was further tested in 1841 when Theodore Parker delivered an ordination sermon entitled *The Transient and Permanent in Christianity*. Parker used this opportunity to outline Transcendentalist principles as well as a naturalistic religion that retained the "valid core" of Christianity while discarding "unnecessary" church practices. According to Parker, those things that varied in religion—the transient—were creeds, confessions, and doctrines, including the scriptures and the divinity of Christ. What was permanent in Christianity was its essence, a pure morality described by Parker as "the divine life of the soul" as manifested in "love to God, and love to man" (Robinson 1985, 81). Like Emerson, Parker placed religious intuition above the Bible.

Parker extended the liberal principles of reasoned scriptural interpretation, dogmatic skepticism and religious individualism that had guided the Unitarian break from Calvinism. But doing so put him at odds with the liberal tradition that had been his home. While declaring himself to be a Unitarian, he went beyond what many of his Unitarian colleagues considered to be acceptable boundaries of their tradition. As a consequence, the mainly Unitarian Boston Association of Ministers asked for his resignation. Parker refused, further testing his colleagues' commitment to the ideals of free inquiry and noncreedal thought. Ultimately the association decided not to pursue excommunication, and thus Parker "won" a victory of sorts for liberalism.[2]

His victory was somewhat tempered by the AUA's declaration in 1853 that "The divine authority of the Gospel, as founded on a special and miraculous interposition of God for the redemption of mankind, is the basis of the action of this Association" (Howe 1989, 55). Because the AUA was an organization of individuals and not a delegate body of Unitarian churches, it had no way of enforcing this quasi-creed. Over the course of the next several decades, the 1853 declaration was gradually forgotten and the schism threatened by the Transcendental "rebellion" was averted.

Traditions and Changes

The last third of the nineteenth century was a time of increased organizational activity and membership growth for the denomination. Unitarianism spread to the west coast, and the First National Conference of Unitarian Churches was held in 1865. At the same time, disagreements and questions about Unitarian identity persisted among those with different theological positions. Some of the more conservative members, searching for a more structured, evangelical mode of worship, left Unitarianism for more traditional Protestant bodies. Many radical members at the other end of the theological spectrum were also dissatisfied with organized Unitarianism.

Several years after the first Conference, a small group of radicals acted on their dissatisfaction by creating "a forum for the expression of more advanced ideas than [Christian-based] Unitarianism seemed ready to accept"—the Free Religious Association (Wright 1989, 72). Consensus on a theological identity remained elusive even within the F.R.A., for its members—many of whom maintained their denominational standing—split themselves between the "intuitional" school of free religion which was influenced by Transcendentalism, and the "scientific" school of free religion which subjected statements of faith to scientific analysis. F.R.A. members met regularly for about ten years before the association quietly ended, after their lively debates about unstructured, free religion had helped to define the boundaries of the denomination.

Issues of Unitarian identity were further sharpened during the first three decades of the twentieth century by religious humanism, a movement "of a piece with Transcendentalism and Free Religion" (Robinson 1985, 152). Participants in this influential movement centered religion on humanity rather than on God and advocated "science against supernaturalism, democracy against tyranny, reason against superstition, [and] experience against revelation" (Parke 1989, 111). Despite their obvious differences with Unitarian theists, religious humanists enriched the denomination through their emphasis on human values. What ultimately undermined the humanist movement was its inability to reconcile belief in the perfectibility of humanity with the human tragedies taking place in the war-torn 1930s. Many Unitarians attacked humanism as an inadequate vehicle for sustaining religious belief and ethical action. Furthermore, individuals within and outside the denomination criticized liberal religion—and liberalism itself—for allowing individualism and freedom to develop selfishly, unattached from a commitment to society and justice.

The denominational introspection stimulated by humanism did

Chapter 3

not resolve the difficulties of balancing individual needs and organizational demands. In the decades leading up to the 1961 merger with Universalism, the issues of individualism, unity, freedom of thought, and moral commitment continued to be sources of denominational focus. These matters are still under negotiation today.

Universalism[3]

Both the early Unitarians and Universalists struggled against the Calvinism of the established churches, but the religious emphases and social origins of these two movements were very different. Unlike their fellow liberals, Universalists believed in an all-inclusive, radical vision of universal salvation. The position that everyone goes to heaven after death set them apart from Unitarians and evoked "violent opposition from evangelical and Calvinist groups who saw the abandonment of doctrines of eternal punishment as an invitation to moral degeneracy and possibly damnation" (Robinson 1985, 48). In 1779 when the first Universalist church was organized in Gloucester, Massachusetts, both the preacher and the members of the congregation were denounced as heretics. Excluded from the Christian mainstream, they were also considered political dissidents because of their relations with various sects dedicated to the separation of church and state. As a result, early Universalist history involved struggles for both theological tolerance and political rights.

Universalists in general had little formal education, and usually developed their religious beliefs on their own by reading the Scriptures or by talking with friends and neighbors. Learned guidance was considered unnecessary, for "In their view, the Holy Spirit operated freely among men and needed not the trappings of the schools" (Miller 1979, 5). Furthermore, many Universalists feared that formal (understood as uniform) training for preachers threatened the diversity of the early movement.

Traveling preachers, "strolling mendicants" who lacked official clerical status, helped spread Universalism up and down the northeast/central seaboard area. Denominational organization began in 1790, when a unifying general meeting of the perhaps two dozen organized Universalist societies was held in Philadelphia. The wide variation in delegates' thinking was reflected in the very general quality of the

Traditions and Changes

meeting's articles, and "given the diversity of views . . . (a characteristic of Universalism from the beginning), no part of this plan [or these articles] was binding" (Howe 1993, 12).

The Convention of Universalists gradually shifted its annual meetings to New England, where many denominational leaders and members were located. At the 1803 New England Convention (as the annual assembly was now called), three articles of faith were adopted, but only after considerable debate. Disagreement did not center on what the articles affirmed (scriptural revelation, universal salvation, and "good works"), but only on the issue of whether any creedal statement at all was tolerable. The accepted solution was the addition of the "Liberty clause" which encouraged member churches and societies to adopt as well "more particular articles of faith . . . as may appear to them best under their particular circumstances provided that they do not disagree with [the] general Profession . . ." (Howe 1993, 21).

Universalism grew rapidly during the first half of the nineteenth century, to include more than 850 societies and thousands of adherents. For much of this time, a potentially divisive debate was brewing between the *Ultra-Universalists* and the *Restorationists*. The former believed that punishment was experienced on earth and that there was no punishment in the afterlife, while the latter believed that the souls of the dead went through some form of necessary purification in hell before ascending to heaven. The controversy erupted in 1831 when a small group of Restorationists broke from the denomination and created a religious community dedicated to the original doctrines of Revelation.

This group, calling itself the Massachusetts Association of Universal Restorationists, argued "that Regeneration—a general Judgement, Future Rewards, and Punishments, to be followed by the final Restoration of mankind to holiness and happiness, are fundamental articles of Christian faith, and that the modern sentiments of No-Future accountability, connected with Materialism, are unfriendly to pure religion and subversive to the best interests of society" (Howe 1993, 38). After only ten annual meetings these Restorationists quietly ended their Association and mission, perhaps because most Universalists seemed uninterested in the controversy. By 1850 Ultra-Universalism was also on the wane. After the deaths of charismatic personalities associated with the two sides, the restorationist view was gradually accepted by most members of the denomination.

Chapter 3

In the years preceding the Civil War, Universalism seemed engaged "in cautious and often painful transition from pietistic, evangelical and biblical roots to a more liberal and rationally grounded faith" (Robinson 1985, 65). When the American Universalists celebrated their centennial in 1870, they recognized that they shared many ideas and goals with Unitarians. Class and education differences, however, continued to keep them apart. The Universalists appeared too unrefined for the Unitarians, while Unitarian resistance to the idea of universal salvation separated them from the Universalists. Most felt that union was impossible, perhaps because as Thomas Starr King—an important Unitarian leader born and trained in the Universalist tradition—observed, "The Universalist . . . believes that God is too good to damn [them] forever; and . . . Unitarians believe [they] are too good to be damned" (Robinson 1985, 98).

In contrast to the Unitarians who constantly engaged in doctrinal debates (and thus identity questions), Universalists associated themselves with the single defining doctrine of universal salvation throughout most of the nineteenth century. As the century came to an end, though, another meaning of the term *Universalist* gained acceptance among members and began to broaden the identity of the denomination. "In this secondary meaning, *Universalist* came to refer not to the fact of salvation for all but to the all-inclusive quality (or potential) of the Universalist church" (Robinson 1985, 124). This sense of Universalism seemed to inspire a progressive element that sought closer ties between the denomination and other liberal religions, a move that troubled conservative Universalists. Tension was eased at the final General Convention of the nineteenth century when the Universalists simultaneously affirmed the faith's "essential principles"[4] and clarified that no precise form of these principles was a condition of membership. As it had a century earlier, the denomination resolved questions about its identity by reinforcing its characteristic individualism.

In the first decades of the new century, Universalism focused increasing attention on the "Social gospel," a Protestant movement concerned with the conditions of society. Economic turmoil, labor unrest, political scandal, agrarian problems, urban poverty, and the unequal distribution of wealth were addressed through "a message of compassion, hope and reform" (Robinson 1985, 133). The social gospel emphasized connections between religious ethics, politics, and social reform, and encouraged Universalists (and Unitarians as well) to reconceptualize individualism and personal development as responsibility to serve others. The humanist controversy of the 1930s also contributed to this notion of service: problems need to be solved, regardless of whether there is a divine being somewhere out there.

Increasingly, denominational members recognized links between "Universalism as theological doctrine" and "Universalism as a working philosophy aimed at securing the universal harmony of all individuals on earth" (Robinson 1985, 140). This kind of insight was important because Universalists were still struggling to come to terms with the "wrenching" years after World War I when membership declined and many churches closed. Influencing these developments was the fact that Universalism's distinction was fading as other Protestant churches replaced the idea of hell with the idea of universal salvation.

The Merger

Seeking greater relevance, Universalists began to explore and support a theology of social action that underscored global unity and religious universals. In 1946 a small group of ministers called for the "universalizing of Universalism," which would be accomplished by transforming the denomination "into a religion for one world, which, while honoring its Christian origins, nevertheless would welcome the truths of other religions on an equal basis" (Howe 1993, 112). The enthusiasm generated by these internal developments was not shared by all and proved to be temporary. The number of Universalists nationwide continued to decline.

At the same time, Universalists continued a collaboration begun in the 1920s with Unitarians on such projects as joint hymnals and religious education materials. The possibility of merger, which had been raised several times during the preceding century, became a serious point of discussion between committees from the Universalist Church of America and the American Unitarian Association. Finding "no insuperable obstacles," the committees presented to the Universalists' 1949 General Assembly a joint resolution recommending a process that would lead to a federal union based on "freedom of faith and congregational polity" (Howe 1993, 119).

The resolution was accepted and, even though a number of Universalist churches polled on the question of merger expressed concern, merger activities proceeded. As provided in the resolution, the two denominations established both a joint council to oversee combined services in religious education, public relations, and publications, and a joint committee to report on merger activities. In 1955, observing that

Chapter 3

"the Unitarians and Universalists hold enough in common to become one people," this committee recommended speedy consolidation of the two liberal churches (Howe 1993, 120).

In 1960, the majority of both Universalists and Unitarians voted to join together to form the Unitarian Universalist Association (UUA). This merger, made official on May 11, 1961, demonstrated that "Unitarians had moved beyond their humanist-theist controversy . . . Universalists had moved beyond their exclusively Christian orientation . . . [and] both bodies had become more willing to accept diversity within their ranks (Howe 1993, 125). It also revealed that the sort of class distinctions and theological arguments that previously separated the two denominations had faded.

Initial tensions and fears regarding the merger gradually subsided as members formerly associated with each denomination developed a genuine appreciation for the richness of the new religious partnership. Most Unitarian Universalists, including "newcomers" who are unfamiliar with the histories of their chosen denomination, consider themselves members of a unified religious tradition. Unitarian Universalism has come to mean social concern for all people and acceptance of all beliefs, free from mental and spiritual coercion. It is a faith that is continually renewed and reformed by its members.

The "Welcoming Congregation" Program

The Unitarian Universalist Association, committed to a wide range of social justice activities, has actively supported the lesbian, gay, and bisexual communities in their struggle for equal rights during the last three decades. In ten separate resolutions since 1970, the General Assembly has voted to institute nondiscriminatory hiring practices within the organization and to support the placement of openly gay, lesbian, and bisexual ministers; to encourage ministers to conduct services of union for same-gender couples; to create the Office of Lesbian and Gay Concerns within the UUA (now the Office of Lesbian, Bisexual, & Gay Concerns—OLBGC) and to support the membership organization of Unitarian Universalists for Lesbian and Gay Concerns (UULGC); and to advocate for the rights of persons with AIDS and those who are HIV-positive.

The most recent resolution dedicated to the inclusion and affirmation of gay, lesbian, and bisexual persons was enacted in 1989 by the

Traditions and Changes

UUA General Assembly and established the "Welcoming Congregation" program. This initiative involves a self-guided, 15-step process to be used by those congregations interested in expanding their memberships to include lesbian, bisexual, and gay persons. However, more than social outreach was behind the development of the "Welcoming Congregation" program. Its creation also had to do with denominational commitment to the fundamental principles of "the inherent worth and dignity of every person" and "justice, equity and compassion in human relations." As the initiative authors observed, "despite a long and luminous tradition of leadership towards an era of wide justice, inclusion and recognition of the dignity and worth of all, still the fear of same-sex love runs deep among Unitarian Universalists." In a very direct way, the initiative focuses on what it means to be a Unitarian Universalist.

In 1994, the fifth year anniversary of the Welcoming Congregation program, the on-going battle over civil rights for lesbians, gays and bisexuals was covered in the July/August issue of the UUA journal WORLD. Included were articles about hate crimes, anti-gay-rights referenda across the nation, alternatives to the traditional Christian view of sexuality, the national support group called Parents and Friends of Lesbians and Gays (PFLAG), and also a photo essay about same-sex unions. This issue stimulated more letters and phone calls from readers than has any other in the journal's history. A representative sample of the letters was published in the November/December issue of WORLD. According to the editors, the entire collection of letters was split evenly between supporters and critics of the program.

Many of the supporters congratulated the editors for "an outstanding issue" and thanked them for their "high quality and creative work." One subscriber wrote that the issue made him proud to be a Unitarian Universalist and noted that "Even in these days of welcoming congregations, facing down homophobia takes courage, vision, and compassion." The journal's attention to gay-bashing, although "painful," was welcomed by at least one reader as a stimulant to become more socially active. Several praised the leadership role taken by the UUA and the journal regarding gay rights, with one observing that "As usual, UUs are a beacon, lighting a path through the darkness for others."

Negative comments targeted both homosexuality and the UUA. One critic, while supportive of gay rights, decried "their bashing on straight people all the time" and called for an end of "preaching." Another acknowledged that homosexuals "do not deserve . . . disrespect"

Chapter 3

but also registered disgust at the WORLD's "publicly flaunting their abnormality." In one church the issue caused "great distress and damage;" some members resigned, and others experienced discomfort as "homosexualism enter[ed] their intellectual environment." The author of this letter went on to clarify that "the members of the church do not advocate, or condone, hatred of anyone—so long as 'anyone' does not intrude upon the privacy and peace of mind of others." The editors were blasted for publishing "a propaganda blast in favor of homosexuality" and thereby betraying the UU commitment to the "free and responsible search for truth." A different writer requested immediate cancellation of his subscription because he was offended by "the UUA's pushing and forcing acceptance [of homosexual lifestyles] on our churches and their members."

The existence of such a range of opinions among members of the denomination is not surprising. After all, UUs joke among themselves that their church is the one that agrees to disagree and that for members, to question is the answer.[5] Throughout their individual histories both Unitarians and Universalists showed themselves to be nonconforming, liberal, and dissatisfied with traditional religion. In their separate pasts and also since unification in 1961, they have demonstrated a willingness to accept differing views, a commitment to social action, and a desire for self-improvement. This "implicit creed"[6] serves two purposes, purposes that potentially oppose and reinforce each other. Not only does it provide a bond that unites members within the "living tradition" of Unitarian Universalism, it also encourages independence by underscoring the value and autonomy of each individual.

In many ways, Unitarian Universalists are unique. Believing in individual freedom, reason, and responsibility, they encourage understanding and acceptance of differing views and practices. Yet as the letters to the editors of WORLD illustrate, this distinctive shared identity is fluid and contested. For further insight into the contingent stability and ever-present change that characterize the denomination—and community in general, we can "listen" to what members of one New England congregation have to say about the meaning and goals of Unitarian Universalism.

Formalizing the Diversity of Community

The particular congregation that is the focus of the last part of this chapter was formed in 1952 when the Unitarian Church in a small

Traditions and Changes

New England town was incorporated into its Universalist counterpart. Both denominations had influenced the town's Protestant life during the 1800s and early decades of the 1900s, but by the early 1940s Unitarianism had all but disappeared. Unable to keep their church afloat during the Depression, local Unitarians first gave their pulpit furniture and communion set to their Universalist colleagues and then joined other local churches. During this same period, the Universalist Church flourished and solidified its position within the town's mainline Protestant community.

The Universalists were led by a minister who, like many nationwide, had ties to both denominations and wanted to advance the cause of unification. In support of their minister, the congregation voted to merge with the local Unitarians. This group of Unitarians, just a handful of individuals, voted to "join the Universalist Church . . . provided that both Universalist and Unitarian names [were] included in the title."[7] Given that the local Unitarian Church had been dead for years, this action was largely symbolic. There was one practical consequence, however. Because the Universalists hosted the union, the now expanded church was renamed the Universalist Unitarian Church.

This "new" congregation was distinctive because of its name and also because it was formed before the 1961 national merger. Generally, though, the congregation followed national patterns during the next forty years. It experienced both a sharp decline in membership during the early 1970s and a steady subsequent increase. A self-administered survey conducted in 1988 revealed other traits similar to the national UU profile: three out of four members were college graduates, nearly 70 percent were raised in other faiths, and slightly more than half were "newcomers" to the church.

The congregation describes itself as "a community that is searching for truth, struggling for justice, and [one] whose members would live in loving relationship with one another." Members agree to "be tolerant of each other in our varied understandings of the religious life"; to "take responsibility, personally and socially, for the world in which we live"; and to "contribute to the on-going life of the group."[8] By the mid-1990s, the congregation numbered approximately 140 individuals.

Generally speaking, members of this church are proud to be involved in social causes. In recent years, they have provided a "home" for the first rape crisis hotline in the area, developed an evening sandwich program that provides for hundreds of local families, and played a leading role in an antidiscrimination movement that successfully

Chapter 3

blocked a state ballot initiative designed to restrict the civil rights of lesbian, bisexual, and gay individuals. Such activities reveal an important shift in the way these Universalist Unitarians think of themselves.

Like many who belonged to the Universalist Church and to the Universalist Unitarian Church after 1952, current members are oriented towards "making life meaningful" and contributing to the community. However, unlike their predecessors who were clearly integrated into the religious mainstream, members today believe their church is an important sanctuary offering relief and alternatives to townspeople, "a haven in a heartless world."

Between September 1995 and April 1996 I met with dozens of church members and the current minister in informal focus groups to discuss the meaning of their religion and the character of their own church. What united Unitarians and Universalists in the past, and what continues to bind church members together today, are "shared values." However, the following comments demonstrate that individual members interpret and act on such values in different ways.

"It's Not Easy Being a U-U": Congregational Reflections

Unitarian Universalists have a fundamental faith in the individual and also recognize that various responsibilities are attached to their valued freedom. According to a lifelong Unitarian woman, a person who wants freedom and choices must grant those same privileges to everyone else. Part of what this involves is truly listening to others and openly accepting their views and actions. As she wrote in her journal,

> U-U's believe in a kind of freedom which does *not* interfere with that of others, and yet which does not send each individual off alone all of the time to do his or her own thing. Certainly that does happen, but it is not the total experience. We feel free to be by ourselves or just to be ourselves, unfettered by the expectations or stereotypes too often imposed by family, job, community or friends, but it is a freedom which remembers to allow the same conditions to others.

UUs generally acknowledge the importance of freedom of expression, observing that it is a natural result of their distinctive, non-creedal,

Traditions and Changes

and open faith. Many also point out that "members are obligated to form opinions and to act on them." One couple clarified this by saying that "arriving at a particular set of beliefs is not the goal, it is being there and being open that is what [Unitarian Universalism] is all about." This process of involving "all in participating by having their say" is important, for it engenders a sense of ownership in the church community and of the faith. But the result is also important, and repeatedly the desired goal of Unitarian Universalism is summed up in one word: diversity.

Lifelong Unitarian Universalists calmly accept the value of questioning and then doing something about almost everything. Newcomers to the denomination generally find such a proactive, antiauthoritarian stance very exciting, and they sometimes become impatient with old-timers who simply take it for granted. Usually, though, the old-timers succeed in forcing the newcomers to contemplate and internalize the overall process of questioning, challenging, and acting.

Old-timers and newcomers—those born into the faith and those who have joined from other traditions[9]—feel connected. One woman who grew up in the denomination put it this way: "there is an instant bond between [us], connective feelings between common threads of belief, a recognition of the shared tendency towards liberalism." This liberal tendency involves the acceptance of diverse viewpoints and encourages personal expression of religious faith. Another woman who recently joined the church suggested that "what unites [us] is the determination to let people go their own way." For all, such connections are a source of both pleasure and freedom. They also provide the assurance that support and care will always be available, "whatever goes wrong."

Others argued that the "glue" bonding members of the congregation together is "activism, compassion, and social concern." UUs share a desire to make meaningful contributions to the larger community. Members tend to agree that "being a UU pushes one out into the community and into service," and also that for them, "church is where you carry on traditions and get involved in civic activities." One middle-aged man who joined the congregation ten years ago summed things up this way: "One knows one is 'home' in the church by listening to the announcements, by watching how people interact, by seeing the care and respect . . . It's a place where what people do matters."

A sense of humor is a valued trait among UUs, many of whom try not to take themselves "too seriously." When it comes to responding to the common accusation that UUs don't believe in anything, however, most are very serious. Speaking for a small group, one person defended

Chapter 3

the denomination in this way: "UUs *do believe*, in the basic principles. The questioning and continual searching is very important to us, but this is also troublesome to many non-UUs. Its harder to be a UU because there isn't the safety of a strict dogma." Rather, "the safety net is the people." Unitarian Universalism relies on the self-confidence and strengths of individual members.

Members frequently speak of community within the church, describing it as "respect," "caring change," and "something that people have in common." Church community is like family in that "it is what one can call on in emergencies." Community is understood as necessary. For some, this boils down to needing to "have a church," for "the church reinforces one's sense of self and brings out one's better self." Others question whether these important functions are limited to a church setting: "If I didn't have this church community, I would have to find community elsewhere, maybe not even in a church . . ." Most, however, agreed that everyone becomes more alive in community, that community and sharing provide an essential opportunity "for each of us individually to be a person."

In many people's minds, community is a safe place where people can "risk connecting with others" and are free to express themselves. What is not acknowledged as frequently is that the kind of openness encouraged in and by community can foster disagreements. Dealing with difference and disagreement is an important task, and not because quarrels as such threaten the existence of a community. Rather, as one individual observed, what can prevent or destroy true community is an unwillingness on the part of members to commit themselves to working with each other through any and all conflicts and problems. Being tolerant by adopting a "live and let live" approach to others is what community is all about, the same individual pointed out: members of a community cannot come and go as they please. Community is a full time responsibility, requiring commitment, compassion, and sometimes painful adjustment, as well as continual learning on the part of everyone.

Aware of the Welcoming Congregation program and of prejudice and ignorance regarding gay, lesbian, and bisexual persons, the minister encouraged five church members to attend a Fall 1993 Welcoming Congregation workshop organized by the UUA District Office. Shortly after completing the intensive training session, these volunteers offered to initiate the program in their home church—an offer endorsed by the board. The volunteers, now formally recognized as the Welcoming Congregation Committee, organized their first abbreviated version of the Welcoming Congregation workshop for the church leadership (including board members and chairs of committees) in March 1994.

A second workshop was offered in March 1995, and again participants were asked to commit themselves to the full eight hours spread over four weeks. As had happened in the first workshop, the second initially generated discomfort, fear, and anger as individuals explored personal feelings and societal norms concerning homosexuality and bisexuality. At the start, individuals "did not know how much to trust each other," but "this progressed as they let themselves become vulnerable." Both workshops stimulated honest discussion about the effects homophobia and heterosexism have on Unitarian Universalists of all sexual orientations. Those who took part in these two workshops admitted that there was a lag time before the "learnings" and insights of the workshop registered, and that the process of making connections required personal pain and hard work. All agreed that it was worth such discomfort.

Other members of the congregation who had not gone through either Welcoming Congregation workshop broadened their understandings of the experiences of gay, lesbian, and bisexual people by volunteering their time to help defeat an anti-gay measure in the fall 1995 election. For months, the church building served as "command central" for this successful grassroots effort, and this helped to keep congregational attention on the issues of homosexuality, bisexuality, and social justice. The minister, who strongly supported the Welcoming Congregation program, was on an eight-month sabbatical leave during much of 1995. Despite this physical absence, members of the congregation generally agree that the minister consistently led on this issue (by letting others lead) and by allowing members to decide whether to become a Welcoming Congregation.

Not all members of the congregation supported the Welcoming Congregation Program wholeheartedly, even though all subscribed to the goals of diversity and acceptance. Some were uncertain about the need to "single out the les-bi-gay community" for inclusion, suggesting instead that it might be more appropriate to "focus on all communities." Interest in both the Welcoming Congregation initiative and in social justice for gay, lesbian, and bisexual individuals was countered by resentment over the amount of time devoted to these issues. The Welcoming

Chapter 3

Congregation Committee offered to help incorporate gay, lesbian, and bisexual life issues into the church's religious education program, but a few parents seemed uncomfortable with what they interpreted as having to "give up their control over their kids."

Early in 1996 the Welcoming Congregation Committee and the minister proposed that the congregation vote to seek certification as a "Welcoming Congregation" at the church's upcoming annual meeting in May. During the preceding winter, a few congregational members committed to the program were discouraged by what they interpreted as persistent undercurrents of homophobia. But others remained optimistic, largely because the Welcoming Congregation Committee had "done its homework."

By March 1996, all of the 15 action plans recommended for UUA certification as a "Welcoming Congregation" had been addressed, and all but a few were completed. Committee members made themselves available on a regular basis after Sunday services to discuss the program and certification, but church members did not have many questions. In the final weeks leading up to the May meeting and vote, several individuals thought that the real problems would be "getting a quorum [so that a vote can be taken] *and* getting people to vote thoughtfully" because "many will probably vote yes without asking questions."

After an abbreviated service on May 19, 1996, more than half of the members of the Universalist Unitarian Church gathered for their annual meeting. The Welcoming Congregation was the first item on the agenda. There was no discussion, and when the question of whether to seek certification was moved, there was no dissension. The unanimous vote to become a Welcoming Congregation represents to many what Unitarian Universalism is all about, and simply formalizes the de facto openness that characterizes the denomination. For other members, the vote symbolizes the aspirations of their church and stands as a pledge to encourage specific values and actions among members. However this vote is interpreted, the congregation appears ready to grow into whatever it will become.

Conclusions: The Living Tradition of Religious Community

The symbolic and organizational boundaries of the Unitarian Universalist community suggest a collective identity that clearly distinguishes

Traditions and Changes

between members and non-members. However, setting the community's boundaries and defining what Unitarian Universalism means are contested activities, partly due to differences within the community and in part "because there is no bright line between its foreign affairs and its domestic relations" (Austin 1992, 1770). Indeed, as this account of a particular congregation reveals, pressures from without and challenges from within appear inevitable and inevitably produce continuous community change.

In general, the varied histories of Unitarian Universalists are a vital element in the denomination's "sometimes tortured search for an identity," for members ultimately come to know who they are only "by understanding who they have been" (Robinson 1992, 3, 4). "Tales" from the past are part of the cultural capital used by new and old members in defining who they are (Kasinitz and Hillyard 1995). All who belong to this "living tradition" are able to participate in the "common project" of continuous examination and reinterpretation of the present and the past (Bellah et al. 1985), but those who participate do so in different ways and for different reasons. These variations and tensions ensure that the community will have an open-ended identity. Furthermore, members continue to be changed by the very community they foster and negotiate. Unitarian Universalism is the creation of both free-spirited individualists and more conservative traditionalists, and members respond to the denomination's historical emphases on both individualism and community.

Membership and participation in community offers each person "a form of life through which . . . identity is fulfilled" (Bellah et al. 1985, 162). Community also provides the means for individuals to connect their own fulfillment with that of others. Both understanding and supporting community are important for religious communities like Unitarian Universalism because "community is the way in which the church gets things done" (Wuthnow 1993, 6). The work of a moral community like Unitarian Universalism involves shaping the way members comprehend the present and plan for the future, providing support and friendship, promoting an ethic of service, and fostering attachments to the wider society in which members live. But like any community, Unitarian Universalism is also a responsive entity, molded by the behaviors of individual members as well as by wider historical and cultural forces (Allen and Dillman 1994; Bell 1994; MacLeod 1995). Ultimately, then, Unitarian Universalism is always in process, the unfolding product of people's aspirations and actions.

Chapter 3

Notes

1. The following sources are important guides to Unitarian history: *A History of Unitarianism in Transylvania, England, and America* by Earl Morse Wilbur (Boston: Beacon Press, 1945); *The Unitarians and the Universalists* by David Robinson (Westport, CT: Greenwood Press, 1985); and *A Stream of Light*, ed. Conrad Wright (Boston: Skinner House Books, 1989).

2. Historian Perry Miller argues that the Unitarian battle over "Parkerism" was not a local denominational fight but was actually part of a larger national struggle with liberalism as a whole. See Perry Miller, *The Transcendentalists* (Cambridge, MA: Harvard University Press, 1950).

3. The following are important sources for Universalist history: *Universalism in America* by Ernest Cassara (Boston: Beacon Press, 1970); *The Larger Faith* by Charles A. Howe (Boston: Skinner House Books, 1993); *The Larger Hope* by Russell E. Miller (Boston: Unitarian Universalist Association, 1979); and *The Unitarians and the Universalists* by David Robinson (Westport, CT: Greenwood Press, 1985).

4. These five principles included: "The Universal Fatherhood of God; the spiritual authority and leadership of his Son Jesus Christ; the trustworthiness of the Bible as containing a revelation from God; the certainty of just retribution for sin; [and] the final harmony of all souls with God" (Howe 1993, 81–82).

5. These and other jokes by UUs about UUism are found in Lee 1992.

6. Richard Wayne Lee develops this notion of the "implicit creed" in *Unitarian Universalists: Organizational Dilemmas of the Cult of the Individual* (PhD. Dissertation, Sociology Department, Emory University, 1992).

7. Taken from an unofficial history of the church, personal copy.

8. Quotations are from materials compiled in 1988 by the church's Search Committee for the purpose of describing the congregation to applicants interested in becoming the new minister.

9. National surveys conducted in 1966 and 1987 revealed that well over 85 percent of Unitarian Universalists were "converts," or newcomers to the faith.

Chapter Four

CHANGING SPACES AND PLACES
Rent Control in Cambridge

A healthy community voices diversity in so many different ways, big and small. (Frantz and Collins 1999, 309)

Cambridge, Massachusetts, a city of 90,000 residents, controlled rents among its approximately 16,000 rental units from 1970 to 1994. The twenty-four years of Cambridge rent control were filled with conflict and struggle—over policy, politics, community identity, and the social control of space. This is a story about how both a controversial policy and the determination of community groups were shaped by unforeseen events and changing social relations. Details of Cambridge's rent-control years provide a picture of a particular stage in the history of a specific community, but they also have a wider significance.[1] Like the case of the Maine Indian communities presented in chapter 2, this particular story offers valuable insights into the fluid quality of community life. It is also a story that unfolded within a peculiar context. This chapter begins by outlining the controversies surrounding rent control.

The Rent-Control Debate

Throughout the fifty-odd-year history of rent control, debates have raged on the desirability, effectiveness, and legality of using this mechanism for regulating the scarce resource of affordable housing. Often viewed as a "key litmus test for identifying political candidates as conservative or liberal" (Dreier 1989, 50), rent controls have been the focal point in a battle over ideological beliefs and between competing visions of the kind of society deemed desirable and possible.

Chapter 4

However, the rent-control debate is *not* a simple two dimensional argument involving landlords and tenants. Relations between the various interest groups involved in urban housing issues are partly complementary and partly conflictual. Conceptualizing the rent-control debate as a straightforward struggle between two fixed and polarized sides—conservatives/landlords who support a laissez-faire approach and expend little direct attention on social welfare needs of citizens and radicals/tenants who advocate political management over community growth and development and active involvement in social service programs (see Feagin and Parker 1990)—obscures the variable and relational quality of the positions held by rent-control proponents and critics. In actuality, arguments on each "side" of this debate flow between need claims and rights assertions on the one hand and personal autonomy and collective identity on the other.

Rent control is perceived and experienced in very different ways by those who support it (often, but not only, tenants who occupy rent-controlled units) and those who oppose it (frequently, but not exclusively, landlords of rent-controlled properties). Additionally, disagreements concerning the effectiveness and legality of rent control are intensified not only by administrative structures, but also by stereotypical beliefs about landlords and tenants and by related arguments about citizen entitlements (to, for example, affordable housing) and rights (associated, for example, with owning private property).

The strategy of regulating the housing market by limiting rent increases was first introduced during World War I and adopted nationwide with the enactment of the Emergency Price Controls Act in 1942. This particular measure was designed in part to respond to a housing crisis fueled by two phenomena. Increased housing demand was causing rents to rise rapidly, and because of wartime restrictions on the construction of new buildings, the housing supply was not increasing. A somewhat modified version of the Act was passed in 1947, but with its expiration in 1952, most states—the notable exception being New York—phased out rent-control programs (Lett 1976). During the 1970s and 1980s, though, a widespread shortage of rental housing galvanized tenant groups across the country who successfully pushed for some form of rent stabilization in hundreds of communities.

Critics of rent control have said that the policy benefits too few of those who most need such assistance, that it is abused by many who do not need help, and that it forces those who do not use it (i.e., property owners) to pay for it. Arguments against this interventionist form of social planning claim that it discourages new construction (Downs 1983), leads to the undermaintenance, abandonment, demolition and conversion of rental housing (Hayek et al. 1983), and encourages discriminatory and illegal behaviors by both renters and owners seeking to exploit the system (Goetze 1983). Asserting that any short-run benefits associated with rent control are canceled out by its long-term disadvantages, rent control critics maintain that the policy unfairly penalizes owners of rent-control units and fails to help poor tenants because there is no requirement to rent to low-income people (Lowry 1970; Sternlieb and Hughes 1980; Block and Olsen 1981).

Supporters have argued that rent control does accomplish its primary purpose of reducing housing costs to levels more commensurate with tenants' ability to pay. They emphasize that it is a regulatory not a welfare program and that the monitoring of rent levels discourages evictions. In this way, supporters claim, rent control enhances neighborhood stability and contributes to urban diversity. Rent control is here conceptualized as an inclusive policy that makes it possible for a heterogeneous assortment of people to share desirable space by regulating both the costs and profits associated with housing (Achtenberg 1973; Gilderbloom 1981; Zarembka 1990; Capek and Gilderbloom 1992).

Because rent-control systems regulate the allowable rents for individual units in a private housing market and not the real or potential occupants of such units, their regulatory and redistributive effects are, as even supporters acknowledge, "far from perfect" (Achtenberg 1973, 556). Critics assert that rent control fosters a black market in controlled apartments, whereby units are handed on only to those who have the right connections, and that the pressure to obtain and retain a controlled unit contributes to a situation in which apartment space is regularly over- or underused and in which tenants in effect become hostage to their apartments. They argue that rent control violates individual constitutional rights and leads inexorably to the deterioration of the city's housing stock. Additionally, "ill conceived" local rent controls are seen as the cause not only of housing shortages but also of homelessness (Tucker 1987; 1990).

Supporters criticize such studies as politically motivated and methodologically unsound, and dismiss claims of a causal linkage between rent control and housing shortages (Appelbaum et al. 1991). As Achtenberg (1973, 434) noted, reasonable rent control systems have

Chapter 4

been "the most expedient short-term response the legal system has to offer in providing decent housing that the poor can afford." The free-enterprise approach so well established in American culture has not been responsive to the housing needs of all citizens and residents; the private sector cannot be relied upon to provide affordable housing (Capek and Gilderbloom 1992). Instead, "public intervention in the private market [is essential] in order to achieve [such] social welfare objectives" as protecting tenants from displacement, preserving a city's diversity and returning control over development to citizens (Stegman 1986, 50). Thus, advocates argue that rent-control programs should be strengthened in the face of attacks (Zarembka 1990).

Because tenants and landlords generally experience distinctly different economic realities, economic arguments fuel the rent-control debate. But the question "Who benefits?" demands consideration of more than just dollars and cents. As Niebanck (1985, 110-11) has pointed out, those researchers who simply perceive rent control as a "rationally chosen regulator used in situations that require regulating" consistently fail to acknowledge that a "locality's interest in rent control has at least as much to do with underlying cultural, socioeconomic, political, and ideological factors as it has to do with market conditions."[2]

Rent control, a frequent policy goal of tenant movements, represents a challenge to the dominant cultural value that ownership of property confers the right to determine how the costs and benefits of housing should be distributed. Furthermore, studies of the redistributional impacts of rent control laws indicate that lower rents additionally benefit tenants by facilitating greater neighborhood stability and diversity (Capek and Gilderbloom 1992, especially 181-83). More significantly, such findings raise the larger question of "whether rents should be controlled by a handful of landlords responsible to no one or by a representative government body accountable to the community"(Capek and Gilderbloom 1992, 264).

The initial justification for national rent-control policies was "that an emergency housing situation exists which needs to be addressed by the public control of rents" (Lett 1976, 28). However, from the start there was concern about who would use what criteria to define and declare an emergency housing situation. Furthermore, a consensus never developed on how to convert what had been initiated as a temporary, stopgap measure into a permanent regulatory policy. Supporters and critics of rent regulations basically agree on the desirability of housing policies that respond to economic and demographic changes in a community; they disagree that an institutionalized rent-control system is an appropriate means toward that end.

The reality of rent control—as temporary emergency measure and as official urban policy—is that it is both a housing program and "a tool for mobilizing social movement participation for broader goals" (Capek and Gilderbloom 1992, 252). Rent control is simultaneously an "ideological battleground," a "programmatic tool" and a "cultural habit" (Niebanck 1985, 117). Debates over its goals and outcomes are much more than "a hollow clash of extremes" in which "the arguments of either side pass each other, as proverbial ships in the night" (Niebanck 1985, 106). The variable and opposing positions describe a struggle to define the basic rights of individual residents (whether or not they own property) and to determine how people should live together, and they illustrate what Capek and Gilderbloom (1992) identify as a struggle between "community" and "commodity" perspectives on private property rights. These theoretical arguments and generic concerns are part of the history and reality of Cambridge, Massachusetts.

The Strange Career of Cambridge Rent Control[3]

In 1970 the Cambridge City Council[4] initiated citywide rent controls by voting 7–2 to adopt the Massachusetts Rent Control Statute.[5] Preconditions for this local initiative were established during the 1950s and 1960s as the Cambridge economy shifted. The number of blue-collar jobs steadily dropped while employment opportunities in defense work, social science and business consulting, architecture, and research and development increased dramatically. This shift away from manufacturing and industry precipitated an overall decline in the population of Cambridge while triggering a sharp increase in the number of young, frequently single and childless workers.

These demographic shifts intensified pressure on the available housing and threatened existing community neighborhoods. At the same time, federally sponsored urban-renewal projects in the city displaced many long-term tenants. A "siege mentality" among renters intensified as more tenants were forced to move into more expensive units or out of Cambridge altogether. According to one study completed

Chapter 4

in 1960, approximately five hundred persons and families were being evicted annually by rising rents (Mollenkopf and Pynoos 1973).

For years, the bulk of Cambridge rental housing had been owned and controlled by a relatively small number of property owners. These owners tended to work closely with the patronage-based city government to promote the development of luxury apartments and business facilities while ignoring the housing needs and concerns of most of the city's renters (Mollenkopf and Pynoos 1973). During the 1960s, this convergence of economic interests and political power resulted in an upward spiraling of rents.

In response, a cross-class coalition of blue-collar workers, shopkeepers, students, liberal professionals, and radical activists organized to oppose the escalating commercial development, to lobby for low-rent housing construction, and to agitate for citywide controls over rent increases. A collective effort to persuade the city council to pass a rent control ordinance failed in 1968; a successful signature drive for a referendum vote the following year was ultimately thwarted by the council's claim that the home-rule provisions of the state constitution prevented the city from voting on the matter. Switching tactics, the coalition of rent-control advocates focused attention on the state legislature and convinced it to pass the required enabling act in mid-1970. This success at the state level combined with a groundswell of local, pro-rent-control sentiment to intensify pressure on the elected city officials. Shortly thereafter, on September 17, 1970, the councillors voted to enact rent control provisions.

After giving the appearance of supporting rent control, however, the city council did little to ensure its success. In fact, during the first eighteen months of rent control, the property owner/city hall element sought to convert what had been a tenant-oriented system to its own advantage. This conversion was facilitated by loopholes in the 1970 act—such as the provision that the rent-control administrator would be appointed by the city manager. The then–city manager was staunchly opposed to rent control, and the first two-rent control administrators were like-minded. It is widely understood that each of these appointees arranged for the unilateral exemption of many rental property owners from the requirement to register their units with the city (and thus from the assignment of a controlled rent) and granted nearly automatic approval of most landlord requests for higher rents. Maintaining that the city's rent-control system was a failure (without acknowledging its own role in making it so), the lame duck city council voted to repeal the

Changing Spaces and Places

measure two days before the expiration of its term on December 30, 1971.

This vote was quickly reversed and rent control reinstated by the newly elected council on January 10, 1972. Over the course of the next two decades, Cambridge developed a moderately strong, well-entrenched rent control system. The governing city ordinance[6] covered mandatory registration,[7] general and individual rent adjustments,[8] apartment-to-condominium conversions,[9] and eviction proceedings.[10] It set rents using a formula that combined the fair cost of housing with a fair net operating income.[11] A five-member board composed of two tenants, two landlords, and a fifth "impartial" member (i.e., someone who neither owned nor lived in rent-controlled property) was appointed by the city council to decide, in weekly meetings, disputes between tenants and landlords of rent-controlled units and to enforce rent control policies.

For most of the first two decades of rent control, Cambridge voters kept the issue at the top of the political agenda and consistently elected councillors who split evenly on rent-control matters. The ninth ("independent") city councillor contributed to the standoff by alternating between pro- and anti-rent control positions. However, this uneven balance ended in Fall 1989 with the election of a pro-rent control majority of six. The election results galvanized both supporters and critics of rent control and intensified debate over the letter and spirit of the Cambridge ordinance.

Throughout the eighties, positions on rent control polarized as debates became more strident, dysfunctional, and argumentative. Two interest groups emerged as the "gladiators" in the rent-control controversy: the Cambridge Tenants Union (CTU) and the Small Property Owners Association (SPOA). The groups were not parallel, for while CTU was involved in a variety of policy issues, the sole mission of SPOA was the elimination of rent control. Neither group fully represented the range of perspectives held by either tenants or landlords, but both organizations earned public recognition as vital and diametrically opposed players.

CTU was founded in 1986. Many of the approximately five hundred members were longtime activists involved in city housing issues. In the decade preceding the establishment of CTU, these housing advocates aligned themselves with a range of political organizations and community groups concerned with housing issues; they came to see rent control as a necessary part of a more comprehensive approach to city planning. CTU, worried about the displacement pressure on tenants arising from a

Chapter 4

combination of legally increased rents, a resistance among many landlords to rent to low-income tenants and a shrinking pool of affordable rental units, called for better enforcement of rent-control procedures and urged that the overall policy be strengthened.

SPOA, a self-described grassroots organization focused on protecting property rights in Cambridge, was formed in January 1988. Many of the approximately one thousand members owned fewer than a dozen rent-controlled units; all maintained that the rent-control system ignored their individual constitutional rights as property owners. Dedicated to ending rent control, SPOA started by calling for such changes as advance approval of rent increases in the case of planned capital improvements, permanent rent increases in the case of all capital improvements, the establishment of minimum rents, and the development of a means test that would eliminate well-to-do tenants from the system.

CTU operated on the principle that "a landlord's need for profit must be balanced against the tenant's needs for an affordable and decent place to live" (Atlas and Dreier 1980, 1). Insisting that rent control had been approved and instituted as a cost-based system, many in CTU held that landlord concerns about both the purported wealth of some rent-control tenants and the lack of profit among rent-control landlords were simply not germane.

In contrast, SPOA argued that rent control discriminated illegally against landlords by preventing a fair and reasonable (i.e., market) return on their property. SPOA further claimed that the "monster" called rent control masqueraded as a housing policy for the needy when in actuality it was a taxation and subsidy program funded by a minority of citizens (landlords) for the direct financial benefit of the majority (tenants), regardless of need (Cravatts 1990).

Starting from different assumptions, each organization developed competing conceptions of entitlement. Each perceived that the system's administrators and policies unfairly advantaged the other, and both justified their claims on the basis of economic conditions, moral arguments, and legal precedents. The most vocal engaged in intensely emotional exchanges, sharply disagreeing but rarely communicating about the same issue.

As the 1980s ended, the pro-rent-control/pro-tenant majority on the council remained steadfast in its commitment to rent control. However, it recognized the need to respond to the distinct concerns of both supporters and opponents of the system. Thus, the city council commissioned additional studies of the system,[12] established a special council subcommittee on rent control, and began to consider recommendations for administrative changes.

The city council's Rent Control Subcommittee (composed of two pro- and one anti-rent-control councillors) held a series of 15 public discussions in late 1990 and early 1991 that were summarized in a 315-page report. This report also included 18 reform recommendations, as well as a mini-report outlining the council's minority, anti-rent control position. Two additional reports were submitted to the council simultaneously: one proposed a single administrative agency to coordinate rent control, subsidized housing, development, inspectional services, and all other housing-related matters currently handled by separate departments, while the other proposed a new housing policy in the form of an affordable housing trust fund. The first stage of this rent-control reform initiative was completed in May 1991 when the city council passed, in resolution form, the ambitious 18-point program outlined in the subcommittee's lengthy report. However, lack of subsequent action led to the death of virtually all of the proposals.

The struggle between supporters and critics of rent control took a new turn in 1992, a "touchstone year" in Cambridge politics. In April, a bill calling for the abolition of rent control in Boston, Brookline, and Cambridge was filed with the state legislature. Although the legislature declined to get involved in this "local matter," rent-control advocates worried that the bill reflected the sentiments of a growing movement and pressured the city council to reinvigorate the rent-control system. Around the same time, SPOA filed suit against the city of Cambridge (claiming illegal taking and discrimination, and demanding the end of rent control) and commissioned a study of 1990 U.S. and Cambridge census figures (which concluded, not surprisingly, that young white-collar professionals—not disadvantaged groups—benefited from rent control at the expense of property owners and that the critical housing shortage used to justify the adoption of rent control no longer existed).

Tenant activists questioned the statistics, the analysis, and the conclusions of SPOA's study and became disenchanted with the pro-rent-control city council that seemed willing to listen to SPOA. But while supporters of rent control grew more skeptical of the Rent Control Board's administration of policies, they denied that anything was wrong with rent control and ultimately failed to respond creatively to the growing challenge of SPOA. The dramatic consequences of this failure became clear in 1993 when SPOA adopted a new strategy that took the battle over rent control out of the city. Supported by the real estate industry, the

Chapter 4

landlord organization led a successful state-wide petition drive to gather the required number of signatures to include the question of rent control's future (Question 9) on the November 1994 ballot. It is difficult to overemphasize the significance of this development; it meant that voters across the state would decide whether Cambridge, along with Boston and Brookline, would remain rent-controlled cities.

The landlord-real estate coalition won the referendum by a narrow margin. Across the state, 46.3 percent of the voters said "yes" to the question of whether rent control should be abolished; 43.9 percent said "no" and 9.7 percent of those who cast their ballots left this question blank. As expected, reactions to the vote were most pronounced in the three rent-control cities, and especially in Cambridge. Proclaiming a victory for private property rights, SPOA and its supporters asserted that more than two thirds of the Cambridge voters had cast their votes against the policy of rent control. Tenant groups countered with the assertion that 58 percent of the city's voters had indicated their desire to keep rent control.

One longtime community activist emphasized the need for a nuanced analysis of the voting patterns on Question 9: "The lower the town's median household income, the more likely the *No* vote; the higher the income, the higher the *Yes* vote." He also observed that:

> The richest 60 towns in the state voted Yes unanimously. More of the big cities voted No. The same income-related pattern can be observed within cities. There was the usual overrepresentation of higher income people in the electorate. Half the population in rich towns voted; a third in poor towns. More people cast blanks in lower-income precincts. (Cunningham 1995)

These sorts of insights reinforced the perception that local matters were being decided by outsiders, and rent-control supporters in particular seemed troubled by this possibility of state interference in local affairs.

Even as debate over the legality and significance of the Question 9 vote continued, the city council was faced with a fast-approaching deadline. Because rent control was scheduled to end on January 1, 1995, there were only a few weeks in which Cambridge, along with Boston and Brookline, could develop and submit proposals to the state legislature outlining plans for the phase-out of their programs.[13] In Cambridge, a subcommittee of the city council began intensive around-the-clock meetings with members of SPOA and tenant groups to discuss the city's future. These meetings, constrained by the longstanding animosity between landlord and tenant groups, were made even more difficult by councillors' desire both to protect tenants and to win broad popular support.

In late November, six of the councillors voted to endorse a plan that called for a five-year phase out of rent control, protections for elderly tenants, and a restriction that limited occupancy of rent-control units to those who earned less than 80 percent of the state's median income.[14] Both supporters and opponents of rent control accused the councillors of selling them out (which prompted one councillor to comment that they "must have done something right"), and so the plan submitted to the Massachusetts legislature initially had little support. During the next several weeks, SPOA accepted that rent control "could not be ended overnight" and endorsed the Cambridge five-year plan. By the end of December, though, no formal decision had been reached by state officials.

This tense uncertainty ended early in January 1995 when Governor Weld—a wealthy, antirent control Cambridge resident—signed a bill that ended rent control throughout the state. This new law, Chapter 282, also offered temporary protection for up to two years for low-income, disabled, and elderly renters. Specifically, those making 60 percent of the median family income, as well as disabled individuals and individuals 62 years of age or older making 80 percent of the median income, were protected through December 1996. Chapter 282 resolved one set of questions as it officially ended a defining period in the history of Cambridge. But almost immediately new concerns were voiced, and for the next thirty months Cambridge grappled with the variety of issues that emerged after the termination of rent control.

Unexpected Developments, Changing Social Relations

Most people concerned about the end of rent control worried about potential financial difficulties; few made direct connections to health. However, shortly after the passage of Chapter 282, thirty local doctors signed an open letter to the city warning of an impending health disaster. These doctors, reviewing hospital records for MI (heart condition) and depression patients, found that slightly more than four out of ten in each category were living in rent-control units. Citing several major research projects detailing the relationship between stress, isolation, and

Chapter 4

higher death rates, the doctors argued that a sudden loss of rent control might be lethal to some of these more vulnerable tenants. Certain links between home and health have been clearly documented; research on the widespread sadness and depression that followed the urban renewal dislocation of Boston's Old West End residents is well known. The difference here was the emphasis on mortality rates. The doctors' warning caught many by surprise, even though many also acknowledged that they "never thought about the health effects" of ending the policy of rent control.[15]

Other issues are unfolding more gradually and some, like the warning on health, have not been fully explored. City officials feared that the end of rent control would force some Cambridge families to move and thus precipitate a decline in public school enrollments. Although the number of public school students has gone down slightly during the last two academic years, the way that the rent-control phaseout figures in this decline is not clear. Many agree that concerns other than rent cause people to move; it may be that some families have left Cambridge in search of better quality schools.

Perhaps the most common prediction associated with the end of rent control was the following: landlords, in a rush to sell their properties to the highest bidders, would evict their tenants by raising rents and ultimately glut the local real estate market. Since mid-1995, lower interest rates, a healthy economy, and the end of rent control have contributed to a robust real estate market in Cambridge that shows no sign of weakening. The average price for one of the city's three thousand single-family houses has increased substantially, and demand is as high as it has been in years. Condominiums also have been surprisingly strong sellers in the post-rent-control market.

Unexpected responses on the parts of both tenants and landlords help explain this situation. Examples abound of former tenants who, uncertain of their fate after Chapter 282, have entered the residential market as condo and house buyers. Some realtors estimate that one-fifth of the people looking to buy are former rent-control tenants. The predicted market glut has not materialized because landlords who are now able to earn market rents are willing to hang onto their properties. Among landlords who have continued to rent their properties, many maintain that the turnover rate of approximately 20 percent during 1995–96 was only slightly higher than that of previous years.

There are other interpretations of the situation. Tenant advocates describe a "quiet exodus . . . an incredible migration" with estimates that roughly thirty thousand former rent control tenants have moved or are actively looking for new housing. With rent increases of over 100 percent that average well over 50 percent, some longtime renters are struggling with the burdens of life without rent control. Many of the elderly have applied for Section 8 or public elderly housing, but the lists of eligible applicants are long. The waiting period for single-room occupancy units at the local YMCA has jumped from four months to over two years. Although not all agree with the opinion recently expressed by one longtime activist that "a rent increase is a rent eviction," many agree that households granted transitional status under Chapter 282[16] are at risk of losing their homes. Mounting evidence about former rent-controlled units being converted to condominiums and about the loss of longtime neighbors to escalating rents supports the claim that the diversity that has long characterized Cambridge is disappearing.

Another ongoing transition concerns the city's political landscape. The end of single-issue politics prompted some pundits to suggest that Cambridge will finally become a "real city" with a broad civic agenda. No one doubts that rent control "took a lot of time" and prevented other issues from being discussed. One councillor, reflecting on his tenure at City Hall during the last years of rent control and the early years of the post-rent-control era, predicted greater attention to education and public safety issues in general, and specifically, to *how* rather than *how much* money is spent in these areas. Still, the ability of city officials to set new agenda continues to be constrained by concerns over affordable housing.

In spring 1995 Cambridge officials unveiled "CityHome," a projected $20-million, ten-year response to the end of rent control. Included in this broad housing-assistance program is an education component that helps first-time buyers secure bank loans and other financial assistance. Another initiative helps landlords upgrade their property through low-interest loans tied to a schedule of moderate rent increases. The end of rent control coincided with changes at the federal level that promised greatly diminished federal funding for housing; specifically, 1,600 rental units were facing expiring federal use restrictions in 1995–96. CityHome has addressed the "expiring use" crisis by providing important negotiating advice to several tenant groups that have succeeded in purchasing their buildings.

Another level of housing assistance is provided through the Cambridge Affordable Housing Trust. Formed in 1992, the trust leverages financing for affordable housing projects like a recently approved

Chapter 4

proposal to build between 20 and 25 apartments for low-income elderly residents in what is now a vacant and rundown building. In one of its most significant moves to date, the city signed a deal with Harvard to purchase 100 of the 669 former rent-control units owned by the university. The $3.2 million purchase price will be financed mainly through a reduction of Harvard's annual payment to the city in lieu of taxes. In another development, on April 14, 1997, the city council narrowly passed a 1-percent transfer fee; this fee or transfer tax will be charged to buyers of property purchased for $300,000 or more. Earnings from this new tax, anticipated to top $600,000 annually, are earmarked for affordable housing. For some, this is "too little, too late"—for others it is an undesired infringement on the rights of property owners.

It is important to note that each of these developments was accompanied by unforeseen disagreements, changing circumstances, and shifting alliances. Also significant is the ongoing influence of this curious mix of confrontation, continuity, and innovation as Cambridge confronts the reality that the 1994 end of rent control is not the end of the story. In December 1999, Cambridge and Somerville Legal Services proposed a local condominium conversion ordinance to strengthen state restrictions on the process of converting rental apartments into condominiums. SPOA identified the proposal as a poorly disguised attempt to reinstate rent control, while in contrast tenant groups and other supporters considered it a means to preserve the steadily shrinking supply of rental apartments and to help preserve tenants' rights. After first tabling the controversial proposal and subsequently referring it "to committee," in mid-December 2000 the city councillors voted 5–4 to defeat the proposed ordinance. As with most housing-related decisions in Cambridge, this one has satisfied some and angered others while leaving unresolved the key issue of who belongs in the community of Cambridge.

Conclusions: What Is the Community of Cambridge?

Cambridge is no longer the community it was during the era of rent control, in part because some of the predictability associated with rent control has disappeared. The physical and social transformations occurring since the end of rent control have raised pressing questions about who counts as community members and what responsibilities a community has towards its members. Every community needs to respond to these concerns and to the larger issue of inequality, and indications are that Cambridge will address these problems in its own novel way.

While much of its unique character remains, Cambridge also resembles most urban communities nationwide. Involved and invested in multi-faceted transformation, Cambridge is moving into an unknowable future guided by competing visions of the past and informed by conflicting views of obligation and entitlement. Illustrated here is a central paradox: community endures as it changes.

Defined partly by its geographic boundaries, the identity of Cambridge is also intimately tied to its residents—both present and past—who directly and sometimes subtly control the conditions of community membership. The rent control policy that dominated Cambridge life for decades is, ultimately, only one element in a larger context of changing circumstances, evolving meanings, and compensatory reactions that make this community what it is. What unfolds in Cambridge will continue to depend heavily on the systematic, modifying constraints of state and national political and economic developments.

Notes

1. Dorothy Smith has written incisively about such two-sided revelations, as well as the basic importance of studying what seem to be idiosyncratic events or "cases."

> The relation of the local and particular to generalized social relations is not a conceptual or methodological issue, it is a property of social organization. The particular "case" is not particular in the aspects that are of concern to the inquirer. Indeed, it is not a "case," for it presents itself to us rather as a point of entry, the locus of an experiencing subject or subjects, into a larger social and economic process. (Smith 1987, 157)

2. In his review of studies critical of rent control, Niebanck (1985) observed that "not all . . . studies draw the same conclusions but generally they indicate that rent control: restrains average rental increases; discourages new investment in housing; weakens incentives to maintain rental property; and retards expansion of the local tax base" (111). He added, however, that such studies

> fail, for the most part, to produce significant results in two major respects: First, their findings are too abstract, too remote, and too generalized to inform the specific case . . . The second failure of evaluative studies is

Chapter 4

related to their data base. They typically draw upon information that is collected for other, more routine purposes, and they use only those variables on which data are commonly recorded . . . [Such] structural flaws leave analysts—and the users of their analyses—unable to separate causes from effects. (111–12)

See also Gilderbloom 1981 and Appelbaum et al. 1991.

3. Apologies, and also thanks, to C. Vann Woodward (1974).

4. Cambridge is governed by a city manager and by a nine-member city council which elects the primarily ceremonial mayor from its ranks.

5. The relevant piece of state legislation was Massachusetts Statutes, Chapter 842, 1970. This statute was valid initially for four years; it was later extended to 1976 at which time it lapsed. From that time forward, any municipal government desiring to establish a rent-control program was required to file a home-rule petition with the state legislature. Cambridge did so on March 31, 1976 (Clark 1988).

6. Rent Control Enabling Act and Ordinances, The Rent Control Board Regulation, in effect July 1, 1988.

7. All property subject to rent control had to be registered with the Rent Control Board. This included all Cambridge property rented or offered for rent with the following exceptions: rental units in hotels, motels, tourist homes, and the like that are rented for less than fourteen consecutive days; rental units constructed or created by conversion from a non-housing to a housing use on or after January 1, 1969; rental units owned, operated, or rent-regulated by a public agency; rental units in cooperatives; rental units in hospitals, convents, monasteries, asylums, public institutions, school dormitories operated exclusively for charitable or educational purposes, or nursing homes; and rental units in an owner-occupied, two- or three-family house, provided that the owner holds at least a 50 percent interest. See the Rent Control Enabling Act and Ordinances, pp. 2–3 (ref. note 5).

The registration lists in 1991 included an estimated 16,000 units. In that year, the estimated total number of dwelling units in Cambridge was 41,800: 40 percent under rent control; 24 percent owner-occupied and thus decontrolled; 12 percent subsidized under federal Section 8 and 23 programs and under the state Section 707 program and thus decontrolled; and 245 private uncontrolled units. The exact number of regulated units was debatable, however, because major categories of housing (e.g., owner-occupied buildings, which are exempt, and exempt condominiums) were not clearly identified.

8. There were two ways to change the maximum allowable rent of a controlled unit, general or individual adjustments. The Rent Control Board authorized periodic (usually yearly) citywide general adjustments in an effort to incorporate inflation into controlled rents. The latest formula for these across-the-board increases included the consideration of changes in maintenance, insurance, and management costs along with increases in utilities and water.

Changing Spaces and Places

The board also granted rent adjustments to individual landlords and tenants on the basis of documented operating/capital expenses and physical condition of the unit(s) in question. See Rent Control Enabling Act and Ordinances, especially Regulations 70, 72, and 76 (ref. note 5).

9. The Removal Permit Ordinance, No. 966, passed on March 12, 1979, restricted the removal of controlled rental units from the rental market. The Massachusetts Supreme Judicial Court initially upheld and clarified this ordinance in 1982 (Clark 1988, 161), but declared it invalid in 1989 when it agreed with a landlord-plaintiff that the Cambridge City Council had exceeded its authority in passing the ban. The council subsequently succeeded in reinstating a more restrictive condominium conversion ban by home-rule petition, getting the required approval from the state legislature in early 1990. In the six months between the invalidation and reinstatement of the ban, more than 580 rent control apartments were converted and sold as condominiums and thus were removed from rent control.

10. Massachusetts state laws govern such landlord-tenant matters as health-code violations, rent withholding, and eviction proceedings. Relevant state laws have informed all decisions of the Rent Control Board.

11. The system relied on 1967 as the base year in the establishment of fair rents on the assumptions that: this was the last year of "relatively equal bargaining power between landlords and tenants, which resulted in fair rents" (Rent Control Board Handbook, n.d., 22); the inflationary effects of real estate development in Cambridge were not significant until after this time; and in 1967 the expense/profit ratio in rents was 1:1. For all units rented in 1967 and continuously since then, "the actual rent charged in that base year is the starting point for all rent computations" (Clark 1988, 163).

12. The most important commissioned studies include Rosenberg (1989), Devine (1990), and Goetze (1990). Together they can be understood as a reaction to the 1987 report by Abt Associates that was criticized for its incomplete statistical portrait of Cambridge renters. However, in spite of such criticism, the Abt study remained the most comprehensive (if faulty) analysis of the system's participants and beneficiaries. According to Abt Associates, 30 percent of the city's rent-controlled units were occupied by residents earning more than the median income in the Boston area, and 38 percent of all rental households in Cambridge claimed serious housing-costs burdens (i.e., they paid more than one-third of their incomes for rent). These estimates were used by both supporters and critics of rent control to alternately exonerate and condemn the system.

13. The cities were alike in that each had rent-control programs, but the programs were distinct. Any possibility of a unified response to Question 9 was precluded by Boston, which stated it "wanted nothing to do with Cambridge."

14. In November one of the nine elected councillors began serving a year's prison term for violating federal banking regulations, so only eight were involved in the final deliberations on the plan.

15. No follow-up studies have been completed because, as one of the

Chapter 4

original organizers of the physician group explained in an April 1997 phone conversation, securing funding for this kind of research is extremely difficult. She and her colleagues continue to hope that someone, perhaps an enterprising doctoral candidate, will continue the investigation.

    16. There is disagreement on the exact numbers, which range from one to two thousand. The Cambridge Community Development Department estimated that about 1,300 tenants signed up for protection after rent control was outlawed. According to an October 1996 report, 362 elderly tenants and more than 1,000 other low-income and elderly tenants in formerly rent-controlled apartments were at risk. Another estimate issued the following month identified up to 1,500 at-risk, low-income, disabled and elderly residents.

Chapter Five

PUSHING THE LIMITS OF COMMUNITY
Rejuvenation Efforts in Waterville, Maine[1]

> Feelings of community, understood as strong, enduring bonds of value, interest, and mutual concern, cannot be willed into being nor, in a society of a vast mixture of value systems and moral standards, can they be assumed or imposed. (Evans and Boyte 1992, xi)

Community is an interactive process. As the preceding case studies reveal, community is negotiated in a variety of situations involving the social control of space and how people should treat each other. People who share places, values, and goals often end up having very different ideas about what can and should be done. Community negotiations are characterized by engagement, commitment, and compromise, and, equally importantly, by differences and disagreements. This plurality of community traits is in continual flux, constrained by circumstances that affect members' options and choices and constantly reinvigorated by how members define and respond to their situations.

That both individual identity and collective well-being are fundamental to the ongoing, essential tasks of recreating and sustaining community are illustrated in the case of the central Maine city of Waterville. Like many urban areas in the 1990s, this small city has experienced both economic hardship and what has been called the loss of community. What distinguishes Waterville is a grassroots program of community rejuvenation that is striving to build on collective aspirations while maintaining individual freedoms.

Chapter 5

Dreaming in the Old Home Town

Waterville, the Elm City, is located approximately 230 miles north of Boston. My ties to this central Maine community of about 17,000 inhabitants run deep, for this is where I grew up and went to school. Although I left Waterville in 1970 when I began college, I have regularly returned to visit family and friends in the area. As happens with many of us, I remain connected to my old home town.

My childhood memories of Waterville as a safe and happy place have been validated by many longtime residents.[2] Life in the city during the late 1950s and the 1960s is remembered as being secure and prosperous. Parents and city officials were proud of the city's schools, students, and teachers. Thomas College, then a recently founded business school, and Colby College, a nationally respected private college, contributed to the local economy and enhanced the city's cultural offerings. A high percentage of residents owned their own homes and felt confident about long-term employment in the many small businesses and several large manufacturing plants centered in Waterville. Children and adults alike participated in such traditional community activities as the Fourth of July Parade and the Easter Egg Hunt. And in general, voters were interested in city politics and assumed that running the city was a collective affair; for years one could find standing-room-only at city council meetings.

Waterville slowly began to change, at first physically, in the early 1960s. Along with many urban areas across the nation, Waterville participated in urban renewal. The goal of this federal program was to revitalize aging commercial and retail areas through a two-step process of demolition and rebuilding. Far too frequently, though, urban renewal stopped after the demolition. There is a widespread perception that this is what happened in Waterville. The retail area on Main Street (known as "downstreet") was razed, and what replaced the small restaurants, family-owned businesses, and local department stores was an oversized parking lot that still strikes many as "a box canyon going nowhere." Urban renewal notwithstanding, Waterville continued to enjoy economic growth. By the 1970s, Waterville had become a key provider of banking and medical services in the mid-Maine region.

During the 1970s, another more gradual change began to affect Waterville residents. This change was associated with a growing perception among residents that the number and scope of rules and regulations issued by federal, state, and local bureaucracies were increasing. Like most New Englanders, women and men who lived in Waterville

Pushing the Limits of Community

took pride in their independence. Looking back, a shared belief that rules and regulations about what could be built, how, where, and for what purposes were increasing seems to have constrained the actions, and ultimately, the thinking of many citizens. One area resident described the demoralization this way:

> Take the classic New Englander, and add government bureaucracy and restrictions. In face of the restrictions and proclamations about what to do, the New Englander backed up and stopped doing anything. Cramped and unhappy, when their freedom was taken away, they didn't test the constraints.

Traditional Maine self-reliance was no longer important in the full range of ways it had been. It was replaced in many individuals by a dependent attitude and a general assumption that things would be taken care of by someone else.

As the 1980s unfolded, the sharing and caring that characterized community life in previous years disappeared. While pride of ownership remained strong, Waterville seemed to become a place of isolated projects. The city's sense of economic security was somewhat eroded by the national recession of the 1980s, but compared to other urban areas in the state, Waterville's base of businesses and manufacturing jobs remained fairly stable throughout the decade. Ironically, it was just when other parts of the state were beginning to recover from the recession in the early 1990s that Waterville's economic downslide accelerated.

The groundwork for Waterville's decline in the 1990s was laid decades earlier. By the end of the 1970s, all the major manufacturers in the area—including Scott Paper (pulp and paper products), Keyes Fibre (paper products), and Hathaway Shirts—had been purchased by larger international corporations with headquarters in other parts of the world. Management of these companies ceased to be a local affair as many of the upper-level managers, who had numbered among the city's wealthier residents, were either transferred or terminated. The collective sense of community pride and company loyalty also disappeared as downsizing began and as hundreds of local jobs were eliminated.

According to several individuals who have lived more than forty years in Waterville, the late 1970s and early 1980s saw an emigration among the city's "upper class." At the same time, the relative strength of Waterville's social services served as a magnet for low-income families from the surrounding, economically depressed towns. These demographic shifts had a negative effect on the city's tax base. The city's

Chapter 5

schools and non-profit sector suffered as the pool of available resources shrank.[3] Another blow occurred in the early 1990s with the sale of the local chain of drug stores to a national conglomerate, which ended employment for another hundred and fifty area residents.

The local political situation enhanced feelings of hopelessness and helplessness. Community involvement in city hall affairs declined during the 1970s in response to a string of mayors who seemed interested in pursuing their own agendas. More recently, political scandals triggered further citizen disengagement; a city administrator left office amid charges of unethical behavior, and one mayor was convicted of embezzling money from a local business. Many despaired of Waterville's lack of leadership but few took it upon themselves to step forward to help, largely because of the perception that as individuals they were unable to make a difference. The announcement from Washington, in early 1995, that Congress had awarded $30 million for the construction of a second bridge across the Kennebec River between Waterville and neighboring Winslow—a project that many local residents opposed—confirmed what a growing number of people believed: they really were powerless.

Many Waterville residents readily recall the prosperity and initiative that characterized Waterville in previous decades. They compared their situation in 1995 to that of the "good old days" and to what was happening in other nearby cities. Whereas neighboring Augusta had carefully invested in community and economic development and was beginning to see the payoffs, nearly one of every ten workers in Waterville was jobless. By 1995 Waterville's unemployment rate of 9.7 percent was nearly 3 percentage points higher than the state average. People who lived in Waterville felt discouraged, frightened, and isolated.

It was in this environment of collective demoralization that Faye Nicholson began to work on community in Waterville. She and her husband Jim, who owned a local accounting business, were—like most other long-term residents—concerned about Waterville's economic slump. One night in December 1994, as the couple drove home from the movies, they began talking about what they might be able to do. Both wanted to help the local economy recover and both believed that local businesses weren't as bad as many people thought. Before they pulled into their driveway they had come up with a simple plan for a "buy local" advertising campaign.

Their newspaper advertisements recommending that townspeople help themselves by supporting local businesses touched a sensitive nerve. "All we did was bring up the possibility of doing things locally," Faye recalled, and then "people came in and talked and talked and talked." The "buy local" slogan stimulated discussion, initially about consumer issues; Faye's response was to listen. In order to accommodate the growing number of men and women who wanted to air the resentments, hopes and fears triggered by their advertisements, Jim and Fay set up a basement office in the building housing their accounting firm. Over the next several months, Faye had private discussions that lasted from one to four hours with more than twelve dozen individual visitors. Early on, one visitor gave Faye a traditional Native-American handicraft known as a dream catcher. This gift, Faye felt, helped her understand the significance of her listening: she was catching dreams.

Faye's records of these open-ended conversations confirmed her perception that they moved through three stages with remarkable consistency. Invariably, they began with concrete complaints about local businesses; two common ones concerned the limited range of sizes in women's clothing and the unfriendly attitudes of shop-owners and salespeople. Attention would then shift to a more personal level, to individual stories of how family life had been disrupted by the recession and to confessions of lost hope and great fears. After bottoming-out, however, discussions would take on a more optimistic tone as they broadened to include ideas about the future and about the community life that each visitor wished to experience someday in Waterville.

This recurring format involved a transition from blaming others, to fearing for self, and finally to the articulation of shared needs and ways to fulfill such needs. Faye was in a position to notice that many area people "were in the same place, with similar priorities" about family, education, and jobs. They were tired of living what they called "reactive" lives. The recession pushed many to recognize the importance of cooperation and participation in a rapidly changing environment. Virtually all talked about feeling disenfranchised and wanting to take an active role in transforming Waterville.

Early on in her "dream catching," Faye identified others in the community who believed that Waterville could heal itself and who were committed to making the effort to do so. A core group of independent, concerned individuals—which included professionals involved in medicine, finance, and education; housewives; independent businessmen and business executives; retirees; social service providers; and members of city government—began regular meetings with Faye and Jim to discuss their dreams and the future of Waterville. This advisory collective

Chapter 5

saw their challenge as figuring out how to "make the dream real." Towards this end, in March 1995 the group took the necessary steps to organize itself into a non-profit corporation with a board of directors and Faye as president. It also took a name: REM was born.

The name REM is symbolically important. It refers to the stage of sleep characterized by Rapid Eye Movement; during R.E.M. sleep the human brain is at its most creative. Additionally, as REM members explain, the psychic chaos that results when R.E.M. sleep is disrupted is analogous to the social chaos that occurs when community is not nurtured. Thus, REM is a reminder of the creativity and critical power of community. More officially, REM stands for "Reviving Energy in Maine (ME)." All of these meanings (as well as the significance of the state's abbreviation) are captured in the stated mission of REM: "to provide and sustain a structure and a process, the forum and the form, through which the people of this region will verbalize, visualize, actualize, and then perpetuate their dreams for the future."

Word got around that "Faye, the Dream Catcher" had a genuine desire to record and share the thoughts, fears, and hopes of the townspeople, and participation increased. Individuals who had already spoken with Faye directed others to her office, and Faye, following the recommendations of many visitors, began to seek out additional members of the community who were known to have particular insights and connections. Faye continued to compile the hopes and ideas "that were in people's minds and hearts" into a futuristic narrative named "The Dream," and a sense of ownership in the project grew.

This twelve-page document represents the needs and desires shared by community members, and it was and still is available to everyone. Faye has been quick to point out, though, that the very nature of "The Dream" means that it will never be finished. There is ongoing discussion of individual suggestions and collective aspirations, and an open-ended request for additional contributions from community members. This listening and sharing process seems to encourage hope as it fosters participation.

Throughout 1995 excitement grew. The diverse individuals who created the grassroots movement now known as REM moved forward, soliciting ideas and requesting commitment from area residents. A growing number of volunteers responded to the call to help the mid-Maine region recover. Committees were organized and responsibilities were delegated. Letters and newspaper articles were written and phone calls were made. Local businesses donated money and equipment, and many professionals freely gave their time and expertise to REM activities.

The several hundred REM members organized an exciting fall event that brought together more people, more ideas, and more energy for community renewal. At the October 1995 rally, the REM Board of Directors announced the result of its national search for a consulting group that could assist REM in building the family-focused and education-oriented community so many had said they wanted. A contract was signed with the Center for Consensual Democracy (CCD), a Maine-based team of consultants known for innovative community work in the northern Maine town of Limestone.[4] For more than forty years that community's social and economic life revolved around nearby Loring Air Force Base; the scheduled 1994 closing of the base threatened the very existence of the town.

The Center began helping Limestone in fall 1993, using a computer-assisted methodology originally developed to enhance private-sector strategic planning. This approach—which builds on the interrelated ideas that organizations and communities must either grow or die, growth is developmental, and change is continuous—enabled citizens of Limestone to organize an effective community association, develop a comprehensive community plan, and create viable action plans. Within two years, Limestone had rejuvenated its economy and realized the community's dream of opening a science and mathematics magnet school for teenagers from across the state.

REM was also attracted by the Center's dedication to the development and practice of consensual democracy. This voluntary form of self-governance is open to all who wish to be involved in identifying and addressing common community interests. It supports the traditional, elected (or sovereign) government while simultaneously providing independent forms of structured democratic process. Consensual democracy derives its political power not from the law of the state but rather from the freely given consent of its constituency—i.e., all individuals committed to addressing the concerns that affect the community's quality of life. Furthermore, it offers the potential for new solutions to civic problems because it is powered by the personal commitments of those who participate. A consensual democracy takes action via cooperation, synthesis, and consensus, not the "rule" of a majority, in the pursuit of a better quality of community life.[5] Consensual democracy as theory and process offered REM a framework and focus for its collective energy.

Chapter 5

In the last months of 1995, REM pushed forward with its plans for community revitalization. A request was made for nominations of individuals who represented the area's diversities of occupation, age, gender, education, income, ethnicity, and opinion, and who also were known for their interest in community building. Fifty area residents were selected for "the Dream Team." With guidance from the Center, REM planned a forum in which the Dream Team would lead Waterville and the surrounding towns of Winslow, Fairfield, Belgrade, Oakland, China, Benton, Vassalboro, Rome, and Sidney in envisioning the area's future. This conceptual barn raising was intentionally planned as a very public affair; all area residents were invited to observe and contribute to an agreement on the what, how, and when of the mid-Maine region's transformation.

The visioning process, called the Community Catalyst, was held in the Waterville Opera House in early January 1996. During six sessions over three long days, Center facilitators prodded and supported members of the Dream Team as they debated what futures were desirable and how they could best be achieved. The achievement of the first day was a collectively written, publicly signed strategic vision of the mid-Maine region in the year 2020. This vision statement summarizes the best the area can and should be, based on the history, varied resources, and aspirations of residents. It describes "a vibrant, family-oriented, regional community actively engaged in and responsible for shaping [it's] future" where "educational, religious, government, social and business organizations collaborate in supporting lifelong learning and growth." A cornerstone of the area's identity is the creative and performing arts. It describes a place where "everyone feels secure"; where inclusion, individuality, and diversity are valued; and where "interaction and respect among people of all ages and backgrounds" are promoted. The region maintains "a vigorous economic environment while preserving a small-town atmosphere," its architecture, and its natural environment.

The second day was devoted to thinking about how mid-Maine's current citizens might allocate community resources to achieve this vision. More than 430 ideas for separate initiatives or projects were generated: some seemed frivolous ("have an ice-cream festival"); others addressed society-wide problems ("end homophobia," "eliminate child abuse and neglect"); yet most were practical and possible ("create a regional youth symphony," "streamline permit process for business startup and expansion," "provide adequate winter clothing for all children"). The Dream Team then identified and grouped into objectives those projects that seemed to be vital for achieving the vision.

The final day involved prioritizing the objectives and organizing volunteer teams dedicated to the accomplishment of the highest priority objectives. The eight top priority objectives include, in descending order of importance:

- Develop a vibrant economy;
- Excel in education;
- Protect human potential;
- Promote arts and entertainment;
- Beautify the environment;
- Empower young people;
- Build community;
- Expand facilities for fitness and recreation.

Achieving such objectives is an enormous task, for each represents a constraint currently blocking the fulfillment of the vision. Success will be possible, the Center cautioned, only with "a disciplined, coordinated regional effort . . . [of skilled professionals and committed volunteers] working together, with respect and mutual support." Recognizing this, the Dream Team considered that its work was completed in the last Sunday session only after team leaders were selected and an agenda was set for the next day's initial leaders meeting of the eight objective teams.

The Community Catalyst was both exhausting and rewarding. Many of the local residents who wandered in and out of the sessions, including the mayor, were impressed that fifty people willingly spent three days working together. The vision statement that emerged out of the contributions of all Dream Team members is a powerful testament to that determined cooperation. Members remain committed to this vision of what the future can be, and the vision statement serves as the motivating force behind REM's ongoing community works.

The Community Catalyst did indeed provide valuable stimulation. The level of activity sustained in the months following the catalyst has affirmed the observation that "this REM stuff doesn't let up." Each of the eight Objective Groups, also referred to as the Point or Action Groups, meets once a month in a scheduled time slot. REM's operation (or "custodial") teams—which include the Communications and Convening Committees, the Board of Directors, and the recently established

Chapter 5

Executive Committee—similarly have a monthly calendar slot. Additionally, the first Thursday of each month is reserved for REM Forum, an open community meeting "where citizens from all over the region come to discuss those things most vital to our lives."

Each of these regularly scheduled meetings is open, and all citizens are encouraged to attend whatever meetings they can, whenever they can. Joining REM is easy; all one has to do is sign up. However, membership is not a requirement for attending any REM meetings or activities. What is expected is that all participants will follow the guidelines (developed by REM in consultation with the CCD) that encourage open and focused communication in meetings. These guidelines invite all participants to

> keep our eye on the vision; welcome diversity; honor confidentiality; be brief and direct; contribute as equals; help each other participate/facilitate; maintain focus; challenge or confront ideas, not each other; keep a sense of our history and traditions; make decisions by agreement where possible, and by vote if necessary; respect and support the decisions we make together; work together in the spirit of cooperation rather than competition; and enjoy the process!

A sampling of REM's accomplishments following the catalyst reveals the varied nature of its mission of community building. During the first months of 1996 REM was instrumental in the creation of a nonprofit corporation, Waterville Regional Arts and Community Center (WRACC), which has the dual goal of fostering the performing and nonperforming arts and providing support for civic groups. A successful fundraiser enabled WRACC to purchase a former Main Street department store for the community, and in August the organization moved into the newly renovated Community Center. REM representatives accepted an invitation to participate in the NGO forums at Habitat II (the second United Nations Conference on Human Settlements), held in Istanbul, Turkey, in June. The recipient of the first annual REM Award for exemplary community spirit was honored in October 1996.

In response to its rapid growth (as of mid-2000 there were well over a thousand members) and expanding responsibilities, REM has tried to streamline its organizational structure. A Constitution and By-Laws Committee was convened to create a regulatory framework that will allow REM to achieve its interrelated goals of building community

Pushing the Limits of Community

and consensual democracy. The board created an executive committee that will meet weekly to make decisions until the by-laws are established; members include the president and vice-president of the board, the chair of the communications committee, the leader or "point person" of the highest priority objective team, and one at-large individual. Also, the organization as a whole is developing a strategic policy to ensure that all fundraising events include education and community-building components.

Much is being done to keep everyone in the mid-Maine region informed of REM actions and goals. In March 1996 the Communications Committee completed the first issue of *The REM Record*, a monthly newsletter focused on community building that is sent to all REM members and available at no charge to non-members. By the time the second issue of the *Record* was distributed in May, the paper had doubled in size and circulation. In early 1997, the paper switched to a newsprint/tabloid format; budget constraints have since restricted its publication to a quarterly schedule. As important, REM's relationship with the daily local newspaper evolved to the point where the two publications now regularly collaborate on announcements, stories, and editorials.

Several computer experts in the area volunteered their time to set up an electronic database and communications network for REM members. The governor, along with state and U.S. senators and representatives, receives regular reports about what is happening in the mid-Maine region. And closer to home, Faye and other members of REM's board have met with elected officials from a number of Maine communities that have expressed interest in developing their own versions of REM.

The objective groups have made progress on several key initiatives generated by the Dream Team during the Community Catalyst. For example, the Beautify the Environment Team (Team 5), focusing its efforts "on developing ideas to change the Concourse [parking lot] from a stumbling block to a steppingstone for downtown development in Waterville," arranged a walking tour with an architectural historian from the local college. This walkabout was held on a frigid Saturday morning in February 1996, and the three dozen volunteers who showed up offered a variety of suggestions to present at a REM-sponsored meeting with city architects. City officials and REM agreed on a final plan for a newly designed concourse in late fall and renovations began in spring 1997. Current team projects include designing the approach to both the historic Two-Cent Bridge and to the traditional symbolic center of

Chapter 5

Waterville, Castonguay Square, and generating ideas for a "waterfront park" on the Kennebec.

Progress is also being made by the "Develop a Vibrant Economy" Team (Team 1). In line with its task to *streamline the permitting process*, the group collected detailed information from everyone who had received a commercial permit between 1994 and 1996 and presented the data to the Economic Development Director of Waterville (who was consulted at all stages of this volunteer project). In late October 1996, the team convened the first-of-its-kind regional Economic Development Summit that brought together business, economic development, and political leaders. A select group of ten from the summit has since met to build upon this valuable collaborative process. Most recently, the team is engaged in a feasibility study to develop a regional business incubator.

Another exciting development emerged out of the collaboration between the "Protect Human Potential" Team (Team 3) and area professionals concerned about violence in the community. In May 1996, REM sponsored a very successful day-long "Focus on Violence" event; teachers and students, parents and children, law enforcement officers, government officials, professionals, victims, and survivors gathered to discuss ways of reducing violence in the mid-Maine community. Powered solely by volunteers and free of charge to the public, this information and training workshop directly addressed this team's most important initiative: *create a climate free of violence and oppression*. A follow-up workshop on preventing youth violence was held in early September.

Along with such successes, though, REM has experienced a variety of problems. Sustaining the necessary high level of energy among REM volunteers is difficult; "burnout" seems to lurk on the horizon. The membership seems to be divided between the "dreamers" (or "talkers") and the "doers" (or "walkers"). While most acknowledge the importance of both for REM, the distinctive styles and needs of the groups have proven to be sources of conflict as well as of inspiration. Furthermore, disagreements often surface when people of different backgrounds and personalities get together. Even if disagreements are unavoidable, and even though a commitment to REM's goals has helped bridge many of them, such tensions have been painful and generally counterproductive.

As a step towards managing conflict within the organization, the REM board informally adopted what it calls the "Pinch Model."

Pushing the Limits of Community

According to this model, everyone makes a commitment to work things through and to refrain from "bad-mouthing" or talking behind others' backs. Supporters of the model believe that any violation of this policy should be met with automatic dismissal; critics strongly disagree. So far a showdown on this issue has been avoided, perhaps because just about everyone appreciates the difficulty of legislating human behaviors. As a member of the Executive Committee pointed out, everyone has to (re)learn how to act, how to be open and trusting, how to find common interests without sacrificing individual needs. Such (re)learning is being nurtured by a recently created "Team Builders Team," which is composed of local psychologists and therapists who volunteer "as a resource for people to discover their talents, resources and the skills to work together effectively." REM's Team Builders Team offered two open workshops in September 1996—one focused on helping leaders and members of REM learn how to build an effective group and keep it moving, and the other taught techniques of conflict prevention and resolution.

To encourage participation, REM has always maintained an "easy in—easy out" approach to its activities, and all meetings are open to the public. However, this "come if you can" attitude, combined with the open-door policy, means that meetings often get bogged down as newcomers are brought up to speed. The need for rules and procedures clashes with the need for flexibility. One way of addressing this, as many committees and teams have discovered, is to allow those who show up at a meeting to set the agenda on the spot. What this often means, though, is that decisions are postponed and action plans reprioritized. The process of inclusive alignment takes time, requires lots of energy, and leads to unpredictable outcomes, and this "lesson" is learned over and over.

Both in and outside the many REM meetings and events, individuals talk about the personal pain and emotional turmoil involved in being truly inclusive and in working with others in "the new, REM way." Cooperating and aligning interests are skills not traditionally valued in our competitive world, and changing how people think and act is usually tricky business. Because REM's goals have more to do with developing a new system than with changing the old system, some have strongly resisted the organization. Still, many acknowledge that the personal growth involved in learning new skills and creating new models of behavior is worth all the "bumps" and discomforts.

Chapter 5

There are high expectations for REM. "People are yearning for an answer, people are in transition," one member observed, and the hope is that REM will provide at least some answers. At the same time there remains a strong current of skepticism. From the start, many discounted the "dreaming" that has been so central to REM. For them, legitimacy was granted only after the successful Community Catalyst and the accompanying national coverage. Among those who initially were wary of Faye and the organization, there are some who now concede that "it can't be all bad."

Another, somewhat related issue concerns the negative reaction to the name of one of REM's principle goals—consensual democracy. Although the operating ideal of consensual democracy is consent (as in people choosing or agreeing to be involved), many people automatically make a connection first to consensus and then to a small and unpopular state "consensus" movement that had a short life and quick death in the early 1980s. Aware of this history, the Constitution and By-Laws Committee is searching for a new name for the process.

Everyone involved in REM understands that there are big challenges ahead. In August 1996, REM's board of directors (the "Custodians") agreed to terminate REM's contract with CCD due to lack of funding. Leadership and guidance have become issues on another level, as well. From the very beginning Faye Nicholson has been synonymous with REM, serving as founder, president, and managing custodian. Faye continues to volunteer upwards of sixty hours a week to the organization, a commitment few others can match. Unfortunately, such dedication is risky in the sense that critics find it easy to dismiss "the REM thing" as a one-person hobby. In truth, REM will not survive without its hundreds of extremely dedicated volunteers who handle everything from publicity and technical set-ups for events, equipment transfers, food service, cleaning details, grant-writing, and fundraising. Acknowledging the value of *all* of REM's "operatives"—also known as the "troops"—has become a goal in all media reports.

A serious, ongoing problem is the lack of a reliable source of funding. Also worrisome is the fact that there has been limited success so far in getting both young people and poor people involved in REM's community-building activities. Much of what has been accomplished to date relates to Waterville in particular, and even though the organization remains committed to the entire mid-Maine region, it recognizes that it has a long way to go before it is accepted as a truly regional force.

Pushing the Limits of Community

A January 1996 *U.S. News and World Report* article about REM and the revival of civic life recognized a tendency among cynics to dismiss REM "as one more example of technocratic, overly managed public life, or worse, as a dubious and self-conscious exercise in nostalgia" (Vol. 120, No. 4, 63). So far, neither description is accurate. Throughout the greater Waterville area, people are getting braver as they reach out, working to break down barriers. Especially between young and elderly residents, communication is improving, and a growing number of individuals are becoming action-oriented. In the words of one volunteer involved in every stage of REM's evolution, "REM was born of the same things which will sustain it . . . [t]he need for autonomy, self-direction, empowerment, integrating and working together for positive change."

It is important to note that REM is not the only game in town. Its activities do not replace the kinds of things that the elected (or "sovereign") governments in the area can accomplish. For example, elected officials were the first to propose an economic partnership with Waterville's "rival" city of Augusta, twenty miles south; details are still being worked out. But what is different now is the hope, and the growing involvement of individuals who are determined to make their community square with a shared vision of "a place where people thrive."

Both hope and involvement were tested in early May 1996 when the parent company of the locally based Hathaway Shirt Company announced plans to stop production. The Waterville plant employed more than five hundred workers; loss of these jobs was a tremendous threat to the area. Immediately, REM called a community meeting at which the mayor began to outline a multilevel campaign to convince the parent company, Warnaco, to postpone closure and to find potential buyers for the Hathaway plant. Within weeks, Senator Olympia Snowe began to mediate negotiations between Warnaco's president and a consortium of Maine businessmen interested in buying the Hathaway name and production facilities (which include the Waterville plant and one in Canada).

Community members joined forces to save the company and the jobs. Hathaway workers mounted a petition drive and supported their union leaders' successful attempt to meet privately with Hillary Clinton at the State Democratic Convention in late May. A purchase agreement was reached in August, but it was only in early November, when the city council approved a transfer of funds that allowed Waterville to temporarily acquire the physical plant, that negotiations were completed.

Chapter 5

Six months after announcing the closure of Hathaway, Warnaco sold the 159-year-old shirt factory to an investor group (CFH Acquisitions) led by a former governor of Maine (John R. McKernan Jr.) and a prominent Maine businessman (Michael Liberty). Hathaway workers and managers, union representatives, and area politicians celebrated what they understood as a community victory with a holiday dance sponsored by the Waterville Elks Club. There was sweet irony in the January 8, 1997, announcement that the company was seeking new workers.

The Hathaway episode seemed to enhance REM's identification as "convenor of community." However, the final months of 1997 tested REM anew. The mayor, after having previously stated the city's commitment to reserve one of its last remaining riverfront properties for a waterfront park proposed by REM, announced that the parcel would instead be sold to a local developer interested in building an expanded community health center. Supporters of this switch argued that it provided an important economic opportunity; critics questioned the economic gain and furthermore claimed that the mayor's action violated the democratic process. After weeks of intense negotiations, all parties agreed that the legality of the mayor's move would be decided by a special referendum vote in early December.

Active involvement of REM members on both sides of the controversy put the organization in the middle of the riverfront referendum and thus posed perplexing questions about the identity and mission of the organization. As a recent REM editorial explained, "It took us [i.e., REM] a while to regroup and refocus." In the same editorial, REM reaffirmed its commitment to "balanced, creative and inclusive community development" and pledged to "work with whatever realities exist following the referendum vote." The vote resolved the issue in favor of the mayor and the proposed developer, and REM subsequently extended a public invitation to "all citizens interested in developing the riverfront to its highest and best use" and requested city council permission to develop a comprehensive plan that will become the basis for further development. In so doing, REM rededicated itself to the uncertain process of developing and sustaining community.

When Is Community Work Done?

Waterville and REM have been located within the context of a national debate about the decay and revival of our nation's civic institutions and social trust. More relevant, though, are lessons about community life that continue to emerge from this self-conscious experiment in community-building. First, community is important in people's lives, but in many different ways. Problematic for some, "community" is a taken-for-granted reality for others. Additionally, any individual's position on community matters, and on *why* community matters, can change. Depending on whether and how one's claims about community are fulfilled, believers can become nonbelievers and skeptics, champions.

A related insight concerns the conceptualization of community. Frequently, geographic place is a primary ingredient of community, as evidenced here by the fact that many residents joined REM because it was "about" the community in which they live. Interestingly, this obvious spatial connection also exists for the many residents who have deliberately stayed away from REM. The people who consider greater Waterville the home they share with others include some who feel they are making a difference and others who believe that REM-like activities are of no consequence. Community, as REM is experiencing, is about more than place. It is also about aspirations and goals, and sometimes the determination to be left alone.

REM illustrates many of the ways community is important in people's lives and also reinforces the crucial role that autonomous individuals can play in a community's well-being. Faye Nicholson has been a driving force in the effort to revive community in mid-Maine, and her very public role has made possible the gradual emergence of other leaders. REM, developed out of the peculiar interplay between "individual" and "community," clearly demonstrates the potential ability of any person to reaffirm community and any community to rekindle individual lives. But there is another side to leadership in a community. What to Faye is a commitment to community, as demonstrated through her dedication to REM, has been interpreted by others (both privately and in public) as hunger for attention and personal agenda-setting. Clearly, it is possible to feel simultaneously at home and alienated in one's community.

Finally, what has been achieved in mid-Maine in the name of community elucidates the roles of action and context in community life. The confrontation between actors and structure, as is repeatedly demonstrated, affects both. The structural situations in which REM members find themselves constrain their options, but ultimately their actions constitute new realities that settle into and thus change the very contexts. For example, the crisis associated with the very real closure of Hathaway

Chapter 5

and the certain loss of hundreds of jobs imposed a specific set of economic factors and a particular time frame. REM responded by defining the situation as a community matter and a matter to be resolved by the community. The politicians and business people who agreed with this interpretation of events worked together to save the historic shirt business and the local jobs, and the Waterville area community is now more economically secure.

Another very different illustration of the formative relationship that exists between structure (or context) and agency (or action) emerged from REM's involvement in the 1997 riverfront referendum. Perceiving a violation of the community's political process, some community members called for a resolution to the controversy through a special vote. During the weeks leading up to the referendum, the issue was framed in contradictory ways. The argument that the community would be strengthened only if its political system was reaffirmed through a denial of the mayor's decision to sell the land to a developer was countered by the claim that the health and strength of the community depended on supporting the mayor's decision. REM, as a community itself and as a community convenor, has had to acknowledge that it is characterized by frustration, conflict, and impermanence as much as by agreement and sharing.

Waterville and REM continue to evolve as each responds to the range of ways people deal with each other. Together, they demonstrate that community is an unending process. The social interactions of these particular communities *are* unique. At the same time, though, they are typical of most communities in that they are shaped by both the various and varying perceptions community members have of their situations and actions, and by changing environmental circumstances.

Notes

1. This chapter draws on material presented in Kempers 1998. Permission granted.

2. Most of the research for this paper was conducted between May 1995 and September 1996, during which time I was a participant-observer in the range of community activities referred to in this chapter. I also conducted dozens of open-ended interviews with a diverse group of local residents; it is from the interview data that I have drawn the descriptive material as well as the phrases and analyses in quotations. I continue to follow Waterville's and REM's community experiment.

Pushing the Limits of Community

3. These dynamics, part of a "persistent and perplexing" pattern of development known as "sprawl," are affecting the state as a whole. See Evan Richert's "Confronting the Issue of Sprawl in Maine" (1997).

4. The Center for Consensual Democracy is located in Woolwich, Maine.

5. See Lloyd P. Wells and Larry G. Lemmel, *Recreating Democracy: Breathing New Life into American Communities* (Woolwich, ME: CCD, 1998).

Chapter Six

"IT AIN'T OVER TILL IT'S OVER" OR "IT'S ONLY JUST BEGUN"
Boston's West End and Celebration, Florida

> [M]aking deep connections with others. This is what we mean by community. (Whitmyer 1993, xx)

The preceding case studies reveal that communities are always in flux due to external constraints, internal pressures, and members' interactions. Moreover, these case studies underscore the importance of defining and analyzing community as a multidimensional concept. There are at least three key dimensions to the phenomenon we identify as community: the ecological, or *community as a spatial unit*; the social-structural, or *community as patterned social interaction*; and the cultural-symbolic, or *community as a state of mind* (Hunter 1974). Although the degree to which these dimensions are present in any given community is variable, all are important. The situation at hand appears to call up, or emphasize as relevant, changing combinations of these defining elements.

The very different communities of Waterville, Cambridge, Unitarian Universalists, and Maine Indians are simultaneously emergent processes and evolving products. Each of these interactive communities is distinguished by history and location, particular and sometimes conflicting goals, and shared experiences and traditions. As people interpret these elements or dimensions they come to understand that "members of a group of people (a) have something in common with each other, which (b) distinguishes them in a significant way from the members of other putative groups" (Cohen 1985, 12).

This dual understanding of similarity and difference is significant in that it helps clarify the boundaries of a community. Such boundaries

Chapter 6

are often expressed in physical, linguistic, religious, or even legal terms, but it is very important to acknowledge that "not all boundaries, and not *all* the components of *any* boundary, are so objectively apparent" (Cohen 1985, 12). Frequently these boundaries, and the resultant encapsulation of a community's identity, exist in symbolic form. Thus it makes sense to think of community as a symbolic entity existing in the minds of people who individually impute meaning to their community (Cohen 1985).

This notion of symbolic communities and the significance of symbolism in community must not be underestimated, as Anthony Cohen (1985) argues so persuasively. Symbols of community are representations that refer to, or reflect, something that may or may not exist. Additionally, such symbols may serve to define and create reality as those who use them supply part of their meaning. The creation and definition of community involve different meanings for different members—what is perceived as important by some may be imperceptible to others—and thus community itself is highly variable. However, a community's diversity is glossed over by its shared "boundary-expressing" symbols: members use the same word and claim to belong to the "same" community. Still, the meanings of these symbols, how they are interpreted, and the ways they are acted upon are actually based on idiosyncratic interests and experiences.

Cohen reasons that (1) boundaries are what distinguish and separate one community from others, and (2) boundaries can change. For example, if the physical or structural bases of a community's identity (or boundaries) are destroyed or "become anachronistic," they can be "replaced by cultural bases expressed symbolically" (81). This sort of boundary adaptation or manipulation, a crucial aspect of community survival, is based on the principal that "the symbolic expression of community and its boundaries increases in importance as the actual geo-social boundaries of the community are undermined, blurred or otherwise weakened" (50). In other words, people can compensate for the weakening, or even destruction, of the physical basis of a community "by bolstering and reinforcing the symbolic statement of the boundary and, therefore, of the terms in which the community can experience a sense of self" (81).

All of this relies heavily on two powerful resources: memories of the past and traditional activities. In their landmark book *Habits of the Heart* (1985), Robert Bellah and his coauthors use the term "community of memory" to describe and explain how "real" community endures.

"It Ain't Over Till It's Over" or "It's Only Just Begun"

Every community, they argue, is defined by its past and its memories of the past. But it is not enough to say that remembering its past through stories helps keep a community alive. These narrative histories, which include "examples of the men and women who have embodied and exemplified the meaning of the community" as well as accounts of "suffering inflicted—dangerous memories" (153), serve often to reaffirm and sometimes to redirect the community. In short, communities evolve as members individually and collectively reflect on their interactions and relationships.

Complementing the dynamic of story-telling are "practices of commitment." This term is used in *Habits of the Heart* to include shared ritual, ethical, and aesthetic activities that "define the community as a way of life" (154). The performance of such traditional activities contributes to a community's survival because this kind of collective engagement permits members to identify across individual differences. Members invest their community with their selves, and their community accommodates these selves without compromising individuality by giving "to each of them an additional referent for their identities" (Cohen 1985, 109). Not only are communities continually evolving, they also, at any given point in time, are characterized by variety and difference.

The importance of place, symbolic community and community symbols, memories and "practices of commitment"—all of this begs for illustrative examples. The remainder of this chapter explores these issues in different contexts. The next section revisits Boston's West End, a community seemingly destroyed more than 35 years ago by urban renewal. However, many former West Enders have remained united by a variety of ideas and events that both perpetuate old ties and develop new ones. The West End case pushes our thinking of what "counts" as community in a world of changing places and illustrates the paradoxical blurring between the destruction and (re)creation of community. To broaden this discussion, the last part of the chapter considers the aims of the planning and design movement known as "New Urbanism" and the planned community of Celebration, Florida.

The "Old" and the "New" West End

In the 1950s, the West End of Boston was one of the city's oldest and most diverse neighborhoods. Two dozen nationalities were represented among the 7,000 people living in about 2,800 households located on a

Chapter 6

48-acre tract bounded by North Station, the Charles River, and Massachusetts General Hospital. The neighborhood was also one of the poorest; its narrow winding streets were lined with multistoried tenements, many of which were badly maintained and unoccupied, and renters in the smaller apartments sometimes shared bathroom and toilet facilities.

By mid-century, many political, economic, and religious leaders of Boston considered the area an overall slum, ripe for clearance and redevelopment. Public accounts described the West End as an "overpopulated," "blighted" and "substandard" neighborhood "in dire need of redevelopment." Beyond redemption, it was a "cancer" that had to be excised before it affected the entire city of Boston ("The West End Preliminary Report" (1953), Boston Planning Board, cited in Kruh 1992). Boston housing officials began to study various proposals in 1950 and three years later formally announced a redevelopment plan that targeted the West End. The approved plan was to create a "new," economically secure Boston by revitalizing the downtown area, and clearing out the West End for the creation of high-rent luxury apartments was an essential step in this urban renewal process.

Securing the required federal and local support took over five years. The first public signs of resistance came in 1956 when a small group of West Enders formed the Save the West End Committee; during its several years of existence, however, it won few local supporters and had little influence. A second wave of protest emerged during a hearing held in October 1957 when more than two hundred residents took turns speaking out against the redevelopment project that called for the destruction of their homes. While sympathetic to the residents, city officials nevertheless continued to move forward and "in January, 1958, the city and the federal government signed the contract that would require the latter to pay two-thirds and the former, one-third of the costs of purchasing the land, relocating the present residents, and clearing the site for the redeveloper" (Gans 1982, 326).

The relocation and demolition project actually began in April 1958 when the city took the West End properties under the power of eminent domain. Families began to move out once the school year ended in June, and by the following summer the buildings of the West End (with the exception of several deemed to be historic) were demolished and the exodus of its residents was complete. In January 1962 the first residents of the "new" West End moved into the luxury apartments in the new Charles River Park complex, a complex still noted for its signs

"It Ain't Over Till It's Over" or "It's Only Just Begun"

along Storrow Drive that read "If you lived here . . . [sic] you'd be home now." Obviously, it would have been simply impossible to recreate the West End. Still, a "more balanced mixture of high-rent and low-rent apartments . . . would have provided an opportunity for some families to remain in a neighborhood they loved and where they had spent all of their lives" (O'Connor 1993, 133). The choices made by Boston officials precluded such an opportunity, and thus, as historian Thomas H. O'Connor observed, "the future of the old West End was gone forever" (1993, 133).

But what *was* it that was gone, destroyed forever? When sociologist Herbert Gans began his year-long study of the West End in 1957,[1] he found friendly relations as well as common values among and between the various ethnic groups. He used the term *urban village* to describe the area's lifestyle, noting that while everyone pitched in to cope with general emergencies, each ethnic group tried to resolve its own members' individual problems. Despite the fact that "outsiders" like the city's politicians viewed the West End as a unified community, it was clear to "insiders" that loyalty to one's kin and close friends overrode any cohesive sense of unity. As Gans summed up, "the concept of the West End as a single neighborhood was foreign to the West Enders themselves" (11).

Group allegiance alone did not account for the generally passive reaction of most West Enders to the urban renewal project. Residents' confusion and collective sense of denial regarding the impending demolition were bolstered by local caretaking agencies who supported the development plans and actively tried to persuade their West End clients that the coming changes would only improve their lives. Additionally, the fact that West Enders were basically excluded from the planning and decision-making processes, and then told of deadlines that were subsequently and repeatedly missed between 1953 and 1958, further explain their disbelief and limited, "muted" protest activities. In theory, federal regulations required the Boston Redevelopment Association (BRA) to assure the West Enders that they would be relocated into safe, clean housing. In fact, however, a majority of the residents had to fend for themselves and arrange for new housing on their own. Aware of no effective way of fighting city hall, most residents simply packed up and left.

Several West End political representatives filed appeals, and a few local teenagers damaged some construction machinery in an attempt to sabotage the project. However, significant opposition to the West End demolition developed only after the area was cleared. Beginning in the

Chapter 6

early sixties, a series of books and articles sharply criticizing the urban renewal began to appear. Independent researchers contradicted the statistics and definitions used by the city of Boston to label the West End a slum, and stories of the hardships endured by hundreds of displaced families were presented in a television documentary and in numerous newspapers and magazines.

Public perceptions began to shift. The West End redevelopment project, once extolled as the best way of improving the lot of its residents, quickly came to symbolize the very worst in urban renewal and planning. As a result, people in other neighborhoods and cities began to challenge government authority, demanding new protections, new techniques of restoration, and new laws. The West End experience contributed to the passage of the Uniform Relocation Act of 1970 and at the international level became the model for the policy that urban renewal must be sensitive to the residents. Ultimately, urban renewal—the policy of "saving" a city by destroying its parts—was abandoned.

Throughout all this, many of the former residents stayed in touch with each other, exchanging memories and comparing their experiences with depression, distress, grief, and anger caused by the destruction of the West End. Unified by the belief that their homes were taken unfairly, many proceeded with their new lives convinced that their old community "never died." There was enthusiastic participation in the summer camp activities established by West Enders for their children, and many former West Enders got involved in organizing and attending annual reunions. These sorts of ritual celebrations continue and have always been very well-attended.

As part of this overall effort to "keep the community together," several West Enders started a quarterly newsletter in 1985 called *The West Ender*. Proclaiming its dedication "to preserving the pride, integrity, tradition and memories of our beloved West End," this newsletter has grown from an initial circulation of 125 to its current subscriber base of well over 4,000 individuals in more than 35 states and several foreign countries. *The West Ender* regularly lists deaths and births as well as a business directory of former residents. Additionally, it reprints articles about the West End that appear in local newspapers and includes in each issue photographs, stories, and historical accounts of past West Ender affairs written by former West Enders themselves. Part of each issue is reserved for trips down "memory lane," and overall the "remember when . . ." theme has been very strong. Still, all this is balanced by the

"It Ain't Over Till It's Over" or "It's Only Just Begun"

many announcements of current and future activities for the families and friends of those who used to consider the West End their home.

Hope has been another unifying force helping to "keep the community alive"—hope in justice for the egregious wrong committed between 1958 and 1960 and for a return to the old West End. This abstract hope was made more concrete in the late 1980s when the city of Boston reappropriated the last undeveloped parcel of land in the West End because its owner failed to develop it as and when he had promised. The BRA, in subsequently announcing its own plans for an apartment complex called Lowell Square to be built on the plot, cited the need to redress the wrong done to West End residents nearly four decades earlier.

Former West Enders saw this as the last-chance opportunity for at least some to "come home." Confident that all or most of the apartments would be reserved for West Enders, a small group that included *The West Ender* founders formed the Old West End Housing Corporation (OWEHC) in 1988 to work with the BRA on the Lowell Square project. Final plans included the allocation of space for a museum dedicated to the old West End and for offices for the OWEHC. Supporters of the OWEHC quickly generated a list of over 300 former West End residents interested in buying into the 183-unit, mixed-market development, and OWEHC representatives were included as guests of honor at the Lowell Square groundbreaking ceremonies in 1994. It began to look as if the resettlement promises of the original West End Urban Renewal Plan would finally be honored.

The initial sense of vindication disappeared the following year, however, when city officials said that federal regulations and a 1993 consent decree regarding new housing mandated an affirmative-action marketing plan and a goal of 41 percent minority residents for Lowell Square. This meant that the city could set aside about half of the units, but only a third of those with the largest subsidies, for the former West Enders. More precisely, they would get first dibs or preference in only 30 percent of the 58 low-income apartments and only half of the 48 moderate-income units; of the 77 market-rate units, all priced out of the range of most West Enders, they had preference in 75 percent.

Angered by what it perceived to be broken promises, OWEHC filed a motion in federal court on September 15, 1995, seeking clarification on whether or not the unique situation of the West Enders exempted them from this mandate. The court's response was that federal guidelines had to be satisfied and that OWEHC and its constituency lacked the necessary

Chapter 6

racial diversity to challenge the guidelines. At this point, Boston City Council members got involved by appropriating funds to hire a lawyer to negotiate with the involved federal and city agencies and the group of former West Enders. These negotiations proved unsuccessful. The West End group turned down the city's "deal" of preference in 101, or 55 percent, of the 183 units, noting both that this really meant that West Enders would have priority in a total of only 23 affordable units and that even former West Enders who were minorities would not gain preference in the subsidized apartments set aside for minority applicants.

Sympathetic to the West Enders claims, the City Council subsequently authorized an additional $25,000 to help West Enders cover the costs of suing the city to enforce their "right of first refusal" to all 183 Lowell Square units. When Mayor Menino vetoed this move, OWEHC's board of directors vowed to come up with the money necessary to continue and to take their case all the way to the Supreme Court if necessary. Once the suit was filed, the conflict escalated. In November 1996 the defendants in the case—the BRA, Lowell Square Associates, and the Archdiocese of Boston—filed a motion asking that the case be dismissed due to lack of merit.

This standoff continued until early 1997, when a U.S. District Court Judge ruled that former West Enders did not have exclusive occupancy rights to the entire Lowell Square development. The OWEHC Board of Directors appealed this ruling, but in January 1998 the U.S. Court of Appeals for the First Circuit upheld the lower court's decision. Still convinced that their cause was justified, OWEHC appealed to the U.S. Supreme Court. In October 1998, marking what was probably the final defeat in a forty-year struggle to reclaim a piece of their old neighborhood, the Supreme Court declined to review the case.

Throughout all this, a core group regularly told newspaper reporters that former West Enders remained "together as a community." An alternate view of the situation, suggesting that this sentiment was more a nostalgic misremembering of the past, was illustrated in a comment from an August 19, 1996, *Boston Globe* editorial: "through their [the former West Enders] eyes, the cramped streets and apartments at the back of Beacon Hill were practically sacred." A more critical view appeared in a November 25, 1997 *Globe* article by Peter Canellos, who pointed out that while there still was widespread sympathy for those who had been displaced during the West End demolition, "outside observers . . . also wonder when a city's tendencies to remember its past becomes a pathology, part of an urban personality that keeps paddling backward."

"It Ain't Over Till It's Over" or "It's Only Just Begun"

These sorts of challenges to the ongoing self-identification of former West Enders as a viable community (albeit one "in exile") triggered spirited responses that reveal the complexity and importance of the unifying memories. In an article by Brian MacQuarrie in the January 10, 1997, *Boston Globe*, 66-year old Vincent Raso had this to say about why he still grieved for the West End: "It wasn't the mortar or the wood that we miss. It was the people, the type of people who were here." This idea that the people were ultimately more significant than the place was captured in a letter by Carmella LoPresti, printed in the June 1998 issue of *The West Ender*: "The greatest gift from the West End was the closeness of family and complete understanding of multiracial and multiethnic people. This tolerance was instilled in us and has been the one lasting effect of our relationship with the West End."

Memories help to keep the past alive for some former residents, but most readily acknowledge that "the West End is no more." It cannot be resurrected and its experience will never be repeated. The buildings are gone, and so in a material sense the old West End is gone. Things are indeed different now, as former resident J. Almeida wrote in the March 1998 *West Ender*:

> Originally built and shaped by working-class immigrants of many nationalities and cultures, snatched and smashed by the wrecking ball of the powers that be, the Old West End of Boston has been rebuilt and reshaped by those who never ever lived there, and those who had have been left hanging with a string of broken promises and everlasting memories.

The long fight appears to be over. However, although the West End as a distinct ecological, social, and cultural entity has disappeared, a West End community spirit lives on. Former residents continue to identify themselves as West Enders bound together by a symbolic past, and memories are powerful. In March 1999 *The West Ender* began charging a $10 annual subscription fee, a move that has made the future of the newsletter more secure. That this in turn will help nurture the community spirit through the retelling of its stories was made clear by Andrew Russo in a June 1997 letter to *The West Ender*: "Although I was born in 1972, long after the wrecking balls had demolished the West End, I often heard stories about it from my grandparents. I am thankful to you for helping me understand better that vibrant community through your newspaper."

Chapter 6

Creating Community?

The story of Boston's West End offers important reminders about the importance of place, the power of symbols, and the significance of memories in community life. During the last two decades, these sorts of reminders have made their way into a loosely unified set of urban planning ideas and design practices. Known as "new urbanism" or "neotraditionalism," this contemporary approach seeks to create and revive community in America by offering alternatives to urban sprawl. Population density and diversity, pedestrian orientation and reliance on public transit, and mixed land uses including the dedication of public open space, all of which foster opportunities for social engagement, are unifying principles among neotraditionalists.

At the heart of this movement is the longstanding belief that a carefully designed and built environment will improve the quality of social life. This assumption that design determines behavior has informed the planning and construction of a wide range of communities in this country's history, from seventeenth century Puritan towns to the secular settlements of the nineteenth century, from post-World War II Levittown to the "new towns" of Reston, Virginia, and Columbia, Maryland. This influential assumption has also been responsible for some colossal planning disasters, especially in the area of housing developments for poor inner-city residents and particularly in the case of Pruitt-Igoe in St. Louis, Missouri.

Completed in 1954, this mammoth public housing development consisted of 2,700 apartment units in 33 separate eleven-story buildings. Almost immediately, residents in this high-rise, low-income project experienced isolation, inconveniences, and injuries, as well as a rapidly escalating rate of crime. By 1970 fewer than half of the units were occupied, and six years later the entire project was torn down. The major lesson of Pruitt-Igoe is that any large-scale design that ignores the various social processes that interact in and with the environment is doomed to failure. While the extent to which new urbanism has incorporated this lesson has not yet been fully established, the lasting success of its community developments ultimately requires understanding that community is a product of various uncontrolled, often unanticipated local and extralocal forces.

The neotraditional vision of planned or intentional community is being tested in Celebration, Florida, a town built in the mid-1990s by

"It Ain't Over Till It's Over" or "It's Only Just Begun"

the Walt Disney Corporation. The company's 1986 decision to create a residential development was based in part on emotion—in the 1960s Walt Disney had talked about his dream of building a model city—and in part on economics—by developing a large chunk of its Florida land holdings, the company would reduce its attraction as a potential takeover target. It was also based on politics—by "de-annexing" the ten thousand acres required for Celebration from its state-chartered municipality called the Reedy Creek Improvement District, the company could generate the kind of local support crucial for its future development projects (Pollan 1997). Convinced that the decision was strategically sound, Disney executives committed themselves to a project that would not only make money, but also would stand as a state-of-the-art example of contemporary community planning. It appears ironic, then, that the designers of this forward-looking project actually looked to the past for inspiration; "the emphasis of the marketing campaign for [the project] was always on old-fashioned values and resurrecting the small town where many Americans either grew up or wished they had grown up or, through the power of revisionist history, thought they had grown up" (Frantz and Collins 1999, 28).

After lengthy meetings with some of the nation's top-quality architects and real-estate developers, in 1991 Disney officials announced general plans for an "old-fashioned" town of twenty thousand houses. The final master plan, a hybrid of neotraditionalism and commercial development, identified education, wellness, technology, environment, and a sense of community as the town's cornerstones. In order to control the creation and quality of both the public spaces and the private houses, the planners developed the *Celebration Pattern Book*. "No detail was left to chance or whimsy" (Frantz and Collins 1999, 66), for there were rules governing just about everything—including the styles and paint colors for the houses, the location of doors and driveways, and the choice and size of shrubs.

Celebration's downtown area, complete with a movie theater, a bank, a post office, a variety of upscale shops and restaurants, and a visitor center, is located next to a small manmade lake. A network of narrow streets flows northward out of this area in a fan-shaped, loosely gridded configuration that favors pedestrian comfort over automobile convenience. Housing in Celebration ranges from relatively inexpensive townhouse apartments to medium-income cottages, and upward to million-dollar homes; and these different categories are deliberately mixed

Chapter 6

together. All of the residences, even the most expensive homes, are located on small lots and all are situated close to the curbs. Every design decision was made to encourage interaction between neighbors.

When the first houses were completed in 1996, thousands of prospective home-buyers entered a series of lotteries arranged by the Disney Development Corporation. Even though the prices in Celebration were nearly a third higher than those in other subdivisions in the area, people from around the nation went to extraordinary lengths to "win" the privilege of purchasing a home in Celebration. Many families were initially drawn by the Disney name, and many others were attracted by the scale and proposed facilities of the neotraditional town; all, however, seemed eager to participate in this experiment in community building. Expectations were high from the start, and from the very beginning this experimental town and its pioneers have been closely watched. Thus, it was no real surprise that when problems with the public elementary school arose, they became a media event.

As Celebration was being conceptualized, designed, and built, considerable attention was focused on developing a world-class educational program and school for the children. Like everything else associated with the town, the curriculum was not ordinary. Key characteristics of Celebration's alternative public school program included: cooperative learning for grades K–12; large classes of mixed age groups; flexible schedules, technology-based, individualized learning plans; and student assessment based on portfolios instead of exams and grades. In 1996, two hundred students began classes. They were held in temporary quarters because the new school building was not yet completed, but the school curriculum was firmly in place. Within months, this controversial approach to education came under fire.

Disenchanted with the school's nontraditional educational philosophy, several sets of parents withdrew their children and moved, and "by the end of the first school year, more than twenty families had pulled their children out of the school" (Frantz and Collins 1999, 136). The formal August 1997 opening of Celebration School, a $20-million showpiece of educational and technological innovations, did little to quell the complaints. A group of more than two dozen dissatisfied parents tried to get Disney officials involved in making changes in the school, but to no avail. Frustrated by what they perceived to be the company's non-response, the group then contacted the local press. As negative stories about Celebration School started to appear on front pages

"It Ain't Over Till It's Over" or "It's Only Just Begun"

and the evening news, a much larger group of residents came out in support of the school.

Tensions mounted between school critics and supporters, and the situation became messier and more political as neighbors stopped speaking to each other (Ross 1999). Disney gradually became more involved—indirectly through the boosterism of its paid "community services manager," and directly by hiring a leading school supporter as its "educational consultant." In Fall 1996, Disney got in deeper through its unsuccessful attempt to secure from disgruntled parents who wanted to move written promises never to reveal why they left Celebration, in exchange for exemption from the contract clause that prohibited profits on the sale of houses held less than one year (Pollan 1997). The company subsequently distanced itself from the fray, and in fall 1997 Disney removed its name from the town banner, saying it was "eager for the public to begin recognizing Celebration as a real, thriving community with its own unique identity" (Pollan 1997, 14).

As the struggle over Celebration School continued, concerned parents began working directly with school administrators to bring about desired changes. This shift was significant. As two participants wrote, residents were now "taking a role in shaping their lives" and "abandoning the comforting notion that Disney would take care of everything" (Frantz and Collins 1999, 296). Another commentator, reflecting on the positive nature of these reported developments, puts it this way: "The angry meetings of parents were proof that Celebration was evolving from a cozy, corporate nanny state peopled by starry-eyed, infantilized Disney true believers into a real community of engaged citizens, which defines its own ideals and copes with its own problems" (Anderson 1999, 76).

Celebration School continues to evolve, with cooperation now characterizing the relations and interactions between parents, school administrators, and teachers. Frustrations remain, but all those involved appear to recognize that it is not up to Disney to solve the problems. In the words of one former resident, "Celebration had been planned as a real community, and so it would have to stand on its own to prove its authenticity" (Ross 1999, 314). Those who have invested in Celebration appear to have committed themselves to the long haul of making their community work.

This determination to succeed has been extended to ongoing construction and building problems. Nearly every home-buyer experienced delays, and when they finally moved in, many discovered—and then

Chapter 6

had to negotiate for necessary repairs to—faulty windows, incorrectly installed cabinets and porches, leaky roofs, and unconnected sewer lines. There *was* a positive side, though. All the delays and mistakes became a bonding source of shared experience, and they further helped "many people recognize that the promise of living in Celebration embodies more than the quality of construction" (Frantz and Collins 1999, 97). Numerous residents have come to feel that Celebration is a caring community that supports its members "in ways that . . . [go] far beyond neighborly expectations of mutual help" (Ross 1999, 241).

In short, Celebration seems to be exploring a sense of itself as a community. Neighborhood friendships and a social-psychological "we" feeling are deepening, and an informal network of clubs, volunteer groups, religious organizations, and civic activities is growing. This growth suggests that community develops when people share a taken-for-granted, unconscious set of daily patterns and relationships, rooted in tradition and connected to a place, that are a prime source of social valuation, and that endure over time (Hunter 1997).

The often messy business of community building cannot be engineered. Celebrationites have discovered that collective hard work and a determined commitment to resolve differences for the sake of unity are essential ingredients of community. Residents of Celebration have demonstrated that they are engaged in something more than a well-orchestrated housing development. They have forged bonds for which there was no planning blueprint and come together in response to foiled expectations and frustrating challenges. Still, the future is unknown, and time alone will reveal the full story of Celebration's community.

Conclusions

Ties that bind people to place, and in community, are powerful. As the West End experience illustrates, when the physical basis on which a community is built actually disappears, such ties can become more symbolic than real. Alternately, the Celebration "experiment" demonstrates that "place"—capable of pulling people together, can be more symbolic than real, at least initially. In both instances, though, the reality of community is tied to members' perceptions, memories, and hopes. Especially important is a collective interdependence and a shared belief that the future of their community is in their hands.

"It Ain't Over Till It's Over" or "It's Only Just Begun"

For former West Enders and for residents of Celebration, community is in part a subjective experience. In both cases, though, the ecological or physical dimension of community remains important; both remain place-oriented, albeit in different ways. Any ongoing cohesiveness among former West Enders rests on memories of experiences in a Boston neighborhood and on the experiences of unsuccessful attempts to reclaim that place. People who bought into Celebration, while sharing a high degree of trust in Disney, were generally attracted to a particular suburban alternative based on traditional, perhaps nostalgic ideas about small town community of past generations. The evolution of each community has involved a variety of accomplishments. And for each, the hard work of community has turned out to be not an end in itself, but a messy, sometimes troublesome means to an always uncertain end.

Notes

1. Gans' study of the old West End resulted in his classic work *The Urban Villagers* (New York: Free Press, 1962/1982).

Chapter Seven

(RE)CREATING COMMUNITY?
The "Virtual" Communities of Cyberspace

> The net can either enhance communities by enabling a new kind of local public space or it can undermine communities by pulling people away from local enclaves and toward global, virtual ones. The second trend is in ascendancy. (Doheny-Farina 1996, 54–55)
>
> [N]ew communication technologies are driving out of fashion the traditional belief that community can only be found locally. (Hampton and Wellman 1999, 476)

Technology can transform individuals, communities, and societies. This fact was recognized by nineteenth-century theorists in the new field of sociology, first in Europe and later in the United States, who attempted to explain how the interrelated phenomena of industrialization, urbanization, and capitalism were changing social life. Ferdinand Tonnies claimed the basic change was away from a communal life based in kinship ties (*gemeinschaft*), toward a less personal social existence organized on shared practical interests (*gesellschaft*). For Max Weber, the shift was from "traditional" to "rational" society. Emile Durkheim argued that social ties rooted in shared ideas and experiences (mechanical solidarity) were being replaced by social connections based on mutual dependence among individuals engaged in highly specialized tasks (organic solidarity).

These themes regarding the distinctiveness of modern social life were elaborated in the United States, starting with the "Chicago School" studies completed at the University of Chicago and including anthropologist Robert Redfield's research which contrasted folk and urban societies. Unifying these very diverse investigations was a largely uncritical, nostalgic yearning for the face-to-face relations that presumably characterized preindustrial rural communities, as well as an informal

Chapter 7

agreement that technologically driven, urbanized living was incompatible with community life. Fears about the erosion and loss of community have been partially assuaged during the twentieth century by studies that have documented community persistence. The field of community studies is being roiled anew, specifically by advances in computer technology. This is because computers and computer-mediated communication (CMC), arguably the most significant new technology since the start of the Industrial Revolution, appear to be introducing dramatic, unprecedented changes in our personal lives and social relationships.

Both critics and supporters of computer technology recognize its transformative potential, and, at the start of the twenty-first century, it is difficult to imagine living without computers. In just one generation, this technology has changed the ways we work, play, learn, move about, save and spend our money, and govern ourselves. Millions of people are now linked online. Wireless technology and CMC have revolutionized the infrastructure we use to exchange information, making it possible to exchange thoughts and ideas instantly across great distances. While it is impossible to make accurate predictions about the future, it appears obvious that for now the interrelated phenomena of CMC and the emerging social formations called cybersociety (Jones 1995) are changing our identities and the ways we think, and are also reworking the processes we relied on in the past to initiate and maintain interpersonal relations. Both directly and indirectly, the development of the online world known as cyberspace[1] is raising new questions about the extent and meaning of community in our lives today.

As illustrated in the preceding case studies, conceptions of community typically or traditionally tend to rely on physical place or locality, as well as on deeply personal, face-to-face exchanges. However, CMC technology has seemingly erased the boundaries of geographic space while introducing countless new opportunities for interaction via communication that is more expansive and less constrained than face-to-face encounters. At the same time, the people who populate cyberspace typically do not meet in the flesh. Social interaction on-line is basically optional, and much of it is limited to written text; still, many people involved in online social exchange systems see themselves involved in building and sustaining community. Have the essential criteria of community broadened or changed? Has common interest or even entertainment replaced physical location as the most vital anchor of community? Is deliberate communication a viable source of community? How

(Re)Creating Community?

important are commitment and stability if joining, participating in, or disengaging from online communities can be so easily accomplished—and with little or no consequence? Finally, in the ephemeral world of CMC where exchanges are frequently anonymous (or pseudonomous) and where identity is so fluid, how "real" are these virtual communities? These are urgent questions. We need to understand CMC and cyberspace because they have the "potential to change us as humans, as communities, as democracies" (Rheingold 1993, 15). As one researcher observed, there is "a sense that we are embarking on an adventure in creating new communities and new forms of community." Furthermore, "that sense is fueled by two motives; first, that we *need* new communities, and second, that we *can* create them technologically" (Jones 1995, 14). This chapter responds to these issues and concerns. It begins with a brief history of computer networking that resulted in the now ubiquitous Internet. In the second section, the most familiar, text-based CMC systems that have fostered the growth of "virtual" communities are described. The third section compares and contrasts observations regarding community in cyberspace. The chapter concludes with a discussion of key implications of CMC—at once a technology, a product, and a creator of social relations—for contemporary community.

A Brief History

Cyberspace is everywhere. It is the mix of computers, communication systems, news and discussion groups, databases, and commercial services, as well as the people who enter this realm in order to find and share information. The system that was developed to unite the millions of cyberspace computers and their users is the Internet. This information-shipping network of networks got its start half a century ago, and its "accidental" history (Rheingold 1993) is a fascinating account of visionary thinking, practical responses, and unanticipated consequences.[2]

The impetus for what has become the Internet began in 1957 with the launching of the first artificial satellite, Sputnik, by the Soviet Union. Humiliated but determined to gain superiority in the space war, the U.S. government authorized the Department of Defense to set up a research program to improve national security. The agency created to oversee this effort, ARPA (Advanced Research Projects Agency), joined forces with a few universities (MIT, Stanford, and Carnegie Mellon) to invest in

Chapter 7

research designed to make computers more intelligent. Computers at that time were huge and very expensive, and their use was limited to number-crunching research projects. Over the next two decades, this fruitful collaboration raised the profile of computers nationwide, and resulted in such varied contributions as

> time sharing, computer networks, landmark programming languages like Lisp, operating systems like Multics (which led to Unix), virtual memory, computer security systems, parallel computer systems, distributed computer systems, computers that understand human speech, vision systems, and artificial intelligence, an endeavor responsible for understanding and emulating human intelligence by machine. (Dertouzos 1997, 37)

By the late 1960s a growing number of research groups around the nation were asking for increased funds from ARPA for computer-related projects. In response to this pressure and as a way of distributing costs, the agency began to encourage computer sharing. The resulting network of users, called Arpanet, was the "granddaddy" of today's internet. At its inception in the early 1970s Arpanet was composed of fewer than two dozen universities and a handful of military sites. It quickly became busier than expected, so members of Arpanet—sponsored by ARPA—began to consider how to expand resource sharing by networking different networks.

Over the next decade, three key developments pushed Arpanet closer to what we now know as the Internet. First, the now standard procedures for communicating between many different networks (the TCP-IP protocol) was established. Second was the emergence of an informal, grassroots approach for establishing standards for the networked system, which would give the Internet its open, democratic character. And third, in the early 1980s as it became possible to link an entire building's computers and workstations into local area networks (LANs), demand for internet connectivity surged.

The system of networked systems was further expanded in the mid-1980s when the National Science Foundation interconnected its various computer research sites. Soon afterward, several other governmental agencies (specifically, NASA and the Department of Energy) and a host of national and international organizations joined on. Subsequent growth of the Internet has been tremendous. In the words of one participant-observer, " . . . [b]y the late-1990s, the baby network that was

(Re)Creating Community?

once destined to have no more than sixty-four *computers* sported over 200,000 interconnected *networks* serving some forty million users—and it is growing at 100 percent per year" (Dertouzos 1997, 40).

The creation of the World Wide Web and browsers (like Netscape and Mosaic) used to navigate the information-laden, interactive home pages of the Web helped insinuate the Internet into our everyday lives. The Web has become the most frequently used means of access to different sorts of Internet information. The need for two kinds of systems guided its development in the early 1990s. The first was a locator system that would indicate the Internet location or address of audio, video, and textual information; and the second was "a simple language for assembling such information into home pages on any kind of computer and a set of conventions for linking and transporting any such information across the Internet" (Dertouzos 1997, 41). The technological result is a web of linked information that any user can explore (aided by any one of a number of search engines) simply by clicking a mouse.

The Internet as originally conceived was intended "to link the core processing capabilities in America's top computer science research centers" (Hafner and Lyon 1996, 232). Almost from the start though, this resource-sharing technology was recognized by its users as a great medium for asking questions and trading comments. Problems that made transmitting these early electronic message communications difficult and unreliable were eliminated during the 1970s as technology improved and as agreements were reached about the technological underpinnings of electronic mail. "Things only got better as the network grew and technology converged with the torrential human tendency to talk" (Hafner and Lyon 1996, 187).

No one person, organization, or government runs the Internet as such. On one hand, thousands of selfless volunteers labor without pay to keep the discussion groups and interactive sites working smoothly. On the other hand, the World Wide Web Consortium, located at MIT's Laboratory for Computer Science, provides the forum in which the 355 member companies try to resolve disagreements about Web codes, format, and philosophy. Today the Internet is used by millions to access purely social realms. People from all walks of life have come to rely on interactive computer technologies for interpersonal communication, and as people connect, "new social spaces" are created. The next section describes text-based communication systems that foster the online interaction that shapes these new places.

Chapter 7

Forming New Spaces and Online Places

The most familiar and frequently used means of communicating in cyberspace is electronic mail. E-mail is a quick and easy way to stay in touch with others. It generally involves one person typing and sending a message directly to another person who can then read the message and maybe respond at her leisure. E-mail can also be used to convey information to an entire group via a discussion list. In this instance, a message sent to a group address is copied and forwarded to all the e-mail addresses on a list; when others respond to the message on the list, a group discussion can be formed. E-mail lists are typically owned by one person or several persons, and it is the owners who decide on membership and content in a discussion group. E-mail communication involves taking turns, which means that the interaction does not require everyone to be at the same place at the same time.

Another form of asynchronous group discussion is found in bulletin board systems (BBSs) or newsgroups. Participants in these technically simple conferencing systems choose topics and organize incoming messages through a commercial online service like AOL. Even though the basic function of BBSs is information exchange, conferencing systems such as the WELL and Usenet[3] repeatedly demonstrate that participants also rely on them for affiliation and support.

Aside from the difference in membership and content control, the major distinction between newsgroups and e-mail systems is like that between pulling and pushing: in conferencing systems and BBSs, "people must select groups and messages they want to read and actively request them" [pulling], while in e-mail, "messages are sent to people without them necessarily doing anything" [pushing] (Smith and Kollock 1999, 6). Both, however, have a "memory" in so far as records of what is communicated are stored, and since the 1980s both communication tools have steadily gained users.

Whereas BBSs and e-mail systems require users to take turns in a process loosely modeled after the U.S. postal system, "text chat" systems are based on the model of CB radio in which people interact in real time (Smith and Kollock 1999). The largest noncommercial chat system, Internet Relay Chat (IRC), is a dynamic, synchronous means of communicating comments and questions about a huge range of topics from and to thousands of users simultaneously. Since the mid-1980s, three basic characteristics have shaped IRC "conversations" and the resulting

(Re)Creating Community?

subcultures: "artificial but stable identities, quick wit, and the use of words to construct an imagined shared context for conversation" (Rheingold 1993, 176). The many users of IRC, gathered into what are called channels (each one of which is focused on a particular topic and has an owner who controls its use), are free to experiment with self-representation and expressive communication.

The people who "hang out" in chat rooms adopt nicknames, invent online identities, and interact with other anonymous characters. Their textual "conversations" also include imagined ("virtual") actions, like "Margot squirms uncomfortably," which are set off textually from the dialogue and serve to create a context for the ongoing exchange. IRC is like an unending stream (as new comments appear at the bottom of the computer screen, previous ones are scrolled off the top), one which participants observe, enter, and leave whenever they desire and with no formal consequences.

Another distinct form of synchronistic CMC is found in the family of networked, interactive programs known as Multi-User Domains (MUDs).[4] These real-time, multiparticipant environments allow people to use computers to play adventure games and maintain contact with other people. Both adventure and social MUDs "attempt to model physical places as well as face-to-face interaction" by presenting users/players with written descriptions of imaginary worlds and allowing them to "build new spaces, create objects, and to use powerful programming languages to automate their behavior" (Smith and Kollock 1999, 7). In short, a MUD "is a kind of virtual reality, an electronically represented 'place' that users can visit" (Curtis 1996, 347).

A MUD system provides a stage but leaves the activities and interactions—whether these involve slaying dragons or teaching scientific principles—up to the participants. MUD interaction is shaped by the four basic commands of *say*, *emote* or *pause*, *whisper*, and *page*, which help players convey nuance, gesture, and general commentary. Additionally, MUDs are user-modifiable, which means that a player can create a character and, with the MUD owner's permission, describe and build a "place" that other players can then be invited to experience. In this way, MUDs enable participants to create sociocultural and "physical" environments (Reid 1995). In the last two decades, the number, variety and complexity of MUDs have all increased; some are used for educational ends, others as a source of community building, and still more as adventure games. In sum, these virtual worlds "are very much about who is in the place at the same time and how they interact" (Rheingold 1993, 149).

The use of audio, video and multidimensional interactive tools is increasing, but text-based communication continues to be the primary mode of online interaction. Still, the emerging cultures of the various CMC technologies are interrelated, and online social patterns "evolve in the context of the complete set of technologies in use" (Bruckman 1996, 324, n. 8). This cross-fertilization makes it difficult to analyze any one CMC technology in isolation. However, given the popularity of and the especially complex interactions between e-mail, news groups, and MUDs, it does make sense to talk about text-based, computer-mediated communication technologies as a single phenomenon.

But Is Virtual Community the "Real" Thing?

Millions of individuals are invested in hundreds of thousands of newsgroups, mailing lists, chat rooms, and MUDs, and the numbers continue to grow. Networked people use the available technologies to create identities, behavioral norms, and relationships within their groups, and since the early days of interactive computing, online social groups have provided not only information, but also support and companionship. The technical characteristics of these computerized networks "enhance connectivity" by making it easier to initiate and cultivate relationships (Wellman and Hampton 1999, 650). "Netters" commonly use the term "community" to describe their online relationships. Scholars of CMC have come to agree with its users that the Internet provides a medium for new forms of relating. Although there is now general recognition that social relationships thrive on-line (Baym 1995; 1998), disagreement remains over whether these thriving relationships and interpersonal interactions actually constitute community in any real sense.

Responses to this debate have employed varying strategies. One direct approach has been to rely on traditional conceptions of community—as place, as shared interests, and as common experiences—to anchor discussions of how or why online "virtual" communities are either similar to or very different from "real" communities. A sampling of this category of responses helps clarify some of the contested issues.

Howard Rheingold, for example, is enthusiastic in his assessment of virtual communities. He writes about the passionate involvement of people who "assemble" in online communities like the WELL (Whole

(Re)Creating Community?

Earth 'Lectronic Link) to do just about everything people do in real life." Using typed words, members of virtual communities

> exchange pleasantries and argue, engage in intellectual discourse, conduct commerce, exchange knowledge, share emotional support, make plans, brainstorm, gossip, feud, fall in love, find friends and lose them, play games, flirt, create a little high art and a lot of idle talk. (1993, 3)

Rheingold is aware that these interactions do differ from their real life counterparts because of both the unique rhythms associated with CMC and the absence of bodies. Additionally, even though all these activities are situated in specific places, Rheingold is quick to clarify that each community place "is a cognitive and social one, not a geographic place" (1993, 61). Finally, because this kind of place requires "an individual act of imagination," Rheingold recognizes that different members of the same cyberspace community are bound to experience it differently. Notwithstanding these differences or the fact that the technology alone is insufficient to create any community, Rheingold concludes that "communities can [and do] emerge from and exist within computer-linked groups" (1996, 420).

Pavel Curtis (1996) similarly relies on the metaphor of place, but he also emphasizes the importance of time in his discussion of MUDding and community. MUDders communicate with each other in "real time" and in an electronically represented "place" filled with rooms, exits, and objects. The social behaviors in a MUD can and frequently do deviate from those in real life, and members' participation in their MUD society is characteristically "somewhat tenuous." Curtis nonetheless believes that "MUDs do become true communities after a time" (366). Players are engaged in social activity and are committed to reaching consensus about standards and rules for their shared environment; many of the usual social mechanisms apply in MUDs. Thus, even though MUDs are "a new kind of social sphere, both like and radically unlike the environments that have existed before" (371), they are communities.

Elizabeth Reid (1995; 1996) also weighs similarities and differences. On the one hand, virtual reality in general is an imaginative experience; on the other hand, it does trigger actual emotional and social responses amongst those who venture into this "place." This situation, while tending to blur "the emotional line between virtual and actual reality," does ultimately foster a common culture among CMC users "that allows [them] to engage in activities that serve to bind them together as a community" (1995, 178, 173).

Chapter 7

In contrast, a number of researchers move away from equating "virtual" with "real" communities by emphasizing the distinctiveness of online communities. Anna DuVal Smith (1999) agrees that many real-life social mechanisms apply on-line, and is convinced that such real-life tools as conflict management can be adapted by the virtual communities of cyberspace. However, DuVal Smith sees these communities as essentially symbolic, "consisting of persistently interacting members with common interests who are linked primarily in symbolic (in this case, electronic) exchange rather than by face-to-face encounters in physical space" (137).

Nancy K. Baym (1999) agrees that while it is possible for an online group to be imagined as a community, this can occur only if stable social meanings are developed. A range of structural factors, in combination with the peculiarities of computer-mediated communication, help ensure a variety of forms of expression, identities, relationships, and behavioral norms; they do not, however, guarantee stability and an emergent sense of community.

One last variation of this "compare and contrast" strategy is found in Stephen Doheny-Farina's *The Wired Neighborhood* (1996). Here, community is defined as a lived, geographically situated experience that involves "continued, unplanned interactions between the same people over a long period of time" (37). Doheny-Farina sees a danger in CMC technology because it can take people away from communities as traditionally defined—places "in which individuals are bound to others through desire and necessity to work together, despite their differences, because they all have a stake in the betterment of their common place" (32). For Doheny-Farina, true community is founded on social and geographic ties and requires a particular commitment that is difficult to find in individuated "virtual communities." Thus, the net's ability to connect everyone electronically exists, ironically, alongside its potential to undermine social connections.

A second, more indirect response to the question of whether online communities are genuine communities focuses attention on the ways in which CMC and computer networking technology can help strengthen and reinvigorate specific physical communities. The basic argument here is that online groups can function as public spaces that are extensions of "real" geographic communities. Ideally, these kinds of computer networks can help build community awareness and enhance participation in community affairs by facilitating information exchange

(Re)Creating Community?

via discussion forums, electronic mail, and internet services. Case studies of the use of online community networks in, for example, the cities of Cleveland and Santa Monica, in rural Montana, and in a low-income housing development in Wilmington, North Carolina, illustrate the empowerment potential of this tool. It is important to note that this potential is not always realized (Doheny-Farina 1996; Schuler 1996; Mele 1999; Uncapher 1999), but the more significant point is that the focus here is not on net-based community, but rather on community use of the net.

Both of these general strategies have generated keen insights while, simultaneously, leaving unresolved the issue of whether online groups deserve the label "community." A third approach to the debate over whether "virtual communities" are real involves rethinking community itself. Some analysts assert a general, nontraditional definition of community and then validate the customized conception with online examples. Philip Greenspun (1999) illustrates this approach when he states that "a community is a group of people with varying degrees of expertise in which the experts attempt to help the novices improve their skills" (62). According to this definition, just about any online group counts as a community; additionally, community in cyberspace is both desirable and possible.

Esther Dyson (1997) offers a slightly different, multifaceted definition of community: it is "the unit in which people live, work, and play" (31), a "set of relationships [and] a shared asset, created by the investment of its members" (33). Wherever people tend to congregate with others who have similar interests, whether in physical places or electronic spaces, communities form. The generality and inclusiveness of such definitions make it possible to sidestep detailed investigations of community characteristics. Dyson and Greenspun do not need to concern themselves with such issues as level of commitment, authenticity of identity, and types of relationships because for them, by definition, "virtual communities" simply *are* real communities.

For others, explicit attention to these sorts of issues is what has led to new understandings of community and more fruitful ways of thinking about online communities. "[L]ooking for *community*, a preeminently social phenomenon, in *places*, an inherently *spatial* phenomenon" (Wellman 1999, xiv) is a mistake; communities are better defined as social networks (Wellman 1988; Wellman and Gulia 1999). More precisely, "it is the sociable and supportive aspect of interaction that

Chapter 7

defines community and not the local space in which interaction may take place" (Hampton and Wellman 1999, 489). This conception of communities as loosely bounded social networks builds on the complementary ideas that community exists in various places and spaces, and that community ties can be supportive, weak, all-encompassing, intimate, or optional.

Barry Wellman and Milena Gulia (1999) rely on this social network definition in their recent assessment of community as it is found on-line. Although evidence is limited, it seems clear to them that ties in cyberspace are like "real-life" community ties: "intermittent, specialized, and varying in strength" (353). However, the structure of the Internet and CMC technology cuts two ways, fostering both "partial" and "more all-encompassing" communities as "cyberlinks between people become social links between groups that otherwise would be socially and physically dispersed" (356). Their conclusion is that online communities are not a substitute for "real life" communities; they are communities in their own right.

According to this view, these computer-supported social networks foster alternative contacts and connections that may reinvigorate or replace face-to-face social relationships. Enthusiasts consider these "new" communities able to create opportunities for different kinds of social interaction by enhancing "the ability to connect with a large number of social milieus, while decreasing involvement in any one milieu." Such innovative connections and involvements probably will require particular types of commitments from the members of these "new" communities; they should also encourage integration by emphasizing achieved over ascribed traits (Wellman and Hampton 1999, 652–53).

Not all are convinced. A large-scale survey completed in early 2000 by the Stanford Institute for the Quantitative Study of Society found that among the 55 percent of all Americans who have access to the Internet, more people are increasingly "home, alone and anonymous," disconnected from family and community. The authors of this study found no evidence that virtual communities can replace traditional face-to-face relationships, and instead found that spending time on the Internet simply translates into less time and fewer connections with real human beings (Markoff 2000). Both the design and the conclusions of this research project have been alternately criticized and defended. Still, the question remains: does the Internet minimize, enhance, or provide alternatives to the kinds of social connections and interactions we know as community?

(Re)Creating Community?

This overview of research findings underscores the argument that applying the term "community" to describe the new social realms that emerge through online interaction is a loaded proposition (Baym 1998). Despite these conflicting perspectives, there seems little doubt that individual experience and social life are being reshaped by CMC. It is true that computers do things for us, but more significantly they also do things "to us as people, to our view of ourselves and our relationships, to our ways of looking at our minds" (Turkle 1999, 646). Thus, the business of predicting the societal impact of the Internet remains very risky.

What Now?

Sociologists have long recognized that social reality cannot be separated from the meanings that social actors give to it. But there are many ways to formulate or give meaning to shared experiences, and this seems especially true in the case of community. As observed by someone intimately involved with issues of CMC and society, "Online as offline, what you bring to a community determines what you get out of it" (Dyson 1997, 34). In complicated ways, CMC is affecting the making, and making sense, of contemporary community.

CMC challenges and obscures the boundaries and meanings of some of our more deeply felt cultural practices, and it requires that we reevaluate our expectations and understanding of community life. Cyberspace is not a purely technological phenomenon because, after all, it forces attention on the lives of the individuals and groups using it. Since computing technology is increasingly focused on the development of new ways for people to interact (Denning and Metcalfe 1998), it can be a vehicle for inclusion. For example, disabled individuals can "see," "hear," "speak," and "move about" with ease in cyberspace.

Clearly, this technology can be invaluable in fostering the kinds of sharing and relationships so often associated with community. But this same technology can also facilitate new forms of social deception and collective disruptions (Gelder 1985; Dibbell 1996; Kolko and Reid 1999) and push individuals further into isolation. Two observations are in order here. First, community involves both sharing and deception, harmony and disruption; all characterize community. This paradox exists because community members regularly perceive and experience their own communities in very different ways.

Chapter 7

The second essential point here is that on their own, CMC and the Internet don't do much. They have an impact only when they are used, by people interacting with others. Moreover, the social effects of CMC technology will become clear only once these innovations are fully routinized, and this has not yet occurred. If it is true that "the one constant of cyberspatial existence is that it is different for everyone" (Reid 1996, 343), figuring out the exact role of computer technology in community life will continue to be an enormous challenge. And mispredictions about computers are legendary (Hafner and Lyon 1996; Bell and Gray 1998). Still, it is possible—and important—to observe a number of established patterns.

First of all, history demonstrates that people consistently and persistently seek to gain and control information, the lifeblood of social institutions and systems. Moving information is the job of communications media, and because computers provide the most efficient and convenient means of processing, organizing, storing, and sharing information, computer technology will remain an important priority. Paralleling this general drive for information is an ever-present desire for communication. Thus a second reasonable observation is that questions about access to textual, visual, and interactive means of communicating will remain important social concerns.

Thirdly, a collection of people on-line constitutes a community only when they share a belief that (their) community is possible. Community is never a simple given; rather, it is an intentional, interactive process that involves reciprocity and requires the kinds of boundaries established by rules, rituals, stable identities, and a common context for communication. The outcome of this process is always unpredictable because the flexibility, liberation, excitement, and connectivity associated with CMC exist in conjunction with their opposites. Finally, because CMC has the potential to generate a range of both anticipated and unintended social consequences, the virtual communities of cyberspace will continue to engage social analysts.

Notes

1. The term *cyberspace* was coined by William Gibson in his 1984 science fiction novel *Neuromancer*.

2. One of the most readable accounts of these exciting events is *Where Wizards Stay Up Late* by Katie Hafner and Matthew Lyon (New York: Touchstone, 1996).

(Re)Creating Community?

3. The origins, growth, and philosophy of the WELL and of Usenet are discussed in chapters 2 and 4, respectively, in Rheingold (1993).

4. As explained by one expert, "MUD originally stood for Multi-User Dimension, the name given by Richard Bartle and Roy Trubshaw to the computer game they designed in 1979. . . . Since the original game was written, many similar programs have appeared, the names of which reflect their indebtedness to the original—MUCK, MUSH, and LPMUD— . . . The name MUD is now used to refer to the entire class of such text-based virtual world systems . . ." (Reid 1995, 165).

Chapter Eight

HOW MUCH DOES COMMUNITY MATTER ANYWAY?

The Liberal/Communitarian Debate

> Community depends for its strength and endurance on how people come to terms with one another's differences, living together as we must. (Perin 1988, 67)

Community does matter. In numerous and complicated ways, community helps to shape people's lives. We all seem to be affected by community, even in situations in which community membership is optional. But *how* important is community? In what ways is belonging—or not belonging—truly significant for individuals? What are the connections between community, personal identity, and social well-being?

These sorts of questions about community have been an important focus in contemporary political philosophy. During the last several decades, theoretical work in this field has explored the ideals of community, freedom, and justice in order to figure out the social, economic and political conditions necessary for a just or "good" society. Under the labels of "liberal" and "communitarian" theory, very different arguments about the nature and significance of both individuality and community are made.

The liberal/communitarian debate that unfolded during the 1970s and 1980s serves as a reminder of the complexities of community and the vital importance of studying community dynamics. Shaping this debate were the liberal preoccupation with individual rights and the communitarian emphasis on shared obligations. Liberals maintained that each of us is free, autonomous, and the source of our own identities. Communitarians disagreed with this idea of "unencumbered"

Chapter 8

selves and argued instead that individual identity can emerge only through interaction with others by participating in communities. While the former approached human existence in terms of freedom and independence, the latter viewed it in terms of connections and social responsibilities. Depending on which position one adopted, community was seen as essentially oppressive or liberating.

This chapter introduces this debate in order to re-evaluate the community examples presented in the preceding chapters. I begin by outlining the contemporary liberal position put forward by John Rawls in *A Theory of Justice* (1971). In the second section I review communitarian responses to Rawlsian liberalism. After identifying key differences and shared concerns, I conclude with a discussion of the usefulness of a combined, "communitarian liberal" position.

Several qualifications should be noted. First, conceptual arguments are understood differently by different people, and this is certainly the case with both liberalism and communitarianism. Each encompasses a range of beliefs and policies, any one of which may be defined in varying ways by adherents and critics; each also has evolved. Here I consciously focus on *some* of the key beliefs and recommended policies. Specifically, my concern is with the distinctive conceptions of individuality and community that shaped the early phase of the debate.

Second, I do not attempt a comprehensive analysis of the liberal-communitarian debate as it continues to unfold. During the last two decades, a tremendous amount has been written on disagreements between liberals and communitarians, and theoretical arguments on both sides have been reformulated. According to some, "the divide that once seemed to separate communitarian and liberal theories of human nature has begun to close" (Etzioni 1995, 4). Although my discussion clearly draws on these developments, I do not attempt to summarize this vast literature or to analyze the evolution of the debate.[1] Instead, my concern is with the relations and connections between community and identity that suggest the practical possibilities of ordering social life around actual shared meanings.

Liberalism, Justice, and Community

The 1971 publication of John Rawls' *A Theory of Justice* marked a renaissance in western political theory as well as a renewal of liberal thought. This work remains critically important, not because everyone accepts his

How Much Does Community Matter Anyway?

theory but because subsequent defenders and critics of liberalism "have formulated their positions in terms that make explicit reference to his theory" (Mulhall and Swift 1992, 1). Rawls' complicated argument has been interpreted in various ways by many different social and political philosophers. My goal in this section is to sketch out a basic outline that highlights ideas about selfhood and community relations that sparked communitarian objections.

We can begin to make sense of Rawls by reviewing some basic claims of classic liberalism that helped to shape Rawls' thinking.[2] Liberal political theory, developed in seventeenth- and eighteenth-century Europe, challenged the old feudal order which emphasized ascription, inherited privilege, and the "rightness" of might. In opposition to centuries-old social patterns which supported the idea that aristocrats were naturally superior to peasants, liberalism offered the contrary idea that every person had an equal birthright to the same natural rights and abstract entitlements. The liberal view of individuals as separate, self-contained holders of specific, natural rights was precisely captured in these famous lines: "We hold these truths to be self-evident, that all men are created equal, that they are endowed by their Creator with certain unalienable rights; that among these are life, liberty and the pursuit of happiness . . ."[3]

Liberal philosophers like Hobbes, Locke, and Rousseau developed social contract arguments to support their moral claim that all of us are born free and equal, and to account for the historical fact that we free and equal people end up governed. Although there were variations, these arguments generally hypothesized a state of nature in which there was no political authority and where each person was self-sufficient "in the sense that there [was] no higher authority with the power to command their obedience, or with the responsibility for protecting their interests or possessions" (Kymlicka 1990, 59). However, in this state of nature the uncertainties and scarcities that characterize social life remained. In such a situation, social contract arguments claimed,

> individuals, without giving up their moral equality, would endorse ceding certain powers to the state, but only if the state used these powers in trust to protect individuals from those uncertainties and scarcities. If the government betrayed that trust and abused its powers, then the citizens were no longer under an obligation to obey, and indeed had the right to rebel. Having some people with the power to govern others is compatible with respecting moral equality

Chapter 8

because the rulers only hold this power in trust, to protect and promote the interests of the governed. (Kymlicka 1990, 61)

The state of nature in which free and equal individuals would agree to a social contract was, according to the liberal theorists, a state in which rational individuals adhered to laws given them by God, and the social contract agreed upon by free and equal individuals would provide a system of rules, laws, and limitations.[4]

Rawls reinvigorated liberal theory with *A Theory of Justice*. In this book he reasserts the priority of equality, liberty, and justice with a political theory of limited government that provides institutional guarantees for personal liberty. He also seeks to correct what he feels is a flaw in earlier social contract arguments. Rawls observes that nature is characterized by inequalities and thus proposes, instead of the "natural state" of classical liberalism, an "original position" which acknowledges, and then transcends, social inequalities. His theory of justice as fairness is based on principles he thinks that ordinary, self-interested, rational men[5] would choose—*if* these men were suddenly and temporarily ignorant of their individual social positions and talents. For Rawls, "principles of justice are understood as what would be contracted to by mutually disinterested individuals motivated to protect and promote their own interests" (Mulhall and Swift 1992, 18).

The basic idea of the original position is a familiar one: if you are asked to divide a candy bar but you don't know which piece you'll get, it makes sense for you to divide it fairly. Rawls is saying that if people don't know where they "fit" in a social hierarchy, they will choose fair principles of justice "to govern the assignment of rights and duties and to regulate the distribution of social and economic advantages" (Rawls 1971, 61).

For Rawls, justice involves bargaining or negotiating under fair conditions. To achieve fair conditions, people need to be similarly situated; this requires that they be unaware of their personal circumstances and how they should live. Such a "veil of ignorance" would eliminate inevitable social inequalities in talents and strengths, inequalities which regularly shift results in favor of those who have more. It would mean that "[i]ndividuals are unaware of, for instance, their intelligence, physical abilities, sex, race, wealth, or values" (Regan 1985, 1082). Rawls' thinking about justice thus emphasizes equality as well as the freedom of all to pursue individual choices. When it comes to justice, what is most important is not what people choose but rather that they have the freedom to choose. If people are free to choose, and equal in his original position sense, they will, according to Rawls, choose the two principles of equal basic liberties and of general equality.[6]

Important assumptions about selfhood and relationships between individuals guide Rawls' conceptualization of the original position. An individual's distinguishing qualities, such as virtue, gender, talent, or social position, can be imagined away because they are not considered "essential constituents but only contingent attributes of the self" (Sandel 1984, 9). Rawls seems to think of people "as distinct from their particularity, both their particular natural endowments and social position and their particular conceptions of the good [i.e., that which is worth having]" (Mulhall and Swift 1992, 11).

Further, Rawls and other modern liberals maintain that we are essentially separate persons with distinct aims, interests and beliefs about what is good and worth having, and that we strive individually to achieve our capacity as free moral agents. There is much more in this lengthy, complex book, and many of the ideas have been significantly modified in Rawls' more recent writings.[7] Still, this vision of the person as a disembodied self, with identity and values fixed independently of the communities of which she is a member, remains a key point of disagreement with communitarian critics of liberalism.

Communitarian Responses to Liberalism

More than three hundred and fifty years ago, the English poet and clergyman John Donne wrote that "No man is an Iland, / intire of it selfe."[8] These short lines captured the observation that we humans are social beings, incomplete when isolated. Many others since Donne have contemplated the claim that a person's sense of self is bound up with others' conceptions and formed through interaction with others. This argument that "[t]he development of [individuals'] personalities and talents, their philosophies of life, and perhaps their very existence . . . [depends] on the community of which they are a part" (Van Dyke 1982, 39) has come to be known as *communitarian*.

The label communitarian was first elicited in 1982 by Michael Sandel in his book *Liberalism and the Limits of Justice*. His work was a detailed critique of Rawls' liberalism, which Sandel argued was fundamentally flawed in part because of its wrong ideas about individuality

Chapter 8

and the relations between individuals and communities. Many other analysts and activists have come to be associated with communitarianism, offering distinctive critiques of Rawls' theory of justice and contemporary liberalism. What unites these varied arguments is a "particular, communally oriented conception of the person" (Mulhall and Swift 1992, 162).

According to the liberal view, "individuals are not defined by their membership in any particular economic, religious, sexual, or recreational relationship, since they are free to question and reject any particular relationship" (Kymlicka 1990, 207). Community membership is seen as a choice made by an individual rather than an essential element of identity. Communitarians, in contrast, conceptualize "the self" as situated or embedded in social practices and relations. Each of us is made or constituted by the values and connections we have, communitarians argue, and thus we cannot opt out of or detach ourselves from them.

Whereas liberals start "with the claim that we are separate, individual persons, each with our own aims, interests, and conceptions of the good," communitarians begin with the assertion that we are dependent and connected to others: "the story of my life is always embedded in the story of those communities from which I derive my identity—whether family or city, people or nation, party or cause" (Sandel 1985, 145, 147). Communitarians consider personal identity to be an achieved social product—meaning that our separate identities emerge as we interact and participate in communities. We can act and choose *only* because we are connected to others and, with others, develop shared histories and hopes (Bellah et al. 1985).

Michael Sandel (1982) used the terms "the encumbered self" and "the situated self" to counter Rawls' assumptions that individuals are not defined by and also can detach themselves from social connections and shared histories. His communitarian argument is that we cannot act in a truly independent manner because what we do as individuals is based on communal values and community attachments that help define who we are. This view considers community membership an essential element in the development of individual identity; community is "not merely an attribute but a constituent of . . . identity" (Sandel 1982, 150). Law professor Kenneth Karst helps explain this when he says that involvement in community is the basic source of "the trust in others that we must have if we are to know ourselves, or even be ourselves" (Karst 1980, 185). There is nothing optional about communities—we are community. It is

How Much Does Community Matter Anyway?

our community connections—our encumbrances—that make each of us possible.

The Limits of Dualism

Liberals and communitarians—groups which include legal and moral theorists, social and political philosophers, and sociologists, are concerned deeply if not exclusively with individuality and community. Liberalism and communitarianism seem to offer diametrically opposed claims and explanations. In this section I want to turn away from genuine differences and consider instead the possibility that there exists "also a lot of cross-purposes, and just plain confusion in this debate" (Taylor 1989, 159).

It may be that some communitarians have misread liberalism, missing the point that the liberal conception of the person "is not intended to be true to that experience we have as private individuals, but is intended to model the way in which it is appropriate to think of ourselves specifically when it comes to politics and justice" (Mulhall and Swift 1992, 28). In other words, liberalism and communitarianism may respond to different tasks. The latter seems much more relevant if our goal is to describe how we actually live. The former, on the other hand, does offer a conceptual modeling that pushes our thinking about key social concerns.

As Taylor (1989) sees it, part of the confusion surrounding the liberal-communitarian debate stems from two "quite different" issues being run together. These distinct yet not quite independent issues concern ontology, or explanations of why things *are* the way they are, and advocacy, or moral/political claims about how things *should be*. Because of a "widespread insensitivity to the difference between the[se] two kinds of issue," each side of the debate is oversimplified and misunderstood; furthermore, we are prevented from seeing the debate as "the complex, many-leveled affair that it really is" (Taylor 1989, 163, 182).

It also may be that the most appropriate question is not *which theory works better*? but rather, *what can both teach us*? Liberals emphasize the separateness of people and the importance of individual freedom. Communitarians insist that our identities and interests are constituted by our relations with others. However, there is real interplay between individuals and society, and these two positions are not mutually exclusive. We

Chapter 8

do not have to conclude that there is "a flat opposition of contradiction" between liberal and communitarian positions if we understand Sandel and his fellow communitarians as attempting "to identify the limits of the attractiveness and worth of autonomy, not [attempting] to deny that attractiveness and worth altogether" (Mulhall and Swift 1992, 164).

Increasingly, scholars in many disciplines have come to recognize that while the longstanding social science tradition of focusing on "discrete things themselves" provides a wealth of empirical information about our social and physical world, it often precludes any exploration of the relationships that exist between things and people (Minow 1990). We can get beyond this impasse by recognizing that boundaries between people—and between individuals and communities—are permeable: As Martha Minow explains in her analysis of how the legal system categorizes people by drawing a boundary between different and normal,

> the whole concept of a boundary depends on relationships: relationships between the two sides drawn by the boundary, and relationships among the people who recognize and affirm the boundary. From this vantage point one can see that connections between people are the preconditions for boundaries; the legal rules erecting boundaries between people rely on understanding social agreements and the sense of community. (Minow 1990, 10)

Even the abstract individual referred to in theoretical discussions about law and philosophy is connected to others. According to political scientist Iris Young, the rights that the abstract individual supposedly has imply connections with others. Simply put, she argues, "rights are relationships . . . institutionally defined rules specifying what people can do in relation to one another" (Young 1990, 25).

Awareness of social interdependence is built into socialization theory, which begins with the idea that every human being depends on others for guidance and support in the formation of self. However, while each individual must learn from others how to fit into society, this kind of dependence doesn't automatically minimize or erase an individual's autonomy. As summed up by one well-known sociologist, "[t]he self is a social product, but that person is a unique person" (Selznick 1987, 447).

Our practical experiences reveal that we are simultaneously separate *and* connected. The ways we live our lives are shaped by the tension that exists between freedom and belonging. The formative interaction between these elements—two sides of the same coin of identity—has been eloquently described by legal scholar Milton Regan Jr. His observations are insightful: We are in fact free to associate or disassociate with many of the varied

> communities of which we are a part. Yet even after we leave home or break off a relationship, or change our political affiliation, can't we still say that those abandoned communal experiences continue in some way to be a part of who we are? At the same time, don't we voluntarily enter into new ones that will exert an influence on our identities as well? Self-realization appears to occur not merely through the choice of particular ends, nor through reflection on shared ends that constitute identity, but through a dialectic of choice and reflection. Appreciation of unity with others informs our individual choices, for it suggests what choices of communal affiliation are most consistent with our fundamental identities. These choices in turn influence the grounds of unity available to us in our daily experience. (Regan 1985, 1128)

These varied nuances of the relationships between an individual and communities are made invisible by the adversarial quality of the liberal-communitarian debate. According to Amy Gutmann, the early communitarian critique in particular "invites us to see the moral universe in dualistic terms: *either* our identities are independent of our ends, leaving us totally free to choose our life plans, *or* they are constituted by community, leaving us totally encumbered by socially given ends; *either* justice takes absolute priority over the good *or* the good takes the place of justice; *either* justice must be independent of all historical and social particularities *or* virtue must depend completely on the particular social practices of each society; and so on" (emphasis added; Gutmann 1985, 318–19).

This kind of polarization tyrannizes our common sense and prevents us from seeing that individuals are not limited to communities of which they are members at a given time. Such dualism also constrains the usefulness of both liberal and communitarian theories because neither alone fully describes social reality. Ultimately, it can lead all "to overlook the moral value of establishing some balance between individuals and community, and to underestimate the theoretical difficulty of determining where the proper balance lies" (Gutmann 1985, 321).

Communitarianism of the 1990s strives to resist the extremes of complete solidarity and unconditional independence (Selznick 1992), recognizing community as a dynamic framework within which both

Chapter 8

individuality and social cohesion may develop. The "new" communitarian position understands that individuals are neither wholly unencumbered or completely encumbered, but instead, are *both* strongly influenced by their communities and capable of making independent choices.[9]

Liberal theorizing also has responded to critics, and in doing so, also has moved beyond the limits of dualism. The argument that individual identities, like other social experiences, "are shaped to some degree by the broader common experience of living in a particular culture" (Regan 1985, 1131) has been persuasive. Liberalism is now more likely to acknowledge constraints on autonomy and freedom. While the value of individual freedom is maintained, liberals now offer the qualification that autonomy is conditioned by the pattern of opportunities created by social structures and relationships that are external to every individual (Mulhall and Swift 1992, 165–294).

Tensions persist. Liberalism remains the dominant orientation in the United States, with individualism still institutionalized in our educational, legal, and political systems. However, there are signs that these systems are also recognizing the importance of groups and communities. At the same time, revised communitarian thinking is moving into the political arena. It has been adopted by a fledgling social and environmental movement dedicated "to creating a new moral, social and public order based on restored communities" (Etzioni 1993, 2).

The "Responsive Communitarian Platform" issued late in 1991 and signed by dozens of ethicists, scholars, and policy analysts from both liberal and conservative camps, affirms the importance and interdependence of both individuality and community. It also maintains that the survival of any community depends on "its members [dedicating] some of their attention, energy, and resources to shared projects" (Etzioni 1993, 253). According to these "new" communitarians, the necessary work of restoring community involves balancing individual rights with social responsibilities, responsibilities determined by community need. Additionally, they urge all Americans to reclaim obligations that have been abdicated to the government, and "to make government more representative, more participatory, and more responsible to all members of the community" (Etzioni 1993, 255).

Such calls for civic renewal are appealing. However, others—including many who criticize liberalism for its inattention to social groups and communities—worry about embracing community as the political ideal. One of their concerns with the communitarian agenda is

How Much Does Community Matter Anyway?

that its emphasis on sharing and unity excludes or oppresses anyone experienced as "different." In their search for mutual identification and for the "common" good, communitarians tend to reinforce homogeneity and override alternative (frequently minority) cultures, histories, and points of view. Racist, sexist, and classist behavior can in this way be legitimated. Communitarianism can thus benefit some at others' expense; it can help reproduce a social order that is hierarchical, exclusionary, and alienating (Young 1990; Bell and Bansal 1988).

There is another concern related to the essential conservatism of the communitarian agenda. The emphasis on collective self-help and responsibility seems to suggest that contemporary problems are, if not caused by, at least resolvable through local politics. This emphasis downplays any role or obligation that "the system"—so often equated with "big government"—might have in the creation or solution of problems felt at the level of individual communities. It is not coincidental, critics argue, that communitarianism has gained currency with the ascendance of the Republican party and a conservative intellectual movement.

Finally, some critics charge that the communitarian call for a return to civic values and "civil society"[10] is a thinly disguised attack on poor and working people by cultural elites. Real social change, not just pious assessments about the state of our civic health, is needed. Social participation is important only if the groups and activities address the causes of today's social problems. The call to common ground will be heard, and heeded, only if people have time and psychic energy to respond. As one observer crisply commented, "the best way to return to civil society is to stop moralizing and start fighting for decent jobs and a living wage for working people" (Brodoff 1996).

Community membership remains a vitally important activity for many individuals searching for personal fulfillment; simultaneously, individualism persists as a societal value, considered by many others to be both a sensible means and desired end of "the good life." In response to this tension, communitarian and liberal arguments continue to evolve. Uniting these ongoing attempts to ascertain the role of community membership in individual identity is a belief in community, a shared assumption that community remains relevant and achievable at the close of the twentieth century. However, even this fundamental assumption has not gone unchallenged. As the following chapter explains, postmodernists have raised important questions concerning the very possibility of community in our fragmenting social world.

Chapter 8

Notes

1. Among the leading exponents of the "liberal" position in this debate are John Rawls, Ronald Dworkin, and Thomas Nagel; the "communitarian" argument is associated with Michael Sandel, Alastair MacIntyre, Michael Walzer, and Philip Selznick, among others. Useful discussions of both the literature and the (changing) debate are found in Rosenblum 1989; Taylor 1989; Kymlicka 1990; Mulhall and Swift 1992. Samples of more recent justifications of communitarian thought are found in Etzioni 1995, and important clarifications regarding the meaning of communitarianism are found in the preface and final chapter of Sandel 1998.

2. Rawls was also influenced by utilitarianism, according to which a "morally right act or policy is that which produces the greatest happiness for the members of society" and "the pursuit of human welfare or utility . . . [is] done impartially, for everyone in society" (Kymlicka 1990, 9–10). See chapter 2, "Utilitarianism," in Kymlicka 1990 (9–49).

3. That the writers of the Declaration of Independence limited these "truths" and "rights" to propertied white males is generally understood. Similarly, the U.S. Constitution was produced through an exclusionary process, limited political participation to free white men, and preserved slavery. The most dramatic attempt to expand the doctrine of natural rights to women was made in the 1848 Declaration of Sentiments in Seneca Falls, New York. See Rossi 1974, 413–21.

4. For a feminist critique of the limitations and omissions of social contract theory, see Hirschmann 1992.

5. Rawls excluded women from consideration here by relying on the assumptions that men were heads of households and that only heads of households could and did participate in the governance of their lives.

6. According to Mulhall and Swift (1992, 7), "In Rawls' view, people in the original [i.e., 'ignorant'] position, denied knowledge of their talents and endowments, motivated not by a particular conception of the good but by their interest in their capacity to frame, revise, and rationally to pursue such conceptions, would agree that their society should be regulated by the following principles of justice. First [quoting Rawls 1971, 302]: "Each Person is to have an equal right to the most extensive total system of equal basic liberties compatible with a similar system of liberty for all." Second [again quoting Rawls 1971, 302]: "Social and economic inequalities are to be arranged so that they are both (a) to the greatest benefit of the least advantaged, and (b) attached to offices and positions open to all under conditions of fair equality of opportunity."

7. See particularly his *Political Liberalism* (New York: Columbia University Press, 1996).

8. This famous quotation is found midway through Donne's seventeenth *Devotions Upon Emergent Occasions* (Donne 1955, 538).

How Much Does Community Matter Anyway?

9. It is important to note that in the 1998 preface to the second edition of *Liberalism and the Limits of Justice,* Sandel distanced himself from the "communitarian" label. See Sandel 1998, ix–xvi for a full discussion of this clarification, which is beyond the scope of this book.

10. A fuller discussion of civil society is presented in chapter 10.

Chapter Nine

IS COMMUNITY EVEN POSSIBLE?
Postmodern Considerations

"Our age [1828]," said Channing, "has been marked by the suddenness, variety and stupendousness of its revolutions. The events of centuries have been crowded into a single life. Overwhelming changes have rushed upon one too rapidly to give us time to comprehend them. (Catherine Drinker Bowen 1944, 51)

It seems to be characteristic of our period that norms and truths which were once believed to be absolute, universal, and eternal, or which were accepted with blissful unawareness of their implications, are being questioned. In the light of modern thought and investigation much of what was once taken for granted is declared to be in need of demonstration and proof. The criteria of proof themselves have become subjects of dispute. (Louis Wirth 1936, x–xi)

Reality isn't what it used to be. (Kvale 1995, 19)

Both continuity and change have been continual features of our nation's cultural landscape. As each of these three quotations remind us, questions about the meaning of these forces and about how we live and make sense of our lives also have dominated our national conscience. In response to these questions, liberals and communitarians have explored the significance of community in individual identity and self-fulfillment. Their conflicting positions have sharpened our understanding of the complicated interplay between communities and their members. However, both communitarian and liberal insights are challenged by postmodernist claims that fundamental changes in the ways we experience and explain our world undermine the very *possibility* of collective experience and community theory in our contemporary society.

Chapter 9

If taken seriously, the postmodern challenge is more radical and thus more threatening than the liberal-communitarian debate. Postmodernism criticizes traditional social science for failing to live up to its liberating promises, for masquerading as "objective" while denying its political nature, and for ignoring the spiritual and ethical dimensions of social existence. Two chief concerns for most postmodernists are the basis of knowledge and understanding, and the meanings and possibilities of progress, individual endeavor and collective aspirations (Rosenau 1992). More generally, "[p]ostmodernism, if it is about anything, is about the prospect that the promises of the modern age are no longer believable because there is evidence that for the vast majority of people worldwide there is no realistic reason to vest hope in any version of the idea that the world is good and getting better" (Lemert 1997, xii). What is involved here is "the definition of an era—our era—and, along with it, the relevance and meaningfulness of *our* political, intellectual, and aesthetic practices" (Winter 1992, 792).

Postmodernists criticize what has been taken for granted as "normal" cultural, political, and economic sense. They do so by questioning and rejecting familiar assumptions and concepts. A central claim is that the "grand narratives" or transcultural, ahistorical assertions about the world on which social science knowledge rests are no longer credible. While the meaning(s) as well as the applicability of postmodern thought are highly contested, most postmodernists emphasize the vulnerability, contingency, and absence of foundations in contemporary social life (Bauman 1992). The postmodern enterprise is further characterized by two general and interrelated qualities. The first is an unwieldiness that stems from the lack of any consistent or unified theme. The second is a methodological orientation that explicitly repudiates reason, logic, rationality, and theory, and thus thwarts descriptive analysis. These same characteristics make it difficult to summarize postmodernism.

The first quality of unruly open-endedness stems in part from the fact that postmodernism means many different things to people from an assortment of disciplines. Anthropologists, geographers, economists, historians, specialists in international relations, lawyers, literary critics, political scientists, psychologists, sociologists, urban planners, and a variety of feminists have engaged in wide-ranging discussions of postmodernism (Hollinger 1994; Rosenau 1992). Disagreements within and between these disciplines on this issue of whether postmodernism is a stylistic approach that can be adopted and discarded at will or,

Is Community Even Possible?

instead, "a condition of life to which we are shackled" (Ewick 1992, 756) have enhanced this interpretive range. Clarifications have been made regarding the important differences between "*post-modernity*, a purportedly new state of world affairs, and postmodernism, a theory or cultural attitude toward those affairs" (Lemert 1997, 26). Still, confusion remains since, while "it is worth distinguishing between postmodern*ism*, when the accent is on the cultural, and postmodern*ity*, when the emphasis is on the social," it is impossible to separate the cultural from the social (Lyon 1999, 9). Furthermore, distinctions regarding specific orientations within postmodernism (Lemert 1997, Rosenau 1992) have served to complicate rather than simplify discussions.

The difficulty in summarizing postmodern thinking is directly related to the simple reality that "an infinite combination of alternatives allow different and varying ways to put together the elements that constitute post-modernism" (Rosenau 1992, 14). The divergent, often competing orientations found among those associated with postmodernism ensure that most statements about postmodernism (including my own) will be considered incomplete or otherwise faulty by at least some advocates and critics of postmodernism. Postmodernism—"endlessly dynamic, always in transition," proud of its "readiness to be incoherent" (Rosenau 1992, 17, 20)—is a "capacious and heterogenous" paradigm that is hard to pin down (Natoli and Hutcheon 1993, ix–x).

The second methodological characteristic is potentially more troublesome. As I will explain, postmodernists are critical of Western society as it developed during and after the Enlightenment, and they reject the modern or Enlightenment standards of reason, logic and objective knowledge. This rejection is based on the two-pronged argument that (a) universalizing theories (i.e., modern Enlightenment theories) repress or ignore contradictory evidence and (b) power arrangements rather than allegiance to Truth lie behind all knowledge claims (Donovan 1992; Smart 1992; Hollinger 1994).

Consequently, postmodernists question not only the accuracy of general descriptions of the social world, but also the very ability to describe and thus to represent the social world. They dismiss causal models and the scientific method; emphasize difference, contingency, and multiple interpretations; and devalue theory-building and conventional academic styles of communication. One inevitable outcome of the postmodern claim that "all is contingent" (Bauman 1992, xxii) is that for those engaged in these kinds of analyses "there are no methods, no rules

Chapter 9

of procedure to which they must conform" (Rosenau 1992, 117). The deliberate, self-conscious impermanence of postmodern analyses can lead to a "new" moral relativism that further undermines efforts to "fix" post-modernism as a specific methodology or comprehensive theory.

Keeping all this in mind, I introduce postmodern thinking as it bears on the social scientific study of community.[1] The first part of the chapter will discuss postmodernist arguments regarding the situatedness of truth and knowledge, the concept of multiple or fractured selves, and the denial of intersubjectivity and thus of shared or community experience. This section is followed by a critique of these postmodern claims. The chapter ends by suggesting that a pragmatic conception of community with and without unity, guided by an interactionist approach that emphasizes everyday experience, can better capture both the common traits and the unique characteristics that characterize communities in contemporary society.

Postmodernism and Community

Postmodernism developed in the 1950s and 1960s in western Europe as nations there experienced dramatic social and technological transformations. During this time, western European intellectuals appropriated, transformed, and transcended a variety of theoretical orientations in order to account for these changes. These continental postmodernists, joined in subsequent decades by North American postmodernists, developed a general critique of modernity[2] by drawing on and reinterpreting French structuralism, romanticism, phenomenology, nihilism, populism, existentialism, hermeneutics, Western Marxism, Critical Theory, ethnomethodology, symbolic interactionism, and anarchism. Asserting the failure of modern science to deliver on its promises of certainty, unity, and order, and emphasizing the ambiguity, paradox, and indeterminancy of contemporary social life, postmodernists have attempted to reconceptualize how we experience, explain, and act in our world as the century drew to a close.

Many key elements of postmodernist social and cultural criticism were introduced to North Americans by French philosopher Jean-Francois Lyotard. Lyotard's *The Postmodern Condition*[3] first linked the term *postmodern* to a departure from the universalizing, rationalizing, ordering, and unifying tendencies that have dominated western thinking

Is Community Even Possible?

since the seventeenth century. In this now classic work he argued against relying on grand Reason and absolute Truth, and called instead for acceptance of multiple reasons and partial truths. Lyotard's analysis, adapted and debated by a long list of authors that includes Jean Baudrillard, Michel Foucault, and Jacques Derrida among others, remains a useful introduction to postmodern thinking.

In *The Postmodern Condition*, Lyotard is primarily concerned with the state of scientific knowledge in the most industrialized, i.e., the "postmodern" societies. He develops his analysis of science and the creation and transmission of knowledge by drawing on the analogy of games. As Lyotard sees it, science "plays" its own game by its own rules, and specific rules govern the creation and legitimation (or consensus-building) of scientific knowledge. However, the numerous technological and political changes of the last decades of the twentieth century have altered the "game rules" upon which we have relied to find meaning to our lives.

According to Lyotard, scientific knowledge is in crisis. This is because science and technology have become less concerned with the production of knowledge and more focused on the translation, storage, and communication of knowledge. This shift has affected what is considered to be "knowledge" and also how knowledge is acquired, validated, and used. Within the context of our growing dependence on computers, pressing questions have emerged regarding what knowledge actually is and who determines what needs to be known.

To explore these questions, Lyotard distinguishes between scientific and nonscientific or "narrative" knowledge. The former predominates in contemporary western society while the latter—which includes myths, stories, and legends—is more prevalent in traditional societies. Both forms of knowledge are equally necessary, as each serves to legitimate people's actions and societies' institutions. But they are not the same, for they are subject to different validating criteria. Scientific knowledge distinguishes itself from narratives on the basis of scientific standards of argumentation and proof. Narratives, understood to be based on the criteria of opinion, custom, power, prejudice, and ideology, have long been considered a different and distinctly inferior type of knowledge.

Lyotard minimizes distinctions between these two kinds of knowledge by pointing out that science, like narrative understanding, also relies on myths, assumptions, and political considerations. For example, scientific research and the accumulation of scientific knowledge have

151

Chapter 9

been justified by the idea that knowledge is liberating. However, this idea is not an Absolute Truth; rather, Lyotard claims, it is an assumption (or myth) that emerged out of the specific and particular conditions of the French Revolution. This reliance on values and assumptions reveals to Lyotard the failure of scientific knowledge to adhere to its own legitimating criteria; scientific knowledge *is* narrative knowledge.

Lyotard believes that scientific knowledge itself contains the seeds of its own destruction because all that has been labeled and included as "knowledge" has conformed to the guidelines which define and legitimate science; it is here that the problems begin. The development of scientific knowledge demands assumptions, for at least some elements of speculative scientific statements have to be taken for granted. At the same time, though, the standards and requirements of science require the identification and analysis of all underlying assumptions. The result—labeled postmodernism—is a dismantling and rejection of universalizing theories, and this is an outcome triggered by the necessity of scientific knowledge to legitimate itself.

Lyotard also targets the universality of Enlightenment theories of progress and morality that have helped justify modern social practices; such comprehensive, ahistorical, and transcendent ("foundational") statements are actually social constructions. Announcing the death of modernism's grand theories or totalizing "metanarratives," Lyotard urges a shift to a postmodern orientation that rejects logical certainty and foundational theories of knowledge and that instead, accepts that all knowledge is both context-dependent and open to interpretation. Abandoning the idea of "an archimedian or ahistorical standpoint from which to understand the human mind, knowledge, society, and history," Lyotard suggests instead "multiple minds, subjects, and knowledges reflecting different social locations and histories" (Seidman 1994a, 5).

Lyotard, concerned as he was with the state of contemporary knowledge in *The Postmodern Condition*, did not explore the sociological aspects of his argument (Lyon 1999, 17). Nonetheless, his critique of scientific truth and knowledge has clear implications for theorizing about community. The decentering postmodernism outlined by Lyotard is skeptical of shared understandings and common experiences and ultimately suspicious of meaningful claims about community matters. By rejecting intersubjective understanding, postmodernism "blocks the possibility of generic political identity or cohesive group/community identity" (Donovan 1992, 202). Postmodernism not only denies that

Is Community Even Possible?

community matters; it also considers community an impossibility.

Postmodernism has revealed that what had been claimed as universal and foundational was actually local and historically specific. It describes our world as one "in which, at the least, the promises of progress and social hope are so often pious vanities or, worse, testimony to the desire of the well-settled to hold on to the familiar at all costs" (Lemert 1997, xiv). As political scientist Nancy Hirschmann has observed, "postmodern theory criticizes modernism for representing reality as given and universal when in fact what we call reality is generally a reflection of particular institutions, practices, and events" (Hirschmann 1992, 28).

Postmodernism's systematic taking apart, or deconstruction, of universal theory appears to preclude any meaningful discussion about community because it holds that all theories are suspect. Sociologist Steven Seidman summarizes this core "suspicion" in the following questions:

> How can an individual, knowing subject who has particular interests and biases by virtue of living in a specific society at a particular historical juncture and occupying a specific social position defined by his or her class, gender, race, sexual orientation, ethnicity and religious status, produce concepts, explanations and standards of truth that are universally valid? How can we assert that humans are constituted by their particular sociohistorical circumstances and also claim that they can escape their embeddedness by creating nonlocal, noncontextually valid concepts and standards? (Seidman 1992; 64–65)

This "abandonment of theory" is based on the postmodern assertion that "the pursuit itself of [social] theories rests upon the modernist conception of a transcendent reason" and that this conception, along with associated theories about individuals, communities, and societies, basically rests on "modern ideals carrying with them specific political agendas and ultimately unable to legitimize themselves as universal" (Nicholson 1990, 4). Social theory itself is laden with historical baggage; some postmodernists further argue that because "facts are defined, even invented by [a particular] community . . . [they] have no meaning outside that collectivity" (Rosenau 1992, 90–91). Accordingly, any attempt to generalize "is simply an effort to impose a local, particular prejudice on others who do not share that prejudice" (Seidman 1992, 65).

Chapter 9

Universal criteria do not exist because "general categories and explanations [that claim to be] universally valid representations [are] reflections of a particular standpoint" (Seidman 1992, 67).

The postmodern claim, then, is that there is no "one true story" about anything. All is subject to interpretation, and no one meaning is or should be considered better or more truthful than another. It makes no sense to hold on to concrete categories or to use such categories to order or comprehend our existence. Postmodern thinking emphasizes that "categories of analysis are social constructs whose meanings and consequences shift in different contexts" (Nicholson and Seidman 1995, 24). Both *the self* and *the community* are suspect categories of analysis: "At the level of the self and the social community, postmodernism signals dissolution and fragmentation" (Winter 1992, 794) by pointing out "the futility of certainty" (790). The self, with no "originary causal efficacy," is no longer privileged; so too community dissolves for all is diversity and heterogeneity . . . any discourse of "community" is suspect as a discourse of oppression" (Winter 1992, 785).

Postmodernism aims to "displace . . . and decenter" rationalism by redescribing all human activities as discourse. More than just talk, discourses are systems of language and meanings connected to social activities "that form the objects of which they speak" (Sarup 1993, 64). Consider "sexuality" as an example of discourse: the thinking here is that human sexuality does not exist on its own in some absolute, fixed state, but rather is constructed out of our analyzing and interpreting and acting. The unsettling implication here is that what we actually "know" about something is what we make up about it.

This redescription of how things are has everything to do with the unprecedented social and cultural shifts taking place in our society. The physical and spiritual worlds in which we live increasingly are disjointed and pluralistic, lacking clear centers. Ideas and values seem unrelated to personal experiences, and all appears to be in flux. Postmodernists generally claim that during this transitional time, all beliefs are equal; there is no overriding truth any more than there are fundamental lies. Truth is a social invention, a dependent variable that is limited in scope because

> [a]ny particular truth is relevant or valid only to the members of the group or community within which it is formulated. Knowledge, then, is relative to the community, true in terms of the beliefs of one

Is Community Even Possible?

community but not for other communities; any rules of knowledge apply only inside the community. (Rosenau 1992, 31)

These postmodern views about knowledge and theory pose a sort of legitimation crisis for community studies. The postmodern rejection of social predictions and generalizations seems to deny the kinds of transpersonal experiences that are essential components of what we have come to define as community. Further, postmodernism appears to dismiss even the possibility of community theory. The world as postmodernists see it is dramatically uncertain, for "[a] world without theory means an absolute equality of all discourse, an end to foundational claims" (Rosenau 1992, 89). In sum, our world and our understandings of our social existence are fragmented, insecure, and unpredictable.

Critiquing the Postmodern Critique

By erasing distinctions between truth, error, and nonsense, postmodern arguments open the way to relativism and nihilism. For some, our postmodern condition is an invitation to rethink and redefine reality; others interpret it as a signal of growing social and cultural chaos, while still others simply reject its claims. More to the point, though, postmodern rejections of reason, sense and knowledge leave many questions unanswered. Taken on their own terms, fashionable postmodern analyses seem to undermine postmodernism itself.

For starters, postmodernism is not as innovative or radical as it appears to be. It has a "cut and paste character," and its component ideas have direct links to numerous intellectual traditions (Rosenau 1992, 13–14). Berger and Luckmann earlier pointed out, in *The Social Construction of Reality* (1967), that people create their/our worlds (including laws, beliefs, social roles, rituals, etc.) and then routinely "forget" that they have made them. Postmodernism does go further than the Berger and Luckmann social construction argument by acknowledging that there are multiple ways in which "language determines knowledge and creates power to the extent that it is virtually impossible to see all the ways we are constructed" (Hirschmann 1992, 302). However, this means that ultimately postmodernism deconstructs itself, for "there is nothing for it to hold on to" (Hirschmann 1992, 312). Furthermore, the postmodern stance that "there is no truth, and all is construction—is

Chapter 9

itself the ultimate contradiction. By making this statement postmodernists assume a position of privilege" (Rosenau 1992, 90). By asserting as true their own theoretical view, postmodernists undermine their central assertions about the bankruptcy of theory and truth.

Some postmodern discussions can be as oppressive as the grand theories they critique because they rely on either familiar (modernist) assumptions about what is good for "the people" (Esteva and Prakash 1998) or the "incorrect premise that the Enlightenment narratives are as unequivocal, unilateral and one-sided as the positivists have depicted them" (Mestrovic 1992, 142). Another consequence of the tendency of postmodern academics to leave unexamined three key modernist assumptions—"the myth of *global thinking* . . . the *universality of human rights* . . . [and] the *myth of the individual self*" (Esteva and Prakash 1998, 9–11)—is that postmodernist thinking is fundamentally ethnocentric and exclusionary. One author has criticized postmodernists for "reflecting on reflecting" instead of noticing what people do (Austin 1992), another for simply ignoring that "there are some realities" (Lemert 1993, 500). Because postmodernism tends to ignore material conditions and social interactions, it seems irrelevant to the actual lives people live.

The critical problem with a postmodern social science that affirms multiple realities and interpretations while disclaiming any generalizable knowledge is that it lacks criteria to use in arguing for the superiority or desirability of any particular view. Ultimately, as Pauline Rosenau concludes in her detailed examination of postmodernism and the social sciences, "the problem with post-modern social science is that you can say anything you want, but so can everyone else. Some of what is said will be interesting and fascinating, but some will also be ridiculous and absurd. Post-modernism provides no means to distinguish between the two" (Rosenau 1992, 137). Clearly, what postmodernism needs is "an ethical edge, a critical handle" (Lyon 1999, 88).

Responding to these criticisms, some postmodernists have argued against the common ("and unnecessary") mistake of concluding "that postmodernism's eschewal of any universal, essential, or ahistorical ground on which to build or anchor any claim of epistemic justification signals the end of the theoretical enterprise entirely" (Hutchinson 1992, 779). Such a conclusion is not logical, as sociologist Steven Seidman points out, because the fact that all knowledge is situated does not mean that knowledge is invalid (Seidman 1994).

Arguments between critics and advocates of postmodernism continue. Meanwhile, pressing issues connected to our social condition—

Is Community Even Possible?

including the effects of globalization, ethical choices, and how best to make sense of our world (Lyon 1999, 105)—intensify. Given this, it makes sense to shift attention away from abstract theorizing and towards the ways real people respond to concrete social, economic, and political conditions. It is doubtful, as Lemert (1997) argues:

> that postmodernism, whatever it turns out to be, can be reliably understood by examining what people think it is, and certainly not from what they say about it . . . Postmodernism, if it is anything real, is an actual historical process the facts of which, being arguable like the facts of anything of the near present, cannot be determined by reference to theory alone. (Lemert 1997, x)

Where To Now?

Although the rarified discussions of academic postmodernists seem disconnected from common, everyday life, it may be counterproductive to dismiss postmodernist thinking out of hand. In their thought-provoking book entitled *Grassroots Post-Modernism* (1998), Gustavo Esteva and Madhu Suri Prakash agree that both the terminology and the conceptual framework of "academic postmodernism" are useless to ordinary men and women. This irrelevancy stems, in good part, from the fact that the divergent group of intellectuals claiming to be postmodernists have accepted key "certainties" or myths associated with modernity. These include an affirmation of global thinking, support for universal human rights, and emphasis on individualism, all of which undermine the autonomy of local communities. Notwithstanding, the growing number of "culturally diverse initiatives" indicates that "the so-called illiterate and uneducated non-modern "masses" [are] pioneering radical postmodern paths out of the morass of modern life" (Esteva and Prakash 1998, 3). These authors would retain the term, along with its emphasis on diversity and distinctive modes of life.

However, the postmodern emphasis on fragmentation is only part of the analytical story: despite divisions, commonalities do exist in our social world. This simple observation is encouraging, for as Lyon (1999) observes, "the only real hope for true toleration must be in discovering what "we" have in common as well as in respecting diversity" (Lyon 1999, 99). Furthermore, some elements of postmodernist thinking actually *reinforce* the idea that community matters and that we must undertake context-specific, interactionist community studies if we are to know

Chapter 9

ourselves. This is particularly true of the postmodernist intimation that community is "historically emergent rather than naturally given . . ." (Nicholson and Seidman 1994, 26). Postmodernism implies that there are many starting points and outcomes when it comes to community and communities, and it also suggests that experiences can be both shared and utterly personal. This kind of thinking acknowledges actual experience, which demonstrates that there are varying ways of being in community, and further that *community* itself has culturally specific meanings that have varied over time.

On a different level, the microsociological approaches often used to explore community life are compatible with postmodernist goals, for they move away from the universal and eternal and towards the local and particular. This is certainly true of the context-sensitive approach outlined in chapter 1. This view of community arising out of actions and reactions that both respond to and influence social communication and structure depends in part on personal stories. By tracing continuities among events and placing them in a sequential order within a context, these narratives serve to organize and give meaning to social experiences. These creations "explain a group to itself, legitimate its deeds and aspirations, and provide important benchmarks for non-members trying to understand the group's cultural identity" (Hinchman and Hinchman 1997, 235). Such accounts, while often of particular interest to specific audiences, offer insights about our world by contributing to our understanding of the ways in which communities are formed and maintained.

It is important to remember that narrative accounts—whether told by community "insiders" or academic "strangers"—are representations that do not encompass all the feelings and lived experiences of all community members. They are not neutral stories since, once constituted, each serves as a model for subsequent explanations of the past and for ongoing actions that sustain and transform the community. As summarized by anthropologist Edward M. Bruner:

> Stories give meaning to the present and enable us to see that present as part of a set of relationships involving a constituted past and a future. But narratives change, all stories are partial, all meanings incomplete. There is no fixed meaning in the past, for with each new telling the context varies, the audience differs, the story is modified . . . We continually discover new meanings. (Bruner 1997, 277)

Narratives are frequently powerful, but narrative is often a frustratingly incomplete and ambivalent means of organizing and speaking

Is Community Even Possible?

about the world. As Martha Minow has pointed out in a recent discussion of storytelling in legal studies: "Stories alone do not articulate principles likely to provide consistency in generalizations to guide future action; stories do not generate guides for what to heed or what additional stories to elicit. Stories on their own offer little guidance for evaluating competing stories" (Minow 1996, 35). In a similar vein, while community stories can be concrete and authentic, storytelling has the potential to promote both admirable and undesirable causes.

These are important observations to keep in mind as we consider what people believe themselves to be doing in and because of community. This shift is a pragmatic response to postmodern skepticism regarding community; despite questions about the significance or possibility of community, most of us consider ourselves involved in what members and nonmembers alike call communities. Community exists because we so regularly share with others and because we are interested in our shared connections.

The community narratives presented in chapters 2 through 7 describe very different communities and community matters that have, nonetheless, certain common features. In all of the cases, community members interpret the situations they are in, agree and disagree on how best to define their situations, and debate how to understand their communities. Each community is characterized by both cohesion and dissension. As members of these distinctive communities find themselves questioning, reworking, and sometimes abandoning formerly taken-for-granted aspects of their community identity, shared goals and serious disagreements are often revealed. In sum, individuals are simultaneously part of and apart from their communities even as they reaffirm the desire to work together for community.

Notes

1. Among the many works that have helped me better understand the problems and implications of postmodern analysis are Anderson 1995; Bauman 1992; Benhabib 1992; Borgmann 1992; Corlett 1993; Dickens and Fontana 1994; Eagleton 1996; Hollinger 1994; Lemert 1997; Lyon 1999; Natoli and Hutcheon 1993; Nicholson 1990; Nicholson and Seidman 1995; Rosenau 1992; Sarup 1993; Seidman 1994a and 1994b; Seidman and Wagner 1993; and Smart 1993.

2. Hollinger (1994) claims to be following "common application" in using the term *modernity* to "denote" this following type of society:

Chapter 9

highly differentiated from a structural-functional point of view, dominated by a capitalist (market) economy, with a complex division of labor, industrialization and urbanization, science and technology, political and ethical individualism, liberal utilitarianism, and social contract theory, a certain set of ideas about the self, and a conception of human history that is implicitly teleological and explicitly optimistic. (Hollinger 1994, xiii)

3. Jean-Francois Lyotard, *The Postmodern Condition: A Report on Knowledge*. Trans. G. Bennington and B. Massumi (Minneapolis: University of Minnesota Press, 1984). This work was commissioned by the government of Quebec and completed in 1979.

Chapter Ten

COMMUNITY THEORIZING AND COMMUNITY LIVING
Questions and Lessons

> The idea that we are living in new times is interesting, persuasive, if not seductive, particularly in a cultural context where there has been, for some time now, a cult of the new, a social and economic context in which innovation and novelty have been promoted, their virtues extolled, often through implied associations with ideas of progress and/or development.... [But] if we are living in new times we also appear to be encountering old troubles, familiar possibilities and pleasures. (Smart 1993, 14–15)

Sociologists grappling with the issues of the significance and range of community have been guided by the assumption that community can be a vehicle for social integration and a basis for social interaction. Additionally, most have attempted to better understand both how community members and nonmembers relate in terms of similarities and differences, and how these relationships change. However, "community"—like "family" and "home"—is a generic term used to cover a wide range of conceptions and examples. Its definitions have shifted over time because social scientists, social activists, and ordinary citizens have employed this term to explain or justify changing patterns of social relations.

Given the variety of research questions guiding the sweeping assortment of community studies, it is not at all surprising that different conclusions have been reached about its significance and vitality. While the diversity of topics, examples, and findings is somewhat unwieldy, it has been helpful to organize the materials around the successive themes of community *lost*, community *found*, and community *liberated*. This

Chapter 10

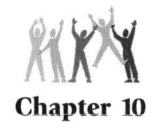

three-stage linear model, initially presented in 1979 by Barry Wellman (Wellman 1979), has since become a standard way of making sense of the intellectual history of community studies. (See, e.g., Flanagan 1995 and Sampson 1999.)

The "community lost" orientation started with nineteenth-century European sociologists and continued in the twentieth century with American urbanists associated with the Chicago School of sociology. Also referred to as the classical view of urban life, this orientation dominated urban and community research through the mid-1900s. The guiding assumption of this view was that the twin forces of industrialization and urbanization were negative forces that disrupted and destabilized social life. More precisely, it was assumed that the rapid shift from the simple agricultural base of rural society to the complex industrial base of urban society transformed how people lived and worked by weakening personal neighborhood ties and emphasizing secondary instrumental relations.

In 1938 Louis Wirth focused these concerns in a famous essay, arguing that population size, density, and heterogeneity interacted to produce a new way of life called urbanism, which precluded the personal, intimate bonds traditionally identified with local community (Wirth 1938). This influential attempt to delineate what is characteristically *urban* emphasized the negative possibilities associated with the dramatic growth of cities, and encouraged researchers to examine such issues as increasing social disruption in urban neighborhoods (Shaw and McKay 1942), growing community impotence and economic dependence (Vidich and Bensman 1958), and the declining significance of local neighborhood as a primary anchor for personal identity (Warren 1988).

By the 1950s, however, new field-based and survey research began to challenge the classic urban claims about the loss of community. This new line of research investigated urban neighborhoods as possible sources of meaningful interpersonal relations and territorial identification in American life, and the findings were generally affirmative. Herbert Gans (1982; 1967) Carole Stack (1974) and Gerald Suttles (1968) were among those researchers who "discovered" that many urban residents were intimately involved in the kind of dense, well-organized social networks associated with traditional neighborhood communities and that, in at least some urban neighborhoods, a localized sense of community had increased (Hunter 1974). "Community saved" was the dominant theme of these mid-century studies that emphasized place of residence and documented the enduring strength of localized community ties.

A third thematic stage emerged in the last three decades as a response to ongoing changes connected to urban living, suburbanization, and technological innovation. The "Community liberated" orientation, with its focus on the ideas that the geographic location of one's residential neighborhood is no longer the controlling factor in many people's lives and that contemporary urbanites have created viable communities that are not dependent on place, has emphasized the face-to-face behavior of everyday life. This microsociological perspective sees community as liberated or unbound from the constraints imposed by physical space, and as essentially composed of primary relationships and social groupings that go beyond, and may not even include, local neighborhood ties.

The communities that most of us feel strongest about are characterized by these kinds of interlocking relationships, or social networks (Wellman and Leighton 1979). But there are other dimensions or functions that characterize the content of community life, and that continue to be acted out in neighborhood communities. Modern society *has* freed people from neighborhood dependence, but it has simultaneously enabled them to create place-based communities of interest (Connerly 1985).

This theme of liberation, of community "without propinquity," has helped to illuminate new opportunities for community in our urbanized reality, and it also has underscored the voluntary quality of contemporary communities. According to this framework, community membership and participation are not connected as much to geographic location or ascription as they are consequences of personal choice and individual satisfaction. If members do not get the rewards they seek in their "communities of limited liability" (Janowitz 1967), they withdraw their commitments and look elsewhere. Association is voluntary, and citizens exercise considerable control over the communities they choose to join.

However, when research attention shifts to include the analysis of institutional networks and large-scale social systems like the economy, a different and more negative view of choice, autonomy, and community transformation emerges. From a macrosociological perspective, both individual and collective control have been severely compromised by the economic and political centralization characteristic of life in the early twenty-first century. As virtually all place-based communities—whether rural or urban, small or large—have become dependent on government for power, water, services, and even food, they have had to

Chapter 10

accept "external" government regulations concerning such resources. This loss of control over their own affairs has "led to an increase in alienation [among community members] and a marked decline in efforts to take care of local problems at a local level" (Whitmyer 1993, 253). Simultaneous with the loss of community relevancy, centralized "big" government appears less able to deal effectively with the localized concerns of separate communities. The only way to escape this precarious situation, it appears, is by reinvigorating an awareness at the national level of the importance of community at the local level.

This overview of sociology's loss, rediscovery, and liberation/transformation of community illustrates the fluid, context-dependent nature of this theoretical concept. The important point here is not to establish which particular interpretation is correct, but rather to recognize that both the focus and conclusions of community studies have shifted in response to changes in community experience. Such changes have been driven, in turn, by evolving political, economic and technological realities. Community studies, with shifting targets and contradictory conclusions, help document the complex evolution of our social life.

Throughout our nation's history, there has been disagreement about the health and benefits of community life. As a people, we have been described as highly individualist as well as deeply attached to the idea of community. According to urban sociologist Claude Fischer, this peculiarly American "contradiction" between individualism and the desire for fellowship has fostered "paradoxical forms of 'voluntary community'" (Fisher 1991, 80). Moreover, Fischer claims, many of us appear ambivalent about the local communities in which we claim membership. Bellah and his colleagues (1991) echo these observations, but go on to argue that the high value assigned to individual autonomy and self-reliance must be balanced by "connectedness" to others and increased citizen participation in public affairs. There are longstanding tensions in American society—between rootlessness and rootedness, freedom and constraint, self-interest and collective well-being, alienation and purposeful living—and American communities both shape and are shaped by these tensions.

Establishing exactly what community is and should be has proven to be a most difficult task. As summarized in chapter 8, no consensus has been reached regarding the importance of community membership in an individual's development or the connections between individualism and community. The liberal-communitarian debate furthermore illustrates that "community" can be used as an ideological weapon to protect and advance particular interests or values.[1] Chapter 9 outlines additional opposing claims of postmodernists and their critics concerning the plausibility of collective understanding, the situatedness of knowledge, and even the ability to reach any conclusions about community. Further insights into the struggle to define the significance and necessary role of community are found in recent discussions on civil society and the related concept of social capital.

Civil society, with origins in Hegelian philosophy, has come to mean "those forms of communal and associational life that are organized neither by the self-interest of the market nor by the coercive potential of the state" (Wolfe 1998, 17). The term is used to refer to the many forms of community and voluntary associations in a democracy that are not controlled by the state but that do serve the public. The concept was revived and revised in the 1980s, partially in response to "a widespread sense that changes in the economy and in the organization of work, family, and neighborhood have outpaced . . . the capacity of older forms of civic and associational life to help individuals and communities cope" and partly as a response to "an anti-government mood that has been part of American life since the later 1970s" (Dionne 1998, 2).

Those involved in the civil society debate, conservatives and liberals alike, tend to agree that there is something missing in contemporary society and that some sort of nationwide social reconstruction is needed. They also tend to agree that supporting churches, neighborhood associations, families, Little Leagues, community groups, and volunteer activities in general is an important step in the direction of reform. There is disagreement, however, over the role government should take in promoting the health of our nation's independent social life and regarding the meaning of many contemporary community and civic activities.

Much of the recent interest in our nation's civil society developed in response to the writing of Robert D. Putnam, and in particular, to his 1995 article titled "Bowling Alone: America's Declining Social Capital."[2] Putnam's central claim is that there has been a widespread, ongoing decline of civil engagement in the last quarter of the twentieth century, manifested in lower rates of participation in voting and volunteering, and in activities connected to schools and churches. People seem to be busier than ever, but also appear to be less connected to others. To use

Chapter 10

Putnam's famous example, more people are going bowling, but they are increasingly dropping out of leagues and bowling by themselves.

Putnam uses the term "social capital" to capture the sum total of civic engagements and interactions. He explains that it includes "features of social life—networks, norms and trust—that enable participants to act together more effectively to pursue shared objectives" and that these "[s]tocks of social capital . . . tend to be self-reinforcing and cumulative" (Putnam 1996, 34, 37). His concern is that the decline in civic engagement, accompanied as it is by an increase in general distrust of others, is eroding America's social capital.

This erosion or weakening of people's connections to the lives of their communities has very serious consequences, according to Putnam. However intangible, social capital is an essential ingredient of economic development and a prerequisite for effective social policy. Therefore, its decline affects the economic and political health of the nation. Moreover, such "civic disaffection, in turn, exacerbates other dangerous trends: sharp social and cultural divisions; growing economic discrepancies; and a wide pattern of group demands for rights and resources with little corresponding commitment to responsibilities and contributions" (Boyte and Kari 1996, 5). The most typical responses to this perceived crisis call for the reinvention of government or, conversely, for the recreation of community.

However, Putnam's analyses and data have been challenged by those who maintain that civil society is in fact "vibrant and lively." The real problem, according to such critics, is that academic arguments and political philosophies "simply miss the rich, nuanced, and complex ways in which average Americans balance the needs of communities with the needs of individuals" (Solo and Pressberg 1998, 83). University-based research is important, but as Boyte and Kari (1996) observe, "*practical* experiences and experiments are the touchstone" of both effective theory and genuine understanding (emphasis added). And there are examples of effective community initiatives that demonstrate the tenacity and strength of civil society and prove that community does work (Dionne 1998).[3]

It is critical that we broaden our focus and balance theoretical examinations of community dynamics with investigations of how ordinary people involve themselves in maintaining old communities and creating new forms of community. We must look at both the actual efforts involved in community work and the ways members themselves

Community Theorizing and Community Living

understand their communities in order to appreciate how and why community matters. The case studies presented in this book provide such an opportunity. They demonstrate that every community faces unique problems, challenges, and opportunities, and reveal important lessons about particular communities and about community in general.

Chapter 2 describes how the collective identity and outlook of the Maine Indians evolved in response to national, statewide, and local changes. The abbreviated review of the complex and lengthy interactions between different community factions and between community representatives and non-native critics, supporters, and government officials helps to illustrate that community boundaries are porous and flexible. There is no rigid line separating a community's "domestic relations" from what could be called its "foreign affairs." Always, community identity evolves through interaction. Additionally, the legal negotiations of the land claim demonstrate that while members were generally motivated to action by expectations, hopes, and fears tied to the best interests of the community, the content of these expectations, hopes and fears varied among members and over time. Ideas about what is desirable or possible are seldom fixed, community alliances shift in the face of new opportunities, and identity is continually negotiated.

These observations about identity and boundaries apply equally well to Unitarian-Universalists. The history of the national religious community, as well as the more recent experiences of the particular congregation introduced in chapter 3, demonstrate that community change can be deliberate and conscious. But only up to a point, because the ultimate direction and final outcome of community change are unpredictable. As the case study indicates, becoming a "welcoming congregation" was not inevitable. Rather, it became a possibility only after members of the community committed themselves to intensive introspection and a collective process of exploring what is involved in being "U-U." For now, at least, the congregation has accepted this new direction.

Although chapters 4 and 5 focus on two very different communities located in two different states, they point to similar issues and dilemmas. Both the story of Cambridge rent control and the story of Waterville's rejuvenation efforts demonstrate that community consensus should never be assumed and frequently remains elusive. Community members may share a general desire to do the right thing, but the specifics regarding both the means to and the "rightness" of the end are often contradictory. Some win and some lose as members struggle to

Chapter 10

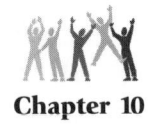

control the direction and interactions of "their" community. Such struggles can be painfully divisive, but generally communities endure such turmoil, balancing change with stability.

One of this book's major themes is that what happens within a community is noticeably shaped by socially created forces outside the community. This is further emphasized in chapter 6, as are the observations that "doing" community is hard work and that hard-working community members do not always get what they want. Extralocal social conditions, like national policy trends and economic pressures, played a dominant role in the destruction of the Old West End. But this community's experience has also been influenced by memories of relations, time, and place; for as Cohen (1985) observed, "the reality of community lies in its members' perceptions of the vitality of its culture" (118).

The irony is that West End supporters and detractors repeatedly claim different memories and competing understandings of past and present interactions. On the one hand, memories, symbols, and physical environment or location are fundamentally important community ingredients. On the other hand, as both Boston's West End and the town of Celebration, Florida demonstrate, nostalgic symbols and careful planning are insufficient by themselves to generate and sustain a community. Hard, interactive work is needed, as is a willingness to persevere in the face of uncertainty.

How does place figure in the matters and work of community? Chapter 7 considers the creation and maintenance of community relationships in cyberspace. One's neighborhood is no longer the only, or even the principal, base of one's important social relationships. Today, many of our community ties are "geographically dispersed, sparsely knit, connected heavily by telecommunications (phone and fax), and specialized in content" (Wellman and Gulia 1999, 187). In a remarkably short period of time, computer systems have connected huge numbers of people and created "new places of assembly that will generate opportunities for employment, political participation, social contact, and entertainment" (Kollock and Smith 1999, 16); thousands of groups of people transact business, discuss hopes and fears, and play games on computer networks. Debates over whether these networked groups have the structure and processes of "real" communities are ongoing and sometimes fierce. But there also is a growing acknowledgment that the social groups or communities of cyberspace "spill out into the *real* world and vice versa" (Smith and Kollock 1999, 19), and that cyberspace is an increasingly crucial location for community theory and practice.

There are some common patterns here. It is in communities that individuals "are met and affirmed, challenged, broadened, and held accountable" (Hirsch 1998, 241). But while people find meanings and establish identities in community, the individuals and groups that form any community do not necessarily reach agreement on these meanings and identities. Additionally, there is an essential taken-for-granted aspect of community that is frequently underestimated; most members simply go about the day-in and day-out business of building connections, finding meanings, and reinventing their social worlds.

The interactions and processes that *are* community respond to the ebb and flow of member's similarities and differences on the one hand, and to external political and economic conditions on the other. Communities are dynamic; they constantly adjust to their ever-changing environments even as they reproduce themselves. The goal of community is to unify diversity in order to achieve common desired ends, but there is no guarantee that efforts expended in the name of community will lead to agreement or success.

Community is accomplished through an interactive process of influence and response that involves individuals, groups, social norms, roles, desires, technology, economics, and politics. The social and environmental context in which such a mix occurs gives shape to the overall product. Also affecting the process of community is the peculiar human tendency to interpret or assign meaning—not merely react—to the actions and situations that confront them. Given the expansive nature of interpretation, this tendency complicates what otherwise might be a straightforward stimulus-response situation. It also ensures that community is a fundamentally uncertain process that unfolds as groups and individuals make choices about actions. Communities can produce new options for members, but there is no certainty about whether this will happen. Community is always acted out but never completed, because it is in negotiation and interaction that the identities, norms, and options of all communities evolve and change.

There is a lot of uncertainty associated with community, specifically regarding how it should be defined, who does or doesn't belong to a specific community, and which particular rules govern a given community's activities. In spite of (or in part because of) such ongoing controversies, it is likely that local community will continue to matter since

Chapter 10

it can provide mutual support for collective betterment. Furthermore, there is considerable evidence that Americans generally remain committed to localities for sentimental and sometimes for political reasons. At the same time, it appears likely that community matters will evolve because increasingly, community is being created in less traditional places—in new spaces and ways.

As new economic, political, and technological realities collide with old expectations and traditions, community "remains essential as a site for the realization of common values in support of social goods" (Sampson 1999, 247). Because of this, achieving common goals demands the kinds of understandings that will emerge from sustained and careful investigations of community issues and individual communities. Perhaps more than ever before, community matters.

Notes

1. I thank my colleague Jason Nwankwo for sharing this insight.

2. The "Bowling Alone" article appeared in the January 1995 issue of the *Journal of Democracy*. Also of importance were "The Prosperous Community" and "The Strange Disappearance of Civil America," which appeared, respectively, in the Spring 1993 and Winter 1996 issues of *The American Prospect*. Putnam's research and conclusions are presented in greatest detail in *Bowling Alone* (New York: Simon & Schuster, 2000).

3. Especially relevant is the research by Carmen Sirianni and Lewis Friedland. Their new book, *Civic Innovation in America: Community Empowerment, Public Policy, and the Movement for Civil Renewal* (Berkeley: University of California Press, 2001), provides multiple examples of innovative community activities and civic engagement.

BIBLIOGRAPHY

Abrahamson, Mark. 1996. *Urban Enclaves: Identity and Place in America.* New York: St. Martin's.
Abt Associates. 1987. "Cambridge Housing Study: Final Report." Cambridge, MA.
Achtenberg, Emily P. 1973. "The Social Utility of Rent Control." In *Housing in Urban America.* edited by J. Pynoos, R. Schafer, and W.W. Hartman, 434-47. Chicago: Aldine.
Allen, John C., and Don A. Dillman. 1994. *Against All Odds: Rural Community in the Information Age.* Boulder CO: Westview.
Andersen, Kurt. 1999. "Pleasantville: Can Disney Reinvent the Burbs?" *The New Yorker* 6 September 1999, 74-79.
Andersen, Margaret, and Patricia Hill Collins, eds. 1994. *Race, Class and Gender.* Belmont, CA: Wadsworth.
Anderson, Walter Truett, ed. 1995. *The Truth about the Truth.* New York: G.P. Putnam's Sons.
Appelbaum, R.P., M. Dolny, P. Drier and J. Gilderbloom. 1991. "Scapegoating Rent Control: Masking the Causes of Rent Control." *Journal of the American Planning Association* 57 (2), 153-65.
Appleby, Joyce, Lynn Hunt, and Margaret Jacob. 1993. *Telling the Truth About History.* New York: W.W. Norton & Company.
Atlas, J., and P. Dreier. 1980. "The Housing Crisis and the Tenants' Revolt." *Social Policy* 10 (4): 13-24.
Austin, Regina. 1992. "Left at the Post: One Take on Blacks and Postmodernism." *Law and Society Review* 26 (4), 751-54.
Barsh, Russel L. 1982. "Indian Land Claims Policy in the United States." *North Dakota Law Review* 58 (8): 7-82.
Bauman, Zygmunt. 1992. *Intimations of Postmodernity.* London: Routledge.
Baym, Nancy K. 1998. "The Emergence of On-Line Community." In *Cybersociety*

Bibliography

2.0: *Revisiting Computer-Mediated Communication and Community*, edited by Steven G. Jones, 35–68. Thousand Oaks, CA: Sage.

———. 1995. "The Emergence of Community in Computer-Mediated Communication." In *CyberSociety: Computer-Mediated Communication and Community*, edited by Steven G. Jones, 138–63. Thousand Oaks, CA: Sage.

Becker, Howard S. 1998. *Tricks of the Trade*. Chicago: University of Chicago Press.

———, and Michal M. McCall, eds. 1990. *Symbolic Interaction and Cultural Studies*. Chicago: University of Chicago Press.

———. 1982. "Culture: A Sociological View." *The Yale Review* [n.s.] 71 (4): 513–27.

Beem, Edgar Allen. 1987."Promises to Keep," Part 2. *Maine Times*, 9 January.

Bell, Derrick. 1987. *And We Are Not Saved*. New York: Basic Books.

———, and Preeta Bansal. 1998. "The Republican Revival and Racial Politics." *Yale Law Journal* 97: 1609–1621.

Bell, Gordon, and James N. Gray. 1998. "The Revolution Yet To Happen." In *Beyond Calculation: The Next Fifty Years of Computing*, edited by Peter J. Denning and Robert M. Metcalfe, 5–32. New York: Copernicus.

Bell, Michael Mayerfeld. 1994. *Childerley: Nature and Morality in a Country Village*. Chicago: University of Chicago Press.

Bellah, Robert N., Richard Madsen, William M. Sullivan, Ann Swidler, and Steven M. Tipton. 1985. *Habits of the Heart*. New York: Harper & Row.

———. 1991. *The Good Society*. New York: Vintage.

Benhabib, Seyla. 1992. *Situating the Self*. London: Routledge.

Berger, Peter L., and Thomas Luckmann. 1967. *The Social Construction of Reality*. New York: Doubleday Anchor.

Berman, Paul, ed. 1992. *Debating PC*. New York: Laurel.

Black, Antony. 1984. *Guilds and Civil Society in European Political Thought from the Twelfth Century to the Present*. Ithaca, NY: Cornell University Press.

Blackwell, James E. 1991. *The Black Community: Diversity and Unity*. New York: HarperCollins.

Block, W., and E. Olsen, eds. 1981. *Rent Control: Myths and Realities*. Vancouver, BC: Fraser Institute.

Bloom, Alan. 1987. *The Closing of the American Mind*. New York: Simon & Schuster.

Blumer, Herbert. 1987. *Symbolic Interactionism: Perspective and Method*. Berkeley: University of California Press.

Borgmann, Albert. 1992. *Crossing the Postmodern Divide*. Chicago: University of Chicago Press.

Bowen, Catherine Drinker. 1944. *Yankee from Olympus: Justice Holmes and His Family*. Boston: Little, Brown and Company.

Boyte, Harry C., and Nancy N. Kari. 1996. *Building America: The Democratic Promise of Public Work*. Philadelphia, PA: Temple University Press.

Brodeur, Paul. 1985. *Restitution*. Boston: Northeastern University Press.

Brodoff, Maureen. 1996. "Return to Civil Society? Let's Get Busy." Letter to the Editor, *Boston Globe*, 4 April, 4.

Bruckman, Amy S. 1996. "Gender Swapping on the Internet." In *High Noon on*

Bibliography

the Electronic Frontier: Conceptual Issues in Cyberspace, Peter Ludlow, edited by 317–25. Cambridge, MA: MIT Press.

Bruner, Edward. 1997. "Ethnography as Narrative." In *Memory, Identity, Community* edited by Lewis P. Hinchman and Sandra K. Hinchman, 264–80. New York: SUNY Press.

Buehrens, John A., and F. Forrester Church. 1989. *Our Chosen Faith: An Introduction to Unitarian Universalism.* Boston: Beacon.

Canellos, Peter. 1997. "Old Boston Grievances Die Hard." *The Boston Globe*, 25 November.

Capek, S.M., and J.I. Gilderbloom. 1992. *Community versus Commodity: Tenants and the American City.* Albany, NY: SUNY Press.

Cassara, Ernest, ed. 1970. *Universalism in America.* Boston: Beacon Press.

Chang Hall, Lisa Kahaleole. 1993. "Compromising Positions." In *Beyond a Dream Deferred* edited by Becky W. Thompson and Sangeeta Tyagi, 162–73. Minneapolis: University of Minnesota Press.

Clark, D. J. 1988. "Rent Control in Massachusetts." *Massachusetts Law Review* (Winter): 160–74.

Clinton, Robert N., and Margaret Tobey Hootoop. 1979. "Judicial Enforcement of the Federal Restraints on Alienation of Indian Land: The Origins of the Eastern Land Claims." *Maine Law Review* 31: 17–90

Cohen, Anthony P. 1985. *The Symbolic Construction of Community.* New York: Routledge.

Cohen, Felix S. 1982. *Handbook of Federal Indian Law.* Charlottesville, VA: Bobbs-Merrill.

Connerly, Charles E. 1985. "The Community Question: An Extension of Wellman and Leighton." *Urban Affairs Quarterly* 20 (4): 537–56.

Corlett, William. 1993. *Community Without Unity.* Durham, NC: Duke University Press.

Cravatts, R.L. 1990. "Rent Control Unfairly Limits Owners' Rights." *Cambridge Chronicle*, 8 November 8.

Cuba, Lee J., 1987. *Identity and Community on the Alaska Frontier.* Philadelphia, PA: Temple University Press.

Cunningham, B., 1995. "History of Rent Control Did Not End with Statewide Vote on Question 9." *Cambridge Chronicle*, 20 April.

Curtis, Pavel. 1996. "MUDding: Social Phenomena in Text-Based Virtual Realities." In *High Noon on the Electronic Frontier: Conceptual Issues in Cyberspace*, edited by Peter Ludlow, 347–73. Cambridge, MA: MIT Press.

Dalton, Harlon. 1987. "Minority Critique of CLS: The Clouded Prism." *Harvard Civil Rights-Civil Liberties Review* 22: 435–47.

Denning, Peter J., and Robert M. Metcalfe. 1998. *Beyond Calculation: The Next Fifty Years of Computing.* New York: Copernicus.

Denzin, Norman K. 1993. "Sexuality and Gender: An Interactionist/Post-structural Reading." In *Theory on Gender: Feminism on Theory*, edited by Paula England, 199–222. New York: Aldine De Gruyter.

Bibliography

———. 1992. *Symbolic Interactionism and Cultural Studies: The Politics of Interpretation*. Cambridge, MA: Oxford University Press.

Dertouzos, Michael. 1997. *What Will Be: How the New World of Information Will Change Our Lives*. New York: HarperCollins.

Devine, A. 1990. "Field Study on Low Rent Units." A Follow-up Report to the Mayor's Green Ribbon Committee to Research and Propose Minimum Rents. Cambridge, MA.

Dibbell, Julian. 1996. "A Rape In Cyberspace; or How an Evil Clown, a Haitian Trickster Spirit, Two Wizards, and a Cast of Dozens Turned a Database into a Society." In *High Noon on the Electronic Frontier: Conceptual Issues in Cyberspace*, edited by Peter Ludlow, 375–96. Cambridge, MA: MIT Press.

Dickens, David R., and Andrea Fontana. 1994. *Postmodernism & Social Inquiry*. New York: The Guilford Press.

Dionne, E.J., Jr., ed. 1998. *Community Works: The Revival of Civil Society in America*. Washington, DC: Brookings Institution.

Doheny-Farina, Stephen. 1996. *The Wired Neighborhood*. New Haven, CT: Yale University Press.

Donne, John. 1955. *Complete Poetry and Selected Prose*, edited by John Hayward. London: The Nonesuch Library.

Donovan, Josephine. 1992. *Feminist Theory*. New York: Continuum.

Downs, A. 1983. *Rental Housing in the 1980s*. Washington, DC: Brookings Institution.

Dreier, Peter. 1989. "Economic Growth and Economic Justice in Boston: Populist Housing and Jobs Policies." In *Unequal Partnerships: The Political Economy of Urban Redevelopment in Postwar America*, edited by G. Squires, 35–58. New Brunswick, NJ: Rutgers University Press.

D'Souza, Dinesh. 1991. *Illiberal Education: The Politics of Race and Sex on Campus*. New York: Free Press.

Durkheim, Emile. 1916/1965. *The Elementary Forms of the Religious Life*. New York: Free Press.

Duster, Troy. 1993. "The Diversity of California at Berkeley: An Emerging Reformulation of 'Competence' in an Increasingly Multicultural World." *Beyond a Dream Deferred*, edited by Becky W. Thompson and Sangeeta Tyagi, 231–55. Minneapolis: University of Minnesota Press.

Dyson, Esther. 1997. *Release 2.0: A Design for Living in the Digital Age*. New York: Broadway Books.

Eagleton, Terry. 1996. *The Illusion of Postmodernism*. Cambridge, MA: Blackwell.

Engel, David M. 1993. "Law in the Domains of Everyday Life: The Construction of Community and Difference." In *Law in Everyday Life*, edited by Austin Sarat and Thomas R. Kearns, 123–70. Ann Arbor: University of Michigan Press.

Erikson, Kai. 1976. *Everything in Its Path*. New York: Simon & Schuster.

Esteva, Gustavo, and Madhu Suri Prakash. 1998. *Grassroots Post-Modernism*. New York: Zed Books.

Bibliography

Etzioni, Amitai. 1993. *The Spirit of Community: The Reinvention of American Society.* New York: Simon & Schuster.

———, ed. 1995. *New Communitarian Thinking.* Charlottesville: University of Virginia Press.

Evans, Sara M., and Harry C. Boyte. 1992. *Free Spaces: The Sources of Democratic Change in America.* Chicago: University of Chicago Press.

Ewick, Patricia. 1992. "Postmodern Melancholia." In *Law and Society Review* 26 (4): 755–63.

Fine, Gary Alan. 1992. "Agency, Structure and Comparative Contexts: Towards a Synthetic Interactionism." *Symbolic Interaction* 15 (1): 87–107.

Feagin, J.R., and R. Parker. 1990. *Building American Cities: The Urban Real Estate Game.* Englewood Cliffs, NJ: Prentice-Hall.

Fenstermaker, Sarah. 1997. "Telling Tales out of School: Three Short Stories of a Feminist Sociologist." In *Feminist Sociology: Life Histories of a Movement*, edited by Barbara Laslett and Barrie Thorne, 209–28. New Brunswick, NJ: Rutgers University Press.

Ferguson, Ronald F., and William T. Dickens, eds. 1999. *Urban Problems and Community Development*, Washington, DC: Brookings Institution.

Fischer, Claude S. 1991. "Ambivalent Communities: How Americans Understand Their Localities." In *America at Century's End*, edited by Alan Wolfe, 79–90. Berkeley: University of California Press.

Flanagan, William G. 1993. *Contemporary Urban Sociology.* New York: Cambridge University Press.

Forman, Charles C. 1989. "Elected Now By Time." In *A Stream of Light: A Short History of American Unitarianism*, 2nd ed., edited by Conrad Wright, 3–32. Boston: Skinner House Books.

Frantz, Douglas, and Catherine Collins. 1999. *Celebration, U.S.A.* New York: Henry Holt.

Gans, Herbert J. 1962/1982. *The Urban Villagers.* New York: Free Press.

———. 1967. *The Levittowners.* New York: Columbia University Press.

Ghere, David L. 1984. "Assimilation, Termination or Tribal Rejuvenation: Maine Indian Affairs in the 1950s." *Maine Historical Society Quarterly* 24: 239–64.

Gibson, William. 1984. *Neuromancer.* New York: Ace Books.

Gilderbloom. John I. 1981. "Moderate Rent Control: Its Impact on the Quality and Quantity of the Housing Stock." *Urban Affairs Quarterly* 17 (2): 123–42.

Gilligan, Carol. 1982. *In A Different Voice.* Cambridge, MA: Harvard University Press.

———, Nona P. Lyons, and Trudy Hamner, eds. 1990. *Making Connections: The Relational Worlds of Adolescent Girls at Emma Willard School.* Cambridge, MA: Harvard University Press.

Godway, Eleanor M., and Geraldine Finn, eds. 1994. *Who is this 'We'? Absence of Community.* Cheektowaga, NY: Black Rose Books.

Goetze, Rolf. 1983. *Rescuing the American Dream: Public Policy and the Crisis in Housing.* New York: Holmes and Meier.

Bibliography

———. 1990. "Cambridge Housing Challenges." Final Report to the City of Cambridge. Cambridge, MA. Cambridge Community Development Department.

Greenspun, Philip. 1999. *Philip and Alex's Guide to Web Publishing*. San Francisco: Morgan Kaufman Publishers.

Gutmann, Amy. 1985 "Communitarian Critics of Liberalism." *Philosophy & Public Affairs* 14 (3): 308–24.

Hafner, Katie, and Matthew Lyon. 1996. *Where Wizards Stay Up Late*. New York: Touchstone.

Hall, Peter M. 1994. "Interactionism and the Study of Social Organization." In *Symbolic Interaction: An Introduction to Social Psychology*, edited by Nancy J. Herman and Larry T. Reynolds, 286–308. Dix Hills, NY: General Hall.

Hampton, Keith N., and Barry Wellman. 1999. "Netville Online and Offline: Observing and Surveying a Wired Suburb." *American Behavioral Scientist* 43, no. 3, (November/December): 475–92.

Hayek, F.A., et al. 1975. *Rent Control: A Popular Paradox*. Vancouver, BC: Fraser Institute.

Herman, Nancy J. and Larry T. Reynolds, eds. 1994. *Symbolic Interaction: An Introduction to Social Psychology*. Dix Hills, NY: General Hall.

Hillery, George A., Jr. 1955. "Definitions of Community: Areas of Agreement." *Rural Sociology* 20: 779–91.

Hinchman, Lewis P., and Sandra D. Hinchman, eds. 1997. *Memory, Identity, Community*. New York: SUNY Press.

Hirsch, Kathleen. 1988. *A Home in the Heart of a City*. New York: North Point Press.

Hirschmann, Nancy J. 1992. *Rethinking Obligation: A Feminist Method for Political Theory*. Ithaca, NY: Cornell University Press.

Hollinger, Robert. 1994. *Postmodernism and the Social Sciences*. Thousand Oaks, CA: Sage.

Howe, Charles A. 1993. *The Larger Faith: A Short History of American Universalism*. Boston: Skinner House Books.

Howe, Daniel Walker. 1989. "At Morning Blest and Golden-Browed." In *A Stream of Light: A Short History of American Unitarianism*, edited by Conrad Wright, 33–61.Boston: Skinner House Books.

Hummon, David M. 1993. "Reading Community." *Contemporary Sociology* 22 (2): 149–50.

Hunter, Albert. 1997. "Community Mislaid: Shifts in Rhetoric and Research on Community from the Chicago School to Today's Communalism." Paper Presented at the American Sociological Association Annual Meeting. Toronto, ON, August.

———. 1974. *Symbolic Communities: The Persistence and Change of Chicago's Local Communities*. Chicago: University of Chicago Press.

Hutchinson, Allan D. 1992. "Doing the Right Thing? Toward a Postmodern Politics." *Law and Society Review* 26 (4): 773–87.

Janowitz, Morris. 1967. *The Community Press in an Urban Setting*. Chicago: University of Chicago Press.

Bibliography

Jones, Steven G., ed. 1998. *Cybersociety 2.0: Revisiting Computer-Mediated Communication and Community*. Thousand Oaks, CA: Sage.

———. 1995. *Cybersociety: Computer-Mediated Communication and Community*. Thousand Oaks, CA: Sage.

Kalberg, Stephen. 1997. "Max Weber's Sociology: Research Strategies and Modes of Analysis." In *Reclaiming the Sociological Classics*, edited by Charles Camic, 208–41. Malden, MA: Blackwell.

Karst, Kenneth L. 1980. "Equality and Community: Lessons from the Civil Rights Era." *The Notre Dame Lawyer* 56 (2): 183–214.

Kasinitz, Philip, and David Hillyard. 1995. "The Old-Timers' Tale: The Politics of Nostalgia on the Waterfront." *Journal of Contemporary Ethnography* 24 (2): 139–64.

Kempers, Margot. 1998. "The Process of Community / Development: Action and Renewal in Mid-Maine." In *Research in Community Sociology: American Community Issues and Problems of Development*, edited by Dan A. Chekki, 91–112. Stamford, CT: JAI Press.

———. 1989. "There's Losing and Winning: Ironies of the Maine Indian Land Claim." *Legal Studies Forum* 13 (3): 267–300.

Kolko, Beth, and Elizabeth Reid. 1998. "Dissolution and Fragmentation: Problems in On-Line Communities." In Cybersociety 2.0: Revisiting Computer-Mediated Communication and Community, edited by Steven G. Jones, 212–229. Thousand Oaks, CA: Sage.

Kollock, Peter, and Marc A. Smith. 1999. "Communities in Cyberspace." In *Communities in Cyberspace*, edited by Marc A. Smith and Peter Kollock, 3–25. New York: Routledge.

Kors, Alan C., and Harvey A. Silverglate. 1999. *The Shadow University*. New York: Harper.

Kruh, David S. 1992. "The West End Story." *The West Ender* 8, no 4 (October): 6–7.

Kvale, Steinar. 1995. "Themes of Postmodernity." In *The Truth about the Truth*, edited by W. T. Anderson, 18–25. New York: G.P. Putnam's Sons.

Kymlicka, Will. 1990. *Contemporary Political Philosophy*. New York: Oxford University Press.

Lee, Richard Wayne. 1992. *Unitarian Universalism: Organizational Dilemmas of the Cult of the Individual*. Unpublished Ph.D. Dissertation. Sociology Department, Emory University.

Lemert, Charles. 1997. *Postmodernism Is Not What You Think*. Malden, MA: Blackwell.

———. 1993. "After Modernity, Since 1979." In *Social Theory*, edited by Charles Lemert, 489–503. Boulder, CO: Westview.

Lett, M. 1976. *Rent Control: Concepts, Realities, and Mechanisms*. New Brunswick NJ.: Center for Urban Policy Research at Rutgers University.

Lowry, I.S. 1970. *Rental Housing in New York City*, Vol.1: *Confronting the Crisis*. New York: Rand Institute and McKinsey Company.

Lyon, David. 1999. *Postmodernity*. Minneapolis: University of Minnesota Press.

Lyon, Larry. 1987. *The Community in Urban Society*. Chicago: Dorsey Press.

Bibliography

Lyotard, Jean-Francois. 1984. *The Postmodern Condition: A Report on Knowledge.* Translated by G. Bennington and B. Massumi. Minneapolis: University of Minnesota Press.

Macleod, Jay. 1995. *Ain't No Makin' It.* Boulder, CO: Westview.

MacQuarrie, Brian. 1997. "West Ender's Dreams Fading." *The Boston Globe,* 10 January.

Mannheim, Karl. 1936. "Preface." In *Ideology and Utopia.* Translated by Louis Wirth and Edward Shils. New York: Harcourt Brace.

Markoff, John. 2000. "A Newer, Lonelier Crowd Emerges in Internet Study." *New York Times,* 16 February, A1, 15.

Marx, Karl. 1869/1968. *The 18th Brumaire of Louis Bonaparte.* New York: International Publishers.

Matsuda, Mari. 1987. "Looking to the Bottom: Critical Legal Studies and Reparations." *Harvard Civil Rights-Civil Liberties Review* 22: 323-99.

McCall, Michal M., and Howard S. Becker. 1990. "Introduction." In *Symbolic Interaction and Cultural Studies,* edited by Howard S. Becker and Michal M. McCall, 1-15. Chicago: University of Chicago Press.

———, and Judith Wittner. 1990. "The Good News about Life History." In *Symbolic Interaction and Cultural Studies.* edited by Howard S. Becker and Michal M. McCall, 46-89. Chicago: University of Chicago Press.

McHugh, P. 1968. *Defining the Situation.* Indianapolis, IN: Bobbs-Merrill.

Mele, Christopher. 1999. "Cyberspace and Disadvantaged Communities: The Internet as a Tool for Collective Action." In *Communities in Cyberspace,* edited by Marc A. Smith and Peter Kollock, 290-310. New York, Routledge.

Meltzer, Bernard N., and Jerome Manis. 1982/1994. "Emergence and Human Conduct." In *Symbolic Interaction: An Introduction to Social Psychology,* edited by Nancy J. Herman and Larry T. Reynolds, 180-87. Dix Hills, NY: General Hall, Inc.

Merry, Sally Engle, and Susan S. Silbey. 1984."What Do Plaintiffs Want? Reexamining the Concept of Dispute." *The Justice System Journal* 9: 151-78.

Merton, Robert K. 1936. "The Unanticipated Consequences of Purposive Social Action." *American Sociological Review* 1: 894-904.

Mestrovic, Stjepan G. 1992. *Durkheim and Postmodern Culture.* New York: Aldine de Gruyter.

Miller, Perry. 1950. *The Transcendentalists: An Anthology.* Cambridge, MA: Harvard University Press.

Miller, Russell E. 1979. *The Larger Hope: The First Century of the Universalist Church in America, 1770-1870.* Boston: Unitarian Universalist Association.

Minow, Martha. 1996. "Stories in Law." In *Law's Stories: Narrative and Rhetoric in the Law,* edited by Peter Brooks and Paul Gewirtz, 24-36. New Haven, CT: Yale University Press.

———. 1993. "Partial Justice: Law and Minorities." In *The Fate of Law,* edited by Austin Sarat and Thomas R. Kearns, 15-77. Ann Arbor, MI: University of Michigan Press.

Bibliography

———. 1990. *Making All the Difference: Inclusion, Exclusion, and American Law.* Ithaca, NY: Cornell University Press.

———, and Elizabeth V. Spelman. 1990. "In Context." *Southern California Law Review* 63, 1597–1652.

Mollenkopf, J. and J. Pynoos. 1973. "Boardwalk and Park Place: Property Ownership, Political Structure, and Housing Policy at the Local Level." In *Housing in Urban America*, edited by J. Pynoos, R. Scharer, and W.W. Hartman, 55–74. Chicago: Aldine.

Mulhall, Stephen, and Adam Swift. 1992. *Liberals and Communitarians.* Cambridge, MA: Blackwell.

Natoli, Joseph, and Linda Hutcheon. 1993. "Introduction: Reading *A Postmodern Reader.*" *A Postmodern Reader*, edited by Joseph Natoli and Linda Hutcheon, vii–xiii. Albany, NY: SUNY Press.

Nicholson, Linda, ed. 1990. *Feminism/Postmodernism.* London: Routledge.

———, and Steven Seidman, eds. 1995. *Social Postmodernism.* New York: Cambridge University Press.

Niebanck, P.L. 1985. *The Rent Control Debates.* Chapel Hill: University of North Carolina Press.

Nisbet, Robert A. 1962. *Community and Power.* New York: Oxford University Press / Galaxy.

Norgren, Jill, and Serena Nanda, eds. 1996. *American Cultural Pluralism and Law.* Westport, CT: Praeger.

Nyhan, Pat. 1986. "Promises to Keep, Part One." *Maine Times*, 2 January.

O'Connor, Thomas H. 1996. *Building a New Boston.* Boston: Northeastern University Press.

O'Toole, Francis J., and Thomas N. Tureen. 1971. "State Power and the Passamaquoddy Tribe: A Gross National Hypocrisy?" *Maine Law Review* 23: 1–39.

Parke, David B. 1989. "A Wave at Crest." In *A Stream of Light: A Short History of American Unitarianism*, 2nd ed., edited by Conrad Wright, 95–124. Boston: Skinner House Books.

Perin, Constance. 1988. *Belonging in America.* Madison, WI: University of Wisconsin Press.

Pollan, Michael. 1997. "Town-Building is no Mickey Mouse Operation." *The New York Times*, 14 December.

Prus, Robert. 1994. "Generic Social Processes and the Study of Human Lived Experiences: Achieving Transcontextuality in Ethnographic Research." In *Symbolic Interaction: An Introduction to Social Psychology*, edited by Nancy J. Herman and Larry T. Reynolds, 436–58. Dix Hills, NY: General Hall, Inc.

Putnam, Robert. 2000. *Bowling Alone.* New York: Simon & Schuster.

———. 1996. "The Strange Disappearance of Civil America." *The American Prospect* (Spring): 35–42.

———. 1995. "Bowling Alone: America's Declining Social Capital." *Journal of Democracy* (January): 65–78.

Bibliography

———. 1993. "The Prosperous Community: Social Capital and Public Life." *The American Prospect* (Spring): 35–42.

Rawls, John. 1996. *Political Liberalism.* New York: Columbia University Press.

———. 1971. *A Theory of Justice.* Cambridge, MA: Harvard University Press.

Ray, Roger B. 1974. "Maine Indians' Concept of Land Tenure." *Maine Historical Society Quarterly* 13 (1): 28–51.

Regan, Milton C., Jr. 1985. "Community and Justice in Constitutional Theory." *Wisconsin Law Review*: 1073–1133.

Reid, Elizabeth. 1996. "Text-Based Virtual Realities: Identity and Cyborg Body." In *High Noon on the Electronic Frontier: Conceptual Issues in Cyberspace*, edited by Peter Ludlow, 327–46. Cambridge, MA: MIT Press.

———. 1995. "Virtual Worlds: Culture and Imagination." In *CyberSociety: Computer-Mediated Communication and Community*, edited by Steven G. Jones, 164–83. Thousand Oaks, CA: Sage.

Reynolds, Larry T. 1994. "Intellectual Antecedents." In *Symbolic Interaction: An Introduction to Social Psychology*, edited by Nancy J. Herman and Larry T. Reynold, 6–24. Dix Hills, NY: General Hall, Inc.

Rheingold, Howard. 1996. "A Slice of My Life in My Virtual Community." In *High Noon on the Electronic Frontier: Conceptual Issues in Cyberspace*, edited by Peter Ludlow, 413–36. Cambridge, MA: MIT Press.

———. 1993. *The Virtual Community: Homesteading on the Electronic Frontier.* New York: HarperCollins.

Richert, Evan. 1997. "Confronting the Issue of Sprawl in Maine." *Rural Connections* 4, no. 2 (Summer/Fall): 1–13.

Robinson, David. 1985. *The Unitarians and the Universalists.* Westport, CT: Greenwood.

———. 1992–94. "Unitarian History and the Unitarian-Universalist Identity: The Work of Conrad Wright." *The Proceedings of the Unitarian Universalist Historical Society*, Vol. XXIII, Part 2.

Rosenau, Pauline Marie. 1992. *Postmodernism and the Social Sciences.* Princeton, NJ: Princeton University Press.

Rosenberg, M. 1989. "The Mayor's Green Ribbon Committee to Research and Propose Minimum Rents: Report to the Chairman. Cambridge, MA.

Rosenblum, Nancy L., ed. 1989. *Liberalism and the Moral Life.* Cambridge, MA: Harvard University Press.

Ross, Andrew. 1999. *The Celebration Chronicles: Life, Liberty and the Pursuit of Property Value in Disney's New Town.* New York: Ballentine Books.

Ross, Thomas. 1996. *Just Stories.* Boston: Beacon Press.

Rossi, Alice, ed. 1974. *The Feminist Papers: From Adams to Beauvoir.* New York: Bantam.

Rouner, Leroy S. 1991. *On Community.* Notre Dame, IN: University of Notre Dame Press.

Sampson, Robert J. 1999. "What 'Community' Supplies." In *Urban Problems and*

Bibliography

Community Development, edited by Ronald F. Ferguson and William T. Dickens, 214–92. Washington, DC: Brookings Institution.
Sandel, Michael J. 1998. *Liberalism and the Limits of Justice*, 2nd ed. New York: Cambridge University Press.
———. 1985. "The Political Theory of the Procedural Republic." In *Constitutionalism and Rights*, edited by Gary C. Bryner and Noel B. Reynolds, 141–55. Provo, UT: Brigham Young University Press.
———. 1984. "Introduction." *Liberalism and Its Critics*, edited by Michael J. Sandel, 1–12. New York: New York University Press.
———. 1982. *Liberalism and the Limits of Justice*. New York: Cambridge University Press.
Sarup, Madan. 1993. *Poststructuralism and Postmodernism*. Athens: University of Georgia Press.
Schlesinger, Arthur, Jr. 1992. *The Disuniting of America: Reflections on a Multicultural Society*. New York: Norton.
Schuler, Douglas. 1996. *New Community Networks: Wired For Change*. New York: ACM Press.
Seidman, Steven, ed. 1994a. *The Postmodern Turn*. New York: Cambridge University Press.
———. 1994b. *Contested Knowledge*. Cambridge, MA: Blackwell.
———, and David G. Wagner, eds. 1992. *Postmodernism and Social Theory*. Cambridge, MA: Blackwell.
Selznick, Philip. 1992. *The Moral Commonwealth: Social Theory and the Promise of Community*. Berkeley: University of California Press.
———. 1987. "The Idea of a Communitarian Morality." *California Law Review* 75: 445–63.
Shaw, Clifford and Henry McKay. 1969. *Juvenile Delinquency and Urban Areas*, 2nd ed. Chicago: University of Chicago Press.
Sirianni, Carmen, and Lewis Friedland. 2001. *Civic Innovation in America: Community Empowerment, Public Policy, and the Movement for Civil Renewal*. Berkeley: University of California Press.
Smart, Barry. 1993. *Postmodernity*. London: Routledge.
Smith, Anna DuVal. 1999. "Problems of Conflict Management in Virtual Communities." In *Communities In Cyberspace*, edited by Marc A. Smith and Peter Kollock, 134–63. New York: Routledge.
Smith, Dorothy. 1987. *The Everyday World as Problematic: A Feminist Sociology*. Boston: Northeastern University Press.
Smith, Marc A., and Peter Kollock, eds. 1999. *Communities in Cyberspace*. New York: Routledge.
Snipp, C.W. 1989. "American Indians and Public Policy in the 1990s: Opportunities and Dilemmas." Paper presented at the Eastern Sociological Society Annual Meeting, Baltimore, Maryland, 17–19 March.
Solo, Pam, and Gail Pressberg. 1998. "Beyond Theory: Civil Society in Action."

Bibliography

In *Community Works: The Revival of Civil Society in America*, edited by E.J. Dionne Jr., 81–87. Washington, DC: Brookings Institution.

Spelman, Elizabeth V. 1988. *Inessential Woman: Problems of Exclusion in Feminist Thought*. Boston: Beacon Press.

Stack, Carol B. 1974. *All Our Kin: Strategies for Survival in a Black Community*. New York: Harper & Row.

Stegman, M.A. 1985. "The Model: Rent Control in New York City." *The Rent Control Debates*, edited by P.L. Niebanck, 29–55. Chapel Hill: University of North Carolina Press, 1985.

Stein, Maurice. 1960. *The Eclipse of Community: An Interpretation of American Studies*. Princeton, NJ: Princeton University Press.

Sternlieb, G., and J.W. Hughes. 1980. *America's Housing: Projects and Problems*. New Brunswick, NJ: Rutgers University Press.

Suttles, Gerald D. 1968. *The Social Order of the Slum*. Chicago: University of Chicago Press.

Svensson, Frances. 1979. "Liberal Democracy and Group Rights: The Legacy of Individualism and Its Impact on American Indian Tribes," *Political Studies* 37: 421–30.

Taylor, Charles. 1994. "The Politics of Recognition." In *Multiculturalism: Examining the Politics of Recognition*, edited by Amy Gutmann, 25–73. Princeton, NJ: Princeton University Press.

———. 1989. "Cross-Purposes: The Liberal-Communitarian Debate." In *Liberalism and the Moral Life*, edited by Nancy L. Rosenblum, 159–82. Cambridge, MA: Harvard University Press.

Taylor, Theodore W. 1984. *The Bureau of Indian Affairs*. Boulder CO: Westview.

———. 1972. *The States and Their Indian Citizens*. Washington, DC: Department of Interior, Bureau of Indian Affairs.

Thomas, W.I. 1923/1994. "The Regulation of the Wishes," *Symbolic Interaction: An Introduction to Social Psychology*. edited by Nancy J. Herman and Larry T. Reynolds, 156–61. Dix Hills, NY: General Hall, Inc.

Thompson, Becky W., and Sangeeta Tyagi, eds. 1993. *Beyond a Dream Deferred: Multicultural Education and the Politics of Excellence*. St. Paul: University of Minnesota Press.

Tilly, Charles. 1996. "Invisible Elbow." *Sociological Forum* 11 (4): 589–601.

Tompkins, Jane. 1996. "'Indians': Textualism, Morality, and the Problem of History." In *"Race," Writing, and Difference*, edited by Henry Louis Gates Jr., 59–77. Chicago: University of Chicago Press.

Tucker, W. 1990. *The Excluded Americans*. Washington, DC: Regnery Gateway.

———. 1987. "Where do the Homeless Come From?" *National Review*. 25 (September): 32–43.

Turkle, Sherry. 2000. "Cyberspace and Identity," *Contemporary Sociology* 28 no. 6 (November): 643–48.

Uncapher, Willard. 1999. "Electronic Homesteading on the Rural Frontier: Big Sky Telegraph and Its Community." In *Communities in Cyberspace*, edited by Marc A. Smith and Peter Kollock, 264–89. New York: Routledge.

Bibliography

Van Den Abbeele, Georges. 1991. "Introduction." In *Community at Loose Ends*, edited by the Miami Theory Collective, ix–xxvi. Minneapolis: University of Minnesota Press.

Van Dyke, Vernon. 1982. "Collective Entities and Moral Rights: Problems in Liberal-Democratic Thought." *The Journal of Politics* 44: 21–40.

van Gelder, Lindsy. 1985. "The Strange Case of the Electronic Lover: A Real-life Story of Deception, Seduction, and Technology." *Ms.* (October), 94–118.

Vidich, Arthur, and Joseph Bensman. 1958. *Small Town in Mass Society*. Princeton, NJ: Princeton University Press.

Vollman, Tim. 1979. "A Survey of Eastern Land Claims: 1970–1979," *Maine Law Review* 31: 5–16.

Warren, Roland L. 1988. "Observations on the State of Community Theory," *New Perspectives on the American Community*, edited by Roland L. Warren and Larry Lyon, 84–86. Homewood, IL: Dorsey Press.

———. 1963/1988. "The Community in America," *New Perspectives on the American Community*, edited by Roland Warren and Larry Lyon, 152–56. Homewood, IL: Dorsey Press.

Waters, Mary C. 1990. *Ethnic Options: Choosing Identities in America*. Berkeley: University of California Press.

Weiss, Penny A. 1995. "Introduction: Feminist Reflections on Community." In *Feminism & Community*, edited by Penny A. Weiss and Marilyn Friedman, 3–18. Philadelphia, PA: Temple University Press.

Wellman, Barry. 1988. "The Community Question Re-evaluated." In *Power, Community and the City*, edited by Michael Peter Smith, 81–107. New Brunswick, NJ: Transaction Books.

———. 1979. "The Community Question: Intimate Networks of East Yorkers." *American Journal of Sociology* 84: 1201–1231.

———, and Keith Hampton. 2000. "Living Networked On and Offline." *Contemporary Sociology* 28, no. 6 (November): 648–54.

———, and Milena Gulia. 1999. "Net Surfers Don't Ride Alone: Virtual Communities as Communities." In *Networks in the Global Village*, edited by Barry Wellman, 331–66. Boulder, CO: Westview.

———, and Barry Leighton. 1979. "Networks, Neighborhoods and Communities," *Urban Affairs Quarterly* 14: 363–90.

Wells, Lloyd P., and Larry G. Lemmel. 1998. *Recreating Democracy: Breathing New Life into American Communities*. Woolwich, ME: CCD.

West, Cornel. 1993. "The New Cultural Politics of Difference." In *Beyond a Dream Deferred*, edited by Becky Thompson and Sangeeta Tyagi, 19–40. St. Paul: University of Minnesota Press.

"West Enders Deserve Better." 1996. *The Boston Globe*, 19 August.

White, Robert H. 1990. *Tribal Assets: The Rebirth of Native America*. New York: Henry Holt.

Whitmyer, Claude. 1993. "Prologue" and "Epilogue." In *In the Company of Others*. 251–56, xvii–xxv. New York: Putnam.

Bibliography

Wilbur, Earl Morse. 1945. *A History of Unitarianism in Transylvania, England, and America.* Boston: Beacon Press.

Williams, Patricia. 1987. "Alchemical Notes: Reconstructing Ideals from Deconstructed Rights." *Harvard Civil Rights-Civil Liberties Review* 22: 401–33.

Winter, Steven L. 1992. "For What It's Worth." *Law and Society Review* 26 (4): 789–818.

Wirth, Louis. 1938. "Urbanism as a Way of Life." *American Journal of Sociology* 4: 8–20.

Wolfe, Alan. 1998. "Is Civil Society Obsolete? Revisiting Predictions of the Decline of Civil Society in *Whose Keeper.*" In *Community Works: The Revival of Civil Society in America,* edited by E.J. Dionne Jr., 17–23. Washington, DC: Brookings Institution.

———. 1991. "Introduction." In *America at Century's End,* edited by Alan Wolfe, 1–13. Berkeley: University of California Press,

WORLD: The Journal of the Unitarian Universalist Association. 1994. Vol. 8, no. 4 (July/August) and Vol. 6, no. 6 (November/December).

Wright, Conrad, ed. 1989. *A Stream of Light: A Short History of American Unitarianism,* 2nd ed. Boston: Skinner House Books.

———. 1989. "Salute the Arriving Moment." *A Stream of Light: A Short History of American Unitarianism,* 2nd ed., edited by Conrad Wright, 62–94. Boston: Skinner House Books.

Wuthnow, Robert. 1993. *Christianity in the 21st Century.* New York: Oxford University Press.

Young, Iris Marion. 1990. *Justice and the Politics of Difference.* Princeton, NY: Princeton University Press.

Zarembka, A. 1990. *The Urban Housing Crisis: Social, Economic, and Legal Issues and Proposals.* Westport, CT: Greenwood.

INDEX

Abt Associates, 79n
Academic postmodernism, 157
Achtenberg, Emily P., 65
Allen, John C., 7, 8, 15n, 61
Almeida, J., 109
American Unitarian Association, 51
  creed, 46
  formation of, 45
America Online, 122
Anderson, Kurt, 113, 159n
Anderson, Margaret, 3–4
Andover Seminary, 44
Appelbaum, R. P., 65, 78n
Appleby, Joyce, 39n
Archdiocese of Boston, 108
Arpanet, 120
Atlas, J., 70
Austin, Regina, 61, 156

Bancroft, George, 45
Bansal, Preeta, 143
Barsh, Russell L., 25, 31
Bartle, Richard, 131n
Bauman, Zygmunt, 148, 149, 159n
Baym, Nancy K., 124, 126, 129
Becker, Howard S., 8, 12, 13, 15n
Beem, Edgar Allen, 25
Bell, Derrick, 15n, 143
Bell, Gordon, 130
Bell, Michael Mayerfeld, 7, 61

Bellah, Robert N., 41, 61, 102, 138
Belonging, concept of, 3–4
Benhabib, Seyla, 159n
Bensman, Joseph, 162
Berger, Peter L., 155
Black, Anthony, 15n
Blackwell, James E., 5
Block, W., 65
Bloom, Alan, 4
Blumer, Herbert, 12
Borgman, Albert, 159n
Boston, Mass., West End, 103–109, 168
Boston City Council, 108
Boston Globe, 108–109
Boston Redevelopment Association, 105
Boundaries, 101–102, 140
Boundary-expressing symbols, 102
Bowen, Catherine Drinker, 147
"Bowling Alone: America's Declining Social Capital" (Putnam), 165–166
Boyte, Harry C., 81, 166
Brodeur, Paul, 25
Brodoff, Maureen, 143
Browsers, 121
Bruckman, Amy S., 124
Bruner, Edward M., 14, 39n, 158
Buehrens, John A., 42

Index

Bulletin board systems, 122
Bureau of Indian Affairs, 25

Calvinism, 43
   Unitarian rejection of, 44
   Universalist rejection of, 48
Cambridge, Mass.
   after end of rent control, 73–76
   CityHome project, 75
   as a community, 76–77
   debate over rent control, 63–67
   end of rent control, 73
   polarization over rent control, 69–73
   rent control, 63–80, 167
   rent control history, 67–73
   rent control in practice, 78n–79n
Cambridge, Mass., City Council, 67
   Rent Control Subcommittee, 71
Cambridge Affordable Housing Trust, 75–76
Cambridge and Somerville Legal Services, 76
Cambridge Community Development Department, 80n
Cambridge Tenants Association, 68–70
Campus culture wars, 4
Canellos, Peter, 108
Capek, S. M., 65, 66–67
Care orientation, 10
Carnegie Mellon University, 119
Cassara, Ernest, 43, 45, 62n
Celebration, Fla., 110–114, 168
Celebration Pattern Book, 111
Celebration School, 112–113
Center for Consensual Democracy, 87
Chang Hall, Lisa Kahaleole, 3
Channing, William Ellery, 44, 147
Charles River Park, Boston, 104–105
Chat rooms, 122–123

Chicago School of sociology, 117–118, 162
Christianity
   Unitarian version, 43–48
   Universalist version, 48–51
Church, F. Forrester, 42
Churches, 41
CityHome project, Cambridge, Mass., 75
City of Memphis v. Greene, 15n
Civil society debate, 165–166
Clark, D. J., 78n, 79n
Clinton, Hillary, 95
Clinton, Robert N., 23
Cohen, Anthony P., 7, 8, 12, 35, 101–102, 103, 168
Collective belonging, 81
Collins, Catherine, 63, 111, 112, 113, 114
Collins, Patricia Hill, 3–4
Coloring of America, 2
Columbia, Maryland, 110
Communitarian theory, 133–134
   and limits of dualism, 139–143
   new, 142–143
   responses to liberalism, 137–139
Community Catalyst, Waterville, Me., 88, 89–90, 91
Community/Communities
   assessment of postmodern critique, 157–159
   boundaries of, 101–102
   as emergent production, 12, 16
   evolution of, 7–8
   extralocal forces in, 168
   human context, 8–11
   impact of technology, 117–119
   and individual identity, 6
   interactive process, 81, 169
   interpreting, 11–14
   key dimensions of, 101
   lessons of Waterville, Me., 96–98

Index

liberal-communitarian debate, 133–145
liberal view of, 134–137
macrosociological perspective, 163–164
nature of, 5–11
network analysis, 10–11, 16
new possibilities for, 6–7
planned versus spontaneous, 6
postmodern critique, 150–155
postmodernist challenge, 147–160
as process, 11–13
reasons for studying, 1–4
relation to individuals, 140–142
religious, 41
research issues and lessons, 161–170
social capital issue, 165–166
studies of, 128–129
symbolic, 102
and tribal land claims, 17–40
in Unitarian-Universalist experience, 58
from urban planning, 110–114
virtual, 117–131
Community-found orientation, 161, 162
Community-liberated orientation, 162, 163
Community life, disagreement about, 164–165
Community-lost orientation, 161–162
Community of memory, 102–103
Community revitalization project, 84–98
Community-saved theme, 162–163
Community ties, 5
Computer-mediated communication, 118–119
  development of, 122–124
  and reality of virtual communities, 124–129
  and real nature of community, 129–130
Condominium conversion proposal, 76
Conflict approach, 16
Conflict management, 92–93
Connerly, Charles E., 163
Consensual democracy, 87
Context of community, 8–11
Convention of Universalists, 48
Corlett, William, 159n
Cravatts, R. L., 70
Cuba, Lee J., 7, 11
Culture wars, 4
Curtis, Pavel, 123, 125
Cybersociety, 118–119
Cyberspace, 117–131, 168–169
  history of, 119–121
  origin of term, 130n

Dalton, Harlon, 40n
Deconstruction, 153
Denning, Peter J., 129
Denzin, Norman K., 12
Derrida, Jacques, 151
Dertouzos, Michael, 120, 121
Devine, A., 79n
Dibbell, Julian, 129
Dickens, David R., 159n
Dillman, Don A., 7, 8, 15n, 61
Dionne, E. J., Jr., 165, 166
Discourse, 154
Disney, Walt, 111
Disney Development Corporation, 112, 113
Diversity, 3–4
Doheny-Farina, Stephen, 117, 126, 127
Donne, John, 137, 144n
Donovan, Josephine, 149, 152
Downs A., 65
Dreier, Peter, 63, 70
D'Sousza, Dinesh, 4
Dualism, limits of, 139–143

Index

Durkheim, Emile, 41, 117
Duster, Troy, 2, 3, 4
Dworkin, Ronald, 144n
Dyson, Esther, 127, 129

Eagleton, Terry, 39n, 159n
Ecological approach to research, 16
Economic decline, Waterville, Me., 83–85
Economic development, Waterville, Me., 92, 95–96
Economic interdependence, 2
Eisenhower administration, 23
E-mail, 122
Emergency Price Controls Act of 1942, 64
Emergent production, 12, 16
Emerson, Ralph Waldo, 45–46
Engel, David M., 15n, 25
Enlightenment theories, 152
Esteva, Gustavo, 156, 157
Ethnicity, symbolic, 7, 15
Etzioni, Amitai, 134, 142
Evans, Sara M., 81
Ewick, Patricia, 149

Fenstermaker, Sarah, 13
Fine, Gary Alan, 13
Finn, Geraldine, 7
First District Federal Court, Portland, Me., 23–24
First National Conference of Unitarian Churches, 47
Fischer, Claude S., 164
Flanagan, William G., 2, 162
Fontana, Andrea, 159n
Forman, Charles C., 44
Foucault, Michel, 151
Frantz, Douglas, 63, 111, 112, 113, 114
Free Religious Association, 47
Friedland, Lewis, 170n
Fuller, Margaret, 45

Gans, Herbert J., 104, 105, 115n, 162
Gates, Henry Louis, Jr., 39n
Gay, lesbian, and bisexual inclusion; *see* Welcoming Congregation
Gellers, Don, 40n
Ghere, David L., 20, 28
Gibson, William, 130n
Gignoux, Edward, 23–24, 33
Gilderbloom. John I., 65, 66–67, 78n
Gilligan, Carol, 10
Global relations, 2
Godway, Eleanor M., 7
Goetze, Rolf, 65, 79n
Grassroots Post-Modernism (Esteva & Prakash), 157
Gray, James N., 130
Greenspun, Philip, 127
Guilds and Civil Society in European Political Thought (Black), 15
Gulia, Milena, 127–128, 168
Gutmann, Amy, 141

Habitat II, 90
Habits of the Heart (Bellah), 102–103
Hafner, Katie, 121, 130
Hall, Peter M., 8, 12
Hampton, Keith N., 124, 128
Harvard College, 44
Harvard Divinity School, 45
Hathaway Shirt Company, 83, 95–96
Hayek, Friedrich A., 65
Herman, Nancy J., 12
Hillery, George A., Jr., 5
Hillyard, David, 61
Hinchman, Lewis P., 10, 40n, 158
Hinchman, Sandra K., 10, 40n, 158
Hirsch, Kathleen, 169
Hirschmann, Nancy J., 3, 144n, 153, 155
Hobbes, Thomas, 135

Index

Hollinger, Robert, 17, 148, 149, 159n
Hootoop, Margaret Tobey, 23
Houlton Band of Maliseets, 25
Howe, Charles A., 49, 51–52, 62n
Howe, Daniel Walker, 45, 46
Hughes, J. W., 65
Humanism, 47–48, 50–51
Hummon, David M., 5
Hunt, Lynn, 39n
Hunter, Albert, 101, 114, 162
Hutcheon, Linda, 149
Hutchinson, Allan D., 156

Identity
    defined by community, 6
    and ethnicity, 7
    importance for community, 81
    liberal versus communitarian views, 138–139
    in Unitarian-Universalist Association, 61
Identity politics, 3
Immigration patterns, 2
Indian Island community, Maine, 22
Internet
    chat rooms, 122–123
    E-mail, 122
    history of, 119–121
    Multi-User Domains, 123–125
    uses of, 122–124
    virtual communities from, 124–129
Internet Relay Chat, 122–123
Intuitional school of free religion, 47

Jacob, Margaret, 39n
Janowitz, Morris, 163
Joint Tribal Negotiating Committee, 33
Jones, Steven G., 118, 119
Justice
    communitarian view, 137–139
    liberal view, 134–137
Justice orientation, 10

Kalberg, Stephen, 9
Kari, Nancy N., 166
Karst, Kenneth, 138
Kasinitz, Philip, 61
Kempers, Margot, 39n, 98n
Keyes Fibre Company, 83
King, Thomas Starr, 50
Knowledge, postmodern view of, 151–152, 154–155
Kolko, Beth, 129
Kollock, Peter, 122, 123, 168
Kors, Alan C., 14n
Kruh, David S., 104
Kvale, Steinar, 147
Kymlicka, Will, 135–136, 138, 144n

Lee, Richard Wayne, 62n
Leighton, Barry, 163
Lemert, Charles, 148, 149, 153, 156, 157, 159n
Lemmel, Larry G., 99n
Lett, M., 64, 66
Levittown, 110
Liberalism and the Limits of Justice (Sandel), 137
Liberal philosophy, 135–136
Liberal political theory, 134–137, 135
    communitarian responses to, 137–139
    exponents of, 144n
    and limits of dualism, 139–143
Liberty, Michael, 96
Local area networks, 120
Locke, John, 135
LoPresti, Carmella, 109
Lowell Square Associates, 108
Lowry, I. S., 65
Luckmann, Thomas, 155
Lyon, David, 149, 152, 156, 157, 159n
Lyon, Larry, 5, 15n–16n
Lyon, Matthew, 121, 130
Lyotard, Jean-Francois, 150–152, 160n

Index

MacIntyre, Alastair, 144n
MacLeod, Jay, 61
MacQuarrie, Brian, 109
Macrosociological perspective, 163–164
Maine Indian land claim, 17–40, 167
    formulating case, 23–25
    gains and losses in outcome, 35–38
    historical and legal context, 18–2a3
    public reaction to ruling, 28–33
    significance of, 38–39
    tribal factions in, 25–28
Maine Indian Land Claim Settlement Act, 28, 38
Maliseets, 25
Manis, Jerome, 11, 16n, 17
Markoff, John, 128
Marx, Karl, 9
Massachusetts
    end of rent control, 73
    tribal land claims in, 23
Massachusetts Association of Universal Restorationists, 49
Massachusetts Institute of Technology
    cooperation on Arpanet, 119
    Laboratory for Computer Science, 121
Massachusetts Rent Control Statute, 67
Matsuda, Mari, 40n
McCall, Michael M., 12, 13
McHugh, P., 17
McKay, Henry, 162
McKernan, John R., Jr., 96
Mele, Christopher, 127
Meltzer, Bernard N., 11, 16n, 17
Memories, 102–103
Menino, Mayor, 108

Merry, Sally Engle, 26
Mestrovic, Stjepan, 156
Metcalfe, Robert M., 129
Miller, Perry, 62n
Miller, Russell E., 48, 62n
Minow, Martha, 9, 18, 40n, 140, 159
Mollenkopf, J., 68
Mosaic, 121
Mulhall, Stephen, 135, 136–137, 138, 139, 140, 142, 144n
Multiculturalism, 3–4
Multi-User Domains, 123–125

Nagel, Thomas, 144n
Nanda, Serena, 18
National Aeronautics and Space Administration, 120
National Science Foundation, 120
Native Americans
    and federal authority, 18
    legal rights and cultural identification, 33–35
    reform efforts of 1960s, 21–22
    tribal land claims, 17–40
Natoli, Joseph, 149, 159n
Neighborhood, 15n
Neotraditionalism, 110
Netscape, 121
Network analysis, 10–11, 16
Networks in the Global Village (Wellman), 10
New England Convention, 48
Newsgroups, 122
New towns, 110
New urbanism, 110
NGO forums, 90
Nicholson, Faye, 84–86, 97
Nicholson, Jim, 84–85
Nicholson, Linda, 153, 154, 158
Niebanck, P. L., 66, 67, 77n
Nisbet, Robert A., 1
Nonintercourse Act of 1790, 23, 24
Norgren, Jill, 18

Index

Nwankwo, Jason, 170n
Nyhan, Pat, 25

O'Connor, Thomas H., 105
Office of Lesbian, Bisexual, and Gay Concerns, 52
Old West End Housing Corporation, Boston, 107–108
Olsen, E., 65
Online communities, 124–129
Original position argument, 136–137
O'Toole, Francis J., 19, 23

Parents and Friends of Lesbians and Gays, 53
Parke, David B., 47
Parker, Theodore, 45, 46
Passamquoddy tribe, 17–40
    formulating land claim case, 23–25
    lifestyle changes, 35
    reservations, 19
    Tribal Council, 20, 23, 24, 26
    tribal factions, 25–28
Passamquoddy v. Morton, 24–25, 28, 32
Penobscot tribe, 17–40
    formulating land claim case, 23–25
    lifestyle changes, 35
    reservation, 19
    tribal factions, 25–28
Perin, Constance, 133
Pinch model of conflict management, 92–93
Pollan, Michael, 111, 113
Postmodern Condition (Lyotard), 150–152
Postmodernism, 147–160
    abandonment of theory in, 153–154
    critique of, 155–157

    critique of community, 150–155
    on discourse, 154
    general irrelevance of, 157
    on knowledge and reality, 154–155
    methodological characteristics, 148–150
    origin of, 150–151
    radical nature of, 148
    on scientific knowledge, 151–152
Post-modernity, 149
Prakash, Madhu Suri, 156, 157
Pressberg, Gail, 166
Process of community, 11
Pruitt-Igoe housing project failure, St. Louis, 110
Prus, Robert, 13
Putnam, Robert D., 165–166
Pynoos, J., 68

Raso, Vincent, 109
Rawls, John, 134–138, 144n
Ray, Roger B., 20
Reagan, Ronald W., 32
Reality, postmodern view of, 154–155
Redfield, Robert, 117
Reedy Creek Improvement District, Fla., 111
Regan, Milton C., Jr., 136, 141, 142
Reid, Elizabeth, 123, 125, 129, 130, 131n
Religion, 41
Religious humanism, 47–48, 50–51
Religious intuition, 46
Removal Permit Ordinance, Cambridge, Mass., 79n
REM Record, 91
Rent control, 63–80, 167
    CityHome project response to, 75

Index

debate over, 63-67
end of, 73
history of, 67073
life after, 73-76
polarization of community, 69-73
in practice, 78n-79n
studies on, 79n
Rent Control Board, Cambridge, Mass., 78n
Rent Control Subcommittee of Cambridge City Council, 71
Responsive Communitarian Platform of 1991, 142
Reston, Virginia, 110
Restorationists, 49
Revive Energy in Maine (REM) project, 86-98
accomplishments, 90-98
conflict management, 92-93
guidelines, 90
objectives, 89
significance of, 96-98
violence-free goal, 92
Reynolds, Larry T., 12
Rheingold, Howard, 7, 119, 123, 124-125, 131n
Richert, Evan, 99n
Robinson, David, 42, 46, 47, 48, 50, 51, 61, 62n
Rosenau, Pauline Marie, 148, 149, 150, 153, 155, 156
Rosenberg, M., 79n
Rosenblum, Nancy L., 144n
Ross, Thomas, 10, 113
Rossi, Alice, 144n
Rouner, Leroy S., 41
Rousseau, Jean-Jacques, 135
Russo, Andrew, 109

Sampson, Robert J., 162, 170
Sandel, Michael, 137, 138, 144n, 145n
Sarup, Madan, 154, 159n
Save the West End Committee, Boston, 103
Schlesinger, Arthur M., Jr., 4
School controversy, Celebration, Fla., 112-113
Schuler, Douglas, 127
Science, and postmodernism, 151-152
Scientific inventions, 2
Scientific school of free religion, 47
Scott Paper Company, 83
Seidman, Steven, 152, 153-154, 156, 158, 159n
Selznick, Philip, 5, 8, 14n-15n, 140, 141
Seneca Fall Declaration of Sentiments, 1848, 144n
Shaw, Clifford, 162
Silbey, Susan S., 26
Silvergate, Harry A., 14n
Sirianni, Carmen, 170n
Small Property Owners Association, Cambridge, Mass., 69-73
Smart, Barry, 149, 159n, 161
Smith, Anna Duval, 126
Smith, Dorothy, 77n
Smith, Marc A., 122, 123, 168
Snipp, C. W., 39
Snowe, Olympia, 95
Social capital, 166
Social Construction of Reality (Berger & Luckmann), 155
Social context, 8-11, 12-13
Social contract arguments, 136-137
Social gospel, 50-51
Social interdependence, 140
Social movements of 1960s, 2
Social sciences, postmodern, 156
Society
communitarian view, 137-139
original position argument, 136-137
as social contract, 136

Index

and state of nature, 135–136
traditional *versus* rational, 117
Sociology
   Chicago School, 117–118, 162
   community-liberated view, 163
   community-lost view, 161–162
   community-saved theme, 162–163
   macrosociological perspective, 163–164
   theorists of 19th century, 117
Solo, Pam, 166
Sparks, Jared, 44
Spelman, Elizabeth V., 9
Stack, Carole, 162
Standing Order churches, 45
Stanford Institute for the Quantitative Study of Society, 128
Stanford University, 119
State of nature, 135–136
Stegman, M. A., 66
Stein, Maurice, 6
Sternlieb, G., 65
Story-telling, 103
Suttles, Gerald, 162
Svensson, Frances, 25
Swift, Adam, 135, 136–137, 138, 139, 140, 142, 144n
Symbolic communities, 102
Symbolic ethnicity, 7, 15
Symbolic interactionism, 11–13
Systems theory, 16

Taylor, Charles, 3, 4, 139, 144n
Taylor, Theodore W., 18, 38
TCP-IP protocol, 120
Technological innovations, 2, 117
Text chat systems, 122–123
Theory of Justice (Rawls), 134–137
Thomas, W. I., 6
Thompson, Becky W., 4
Thoreau, Henry David, 45
Tilly, Charles, 13
Tompkins, Jane, 39n

Tonnies, Ferdinand, 117
Transcendentalists, 45–46
Transient and Permanent in Religion, The (Parker), 46
Trubshaw, Roy, 131n
Tucker, W., 65
Tureen, Thomas N., 19, 23, 40n
Turkle, Sherry, 129
Tyagi, Sangeeta, 4
Typological approach to research, 15

U. S. News and World Report, 95
Ultra-Universalists, 49
Uncapher, Willard, 127
Uniform Relocation Act of 1970, 106
Unitarian Boston Association of Ministers, 46
Unitarianism
   early views of Universalists, 50
   history and beliefs of, 43–48
   merger with Universalists, 51–52
Unitarian-Universalist Association, 167
   at congregational/individual level, 56–60
   formalizing diversity, 54–56
   formation of, 52
   as religious community, 60–61
   roots of, 43
   statement of purposes and principles, 42
   in United States, 42–43
   Welcoming Congregation program, 52–54, 58–60
United Nations Conference on Human Settlements, 90
United States
   coloring of America, 2
   social movements of 1960s, 2
   Unitarian-Universalist Association in, 42–43
United States Department of Energy, 120

Index

United States Department of Defense Advanced Research Projects Agency, 119–120
United States Department of Justice, 23–25
United States Department of the Interior, 24
Universalism
  early views of Universalists, 50
  history and beliefs of, 48–51
  merger with Unitarians, 51–52
  split in, 49–50
Universalist Church of America, 51
University of Chicago, 117–118
Urbanism, 162
Urban planning, 111–114
  new urbanism, 110
Urban renewal, 82
  in Boston's West End, 104–109
  failure of Pruitt-Igoe, 110
Urban village, 105
Usenet, 122, 131n
Utilitarianism, 144n

Van den Abbeele, Georges, 6
Van Dyke, Vernon, 137
van Gedler, Lindsy, 129
Vidich, Arthur, 162
Virtual communities, 117–131, 168–169
  reality of, 124–129
Vollman, Tim, 23, 38, 40n

Wagner, David G., 159n
Walt Disney Corporation, 111
Walzer, Michael, 144n
Warnaco, 95–96
Warren, Roland L., 11, 162
Waters, Mary C., 7, 15n

Waterville, Maine, 81–99, 167
  decline since the 1960s, 82–85
  rejuvenization project, 84–98
Waterville Regional Arts and Community Center, 90
Weber, Max, 117
Weiss, Penny A., 5
Welcoming Congregation program, 52–54, 58–60
Weld, William, 73
Wellman, Barry, 6, 8, 10, 11, 124, 127–128, 162, 163, 168
Wells, Lloyd P., 99n
WELL (Whole Earth 'Lectric Link), 122, 125, 131n
West Ender, Boston, 106–107, 109
West End Urban Renewal Plan, Boston, 107–108
White, Robert H., 39
Whitmyer, Claude, 101, 164
Wilbur, Earl Morse, 62n
Williams, Patricia, 40n
Winter, Steven L., 148, 154
Wired Neighborhood (Doheny-Farina), 126
Wirth, Louis, 147, 162
Wittner, Judith, 12
Wolfe, Alan, 2, 165
Women's rights, 144n
Woodward, C. Vann, 78n
World Wide Web, 121
World Wide Web Consortium, 121
Wright, Conrad, 47
Wuthnow, Robert, 61

Young, Iris Marion, 140, 143

Zarembka, A., 65, 66